Michael Gould holds a PhD from the School of Oriental and African Studies (SOAS), University of London. He has lived and worked in Nigeria and is an honorary chief of the Igbo people.

'This book is an in-depth, scholarly and rigorous reassessment of the traumatic Biafran War and the making of today's Nigeria, based on the author's intimate personal knowledge of the region. One of its many strengths is its profound understanding of post-colonial Nigeria and its peoples. Another derives from the several searching interviews conducted with many of the leading protagonists. Michael Gould has written an excellent and genuinely enlightening book.'

Denis Judd, Professor of History, University of New York in London

'An outstanding account and analysis of the Nigerian Civil War (also known as the Biafran War) ... Its profound research is based on unique personal interviews with many of the principal participants and on archival and other primary sources, which no other author has been able to access ... Michael Gould's outstanding study concludes with important interpretations of Biafra's longevity and how far genocide was a reality or a myth, along with a notable appraisal of the history and impact of the two leaders ... This is a brilliant history of the Nigerian Civil War and, forty years later, stands as the best analysis yet published.'

Anthony Kirk-Greene, Emeritus Fellow of St. Antony's College, Oxford

The Biafran War

The Struggle for Modern Nigeria

Michael Gould

Foreword by Frederick Forsyth

I.B. TAURIS

LONDON · NEW YORK

New paperback edition published in 2013 by I.B.Tauris & Co Ltd
6 Salem Road, London W2 4BU
175 Fifth Avenue, New York NY 10010
www.ibtauris.com

Distributed in the United Stats and Canada Exclusively by Palgrave Macmillan
175 Fifth Avenue, New York NY 10010

First published in hardback in 2012 by I.B.Tauris & Co Ltd

ISBN 978 1 78076 463 4

A full CIP record for this book is available from the British Library
A full CIP record is available from the Library of Congress

Library of Congress Catalog Card Number: available

Typeset by Newgen Publishers, Chennai
Printed and bound by CPI Group (UK) Ltd, Croydon, CR0 4YY

MIX
Paper from
responsible sources
FSC® C013604

This book is dedicated to my late father John,
a member of the Royal West African Frontier Force.

CONTENTS

ILLUSTRATIONS

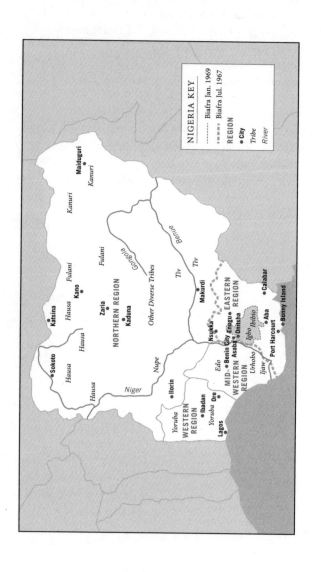

Map 1. Map of Nigeria

Map 2. Map of Biafra

FOREWORD

At the time of writing it has been forty years, but people still remember Biafra.

The rebellion of Nigeria's Eastern Region against the Federal Government many miles away and its declaration of separate independence was supposed to be quashed within ten days by the federal army. So at least London's Commonwealth Relations Office confidently announced.

The war lasted two and a half years, from July 1967 to January 1970. In that period an estimated number of Biafrans died, overwhelmingly children and primarily of starvation, that is generally agreed to be close to a million.

For the last year and a half, the outer world, belatedly made aware of the horror, watched and protested. In vain. There was no intervention.

But those thirty months marked two basic innovations that it took years to realise. Television war coverage came of age, and the developed world, impotent in a hundred million sitting rooms, watched their first African mass famine. Others would follow, have followed, ever since. But this was a man-made famine and no one had ever seen its like before.

Today old-stagers of the war correspondents' circuit watch in awe the technology of the new craft: the brilliant colour images, in high definition, transmitted from the most obscure rock defile or jungle clearing direct to our screens at the touch of a 'send' button. Back then it could take weeks.

Cameramen back-hauled cumbersome kit using old celluloid film. With the film finally 'in the can' (literally a flat disc of aluminium duct-taped shut) the evidence had to reach some kind of airport. From there, perhaps in the hand baggage of a kindly missionary, it had to be flown across the world to the USA or Europe.

That was not the end. A despatch rider would take the discs to the studio for slow development into long wet strings, pegged up to dry. Finally, cut and edited, literally with a guillotine and sticky tape, the sound-track pasted to the edge, hopefully 'in synch', the film would make the evening newscast. It was often screened a week after being shot. In the battle-zone much could have happened, but it was the best we could do.

Much of it was in black and white, for colour 'stock' was expensive. But for all the struggles and all the delays, those filmed reportages out of the Biafran enclave had a traumatic effect on two continents: Europe and North America. They just had not seen anything like it before.

Words can do so much and some still photos have become iconic down the decades. But there is nothing like the moving colour film and the sheer immediacy of instant transmission. People in their sitting rooms had never seen, in the corner, images of children reduced to stick insects. They had not seen the monstrous heads lolling on the wasted necks; the bones jutting like dry kindling; the air-bloated bellies; the mass graves tended by priests and nuns. And they had not heard the constant low wailing of dying babies.

The images shocked, horrified and angered. There were demonstrations; politicians were hounded; donations collected; relief aid flooded in. The world looked, gagged and tried to help.

Today we are all inured. We have seen it countless times. In Ethiopia, Tigre, Eritrea, Sudan, Darfur, Niger. We donate and turn away. But Biafra was the first and it shook the world.

And Biafra was deliberate. The land called Eastern Nigeria was rich and prosperous. It grew food and exported much. But due to its intensive population in a small landmass it had to import protein: fish, meat, eggs, milk. It was the Nigerian blockade that caused the slaughter. Children need protein every day.

One can be sad over a drought, a volcano, an earthquake, a flood, a failed crop. But one cannot rail at it. It is an act of God. But Biafra was deliberate, an act of Man.

The actual ground war was sometimes brutal, often farcical. Despite prodigious quantities of fired-off ammunition, few died of violence. The killer was the hunger.

But why did it happen? How did it happen? Who was behind it? Why could it not be stopped? Who were the main players? Who told us the truth and who lied?

In those forty years an enormous amount has come to light. Some memories have faded, others have been muted by death, and yet others conveniently altered. But the revelations supercede them. Forty years on it is possible to reveal what I could not explain as I sat writing the slim paperback *The Biafra Story* in the heart of it all.

That is why I am confident that Michael Gould can tell us much we did not know before.

Frederick Forsyth
Hertford, 2010

PREFACE

This narrative is an overview account of the Nigerian Civil War. It discusses the ethnicity of the conflict and how it was supported by Britain who backed the Federal Government, and France who sided with the seceded state of Biafra. It argues that at certain times during the war, because of frustration by the international community over both parties' inability to agree a truce, some nations gave Biafra international recognition, and others came very close to doing so. Debatably, part of the international dimension to the war was the great powers' wish to protect and enhance their commercial interests in Nigeria.

Whereas the Federal forces thought and planned for a short conflict, indeed its initial strategy was that this was simply a police action, they totally underestimated the strength and determination of the opposition to succeed. Federal Nigeria, also, had no long term strategy for subduing the recalcitrant state, whereas Biafra's objective was to achieve permanent sovereignty.

Both sides were to suffer from a chronic shortage of arms throughout the campaign, but for totally different reasons. Overt support for arms and armaments was given by Britain to the federation as the conflict ensued, but this was soon tempered by political constraints confirming limits and restrictions on the supply of arms. This forced the federal forces to look elsewhere. They found support for their needs from Russia. Being at the height of the 'Cold War' this caused reverberations of concern among the western powers. Biafra sought arms support from any country and source that was willing to trade with the seceded state. However throughout the campaign she received covert arms support from France. It was these two factors which turned the war from a local conflict into an international one. The lack of consistent arms supply for both sides, throughout the war, was to cause constraints on both parties' ability to gain overall military superiority.

Initially the conflict appeared to have been ethnically inspired, but gradually support from Britain and France arguably turned the war into an international commercial war, for control over Nigeria's natural resources. Both powers realised the future potential and significance of the country's oil resource. Indeed Shell had carried out confidential research into Nigeria's oil reserves and it had found them to be twice the original estimates. This information was to remain confidential to the oil company until after the cessation of hostilities. Neither of Nigeria's antagonists, in the war, was aware of this.

Within the first few days of the campaign the Federal forces were very nearly able to conclusively defeat Biafra. Due to supply problems they stalled their attack and Biafra reversed its misfortune by a daring incursion on the West through the Mid-West region.

Even though this initiative ended in failure, because of its commander's perfidiousness, Biafra became increasingly impervious to the continual Federal onslaughts. Its position was inadvertently strengthened by the media's ability to bring the ravages of this war to the attention of the international community. Not only did this attention swell the coffers of the aid agencies, because of the international communities' concerns for the starving, dying and disease-ridden children of Biafra, but armament support became entwined with aid support for Biafra. This situation became even more confused, and was to cause great embarrassment to Britain, because on the one hand it continued to supply arms to the Federal Government, but on the other its charities were overwhelmed with funds to support the civilian population of Biafra who were being killed and maimed by the opposing military machine armed by Britain.

Inexorably, the Federal forces gained the upper hand and Biafra's frontiers contracted, until it became a fraction in size of its former territory. In spite of this it finally only agreed to an armistice, not unconditional surrender, threatening a guerrilla campaign, if this was unacceptable.

ACKNOWLEDGEMENTS

In writing this book I received tremendous support and encouragement from a large number of people both in Britain and Nigeria. They ranged from librarians, museum curators, academics, politicians, diplomats and military personnel to friends and friends-of-friends and acquaintances. They were all very supportive of my project and freely gave their time to help me write this book. Without their input and support my task would have been very daunting. Most people were able to give valuable information, which helped to fill in gaps and to answer my many questions. To all these people I am deeply indebted. I wish to record my gratitude and thanks. It is important to me that I recognise the support I received from Denis Judd, who mentored me from the start and told me that my thesis was worthy of becoming a book, and indeed gave me confidence at every stage of the writing process to help me achieve my objective. I would also like to acknowledge Tony Kirk-Greene, who enthused over my project and gave me constant support whenever it was sought. James Eneje is another person to whom I was able to turn when support was needed and who was able to act as introducer when I sought to meet various people from his native Igboland. I would also mention Joe Achuzia, who welcomed me into his family in Asaba, and now regards me as a member of that family. Ben Gbulie was also another supporter who gave me his personal insight into the first coup. Finally I would like to acknowledge and thank everybody at I.B.Tauris, especially my editor Joanna Godfrey, who has patiently guided me through the intricacies of the publishing world.

CHAPTER 1

INTRODUCTION

To the North ... dwell the Hausa and Fulani, devout Moslem people governed by feudal emirs. The Western Region is the home of the Yoruba, a tribe known for its profusion of gods and its joie de vivre. To the East, where they are now trapped, the ambitious and clever Ibo people thrived. Brought together forcibly under colonial rule, the three regions developed the hatreds and jealousies of totally different cultures.[1]

At the time of independence in 1960 Nigeria was ruled by Britain and the North's oligarchic elite, together with their coalition partners. After independence it was this same group of people who were left in charge. Admittedly there was a veneer of parliamentary democracy, but rigged and corrupt voting seriously compromised democratic elections. This meant that although there were sincere attempts by well-meaning nationalists to ensure that democracy was potentially possible, the reality was that the parliamentary system left by the British was hopelessly undemocratic and factionalised.

The social upheaval, which led to the civil war, occurred because the accepted system of corruption and preferment, well established during British control, and readily adopted by the new rulers, was simply unsustainable if it was to accommodate all those who felt that they should be part of the ruling elite. It was workable when the British were in control, because the authority and power base was theirs alone. However democratising the system simply undermined the new rulers' power base and made oligarchic rule impossible. There was deep frustration for those trying to get into the centre of government. They could see the oligarchy enriching themselves and their extended families to the detriment and disadvantage of the majority of the community. The problem was that Britain, concerned for her huge vested interests in the country, had chosen the people whom it thought would protect and develop those interests. This is exactly what the ruling oligarchy did, but to the disadvantage of the majority of the population. The following quotation, originally refer-ring to Kenya, could equally apply to Nigeria: 'The shared interests of this alliance were deliberately engineered by the British Government in the dying days of empire, as the colonial government sought to transfer power to a reliable and sympathetic elite.'[2]

The tragedy of the first coup was that because it did not achieve its objec-tive of ridding the country of the ruling elite and, to a lesser extent, of corrupt politicians, but allowed the army to take control, as the army was an exten-sion of the ruling oligarchic elite, the coup leaders simply handed control of the country from one elite group to another. The counter coup was simply the North's opportunity to reassert itself and ensure that its ruling elite was put in charge of the country again. But this time, they were not there by the ballot box, however corrupt that was, but by the power of the gun.

Under British rule the army had remained firmly out of politics. After independence it became increasingly politicised, not for want of becom-ing political, but because that was the only way it could exercise power in support of the status quo and the oligarchic rulers, centred in the north of the country.[3] Lower down in the army hierarchy, well-educated jun-ior officers became increasingly vociferous and increasingly disillusioned with their senior officers and governing politicians who were seen to be enriching themselves at the expense of the rest of the country. This led to the point where they felt that the only hope for Nigeria's salvation was open revolt, for nationalistic and altruistic reasons, certainly not for their own self-aggrandisement or enrichment.[4]

Northerners had historically failed to embrace western ideologies, con-tinuing to favour their Muslim and Middle Eastern heritage, as encour-aged by the British. The North's tragedy was because it failed to adapt to western ways, there was a vacuum in its economic, educational and administrative development. Because the South had readily absorbed western ideology, its people were only too willing to fill this vacuum. This meant that much of the economic and administrative life of the North was controlled by people from the South. This state of affairs cre-ated serious ethnic tensions, leading to a series of riots of killing and property destruction immediately after the second coup, which the mili-tary administration seemed unable or unwilling to control.

The fact was that the North, by persecuting Easterners, created the catalyst for the East to secede from the federation in order to create an independent state. The Aburi meeting was an attempt by the military leaders to reach a compromise to secure the life of the federation by allowing the four regions to step apart, but within the confines of a federal state. If this had been confirmed and carried out by all the parties it is likely that a civil war would not have occurred, but, because the newly appointed military ruler, following the second coup, was encouraged by his senior civil servants and Britain to renege on the Aburi Accord, a war became inevitable.

The seceded state of Biafra regarded the war as a war of survival in order to gain permanent sovereignty, whereas the rest of Nigeria was solely intent on getting the renegade state to return to the federation, and thinking that this would prove an easy matter had no long term plans for achieving its objective. Throughout the war both sides suffered from a chronic shortage of arms but for totally different reasons.

Although, initially, Nigeria regarded attempts to subdue the recalcitrant region as a police action, such was the unpreparedness of both sides for war that Biafra very nearly capitulated after the first few days of the conflict. However, it proved intuitive in reversing this situation, eventually, to become seemingly impervious to continual Nigerian onslaughts. Furthermore, Biafra's position was inadvertently strengthened by the media's ability to bring the ravages of the war to the attention of the international community. The media made great play on portraying dying, starving and disease ridden children in Biafra. This led to the international aid agencies providing increasingly supportive aid. Unfortunately, some aid agencies were not adverse to supplying arms as part of their aid programme to Biafra. This together with 'Attack Markets' and the East's innate creativeness led to the war's longevity.

It proved to be a strange war in some respects. There were no major set battles, as was the case in World War II. It was a war of minor skirmishes, short sharp confrontations and localised incursions with ever changing boundaries, both sides being in the ascendant and descendant in almost equal measure throughout the campaign. In spite of there being some 300,000 troops[5] eventually involved in the war for both sides, total casualties could have been as few as 30,000.[6] It was also a war which featured prolonged periods when little fighting actually took place. Of course there were significant incidents during the campaign which gave the Federal Government greater confidence that they would achieve their objective of retaining the unity of Nigeria. Defining moments such as the debacle at Ore, the capture of Enugu and the fall of Port Harcourt all gave the Federal Authorities belief in an eventual victory. However, equally salutary from the Federal Government's point of view, and which in turn gave Biafra confidence that it could achieve sovereign status, were Mohammed's shambolic attempts to cross the river Niger and take the important trading town of Onitsha, the Abagana incident, which Ojukwu insisted on leaving as a victorious feature for visiting journalists to witness, and the amazing rout of part of Adekunle's division at Owerri.

It was also a war which featured virtually no heavy armaments. During the war's closing stages the Federal Authorities had the benefit of some Russian-supplied heavy guns, but they played very little part in bringing the war to a conclusion. Although random aerial bombing of markets, hospitals and civilians by Federal airmen featured heavily in Ojukwu's campaign to discredit the Federal Authorities on the international stage, the reality was that it had very little effect on the outcome of the war. What, however, was true was the dramatic effect the airlift had on Biafra's ability to survive, especially during the later stages of the campaign. It is also true to say that Von Rosen's Mincom aircraft proved effective in disrupting the supply of oil to Lagos, but their effectiveness was really too late to prevent an eventual Biafran capitulation.

The war also created celebrity generals, especially Adekunle and Achuzia, both of whom gained a reputation for aggressive behaviour towards their troops, but who both enjoyed success and adulation by the public. Such was their popularity that both were removed from their commands for the apparent fear that they might have become threats to the leadership of both sides. Eventually the war came to an end, to the great relief of most people on both sides, and reconciliation and reunion with colleagues and families who had fought on opposing sides became of paramount importance, to the point where on the surface at least the scars of this war quickly healed. As John de St Jorre pointed out, this indeed was a brothers' war.[7]

Chapter content

Chapter 2 considers the background to the conflict and concludes that one of the main reasons for the war was because of the historical divisiveness between the Hausa, Fulani people from the North and the Igbo people from the East. Arguably this division had always been a cause of conflict, which is shown by the rise and fall of various empires from

Nigeria's earliest history. This division was confirmed by the British who because of parsimony, and because of their consul's experience in India, determined on a policy of indirect rule. This policy, whilst acceptable, and welcomed by the North, found little favour in the South, especially the South East, where a system of democracy was the more accepted norm. The question of ethnicity went to the very heart of the origins of the conflict, which was highlighted by Britain's attitude to class, race, religion and education at the end of the nineteenth and the early twentieth centuries. One of the main reasons for the war was the ethnic mix of people, within Nigeria, who had little understanding of their individual diversity. It also considers the country's political development from its earliest days up to and after independence and shows how divisive the parliamentary single vote system proved to be, and how political power gave financial power. The two coups which brought the military into the political arena are analysed and the book finds that the first coup was not ethnically inspired, but was a sincere attempt by the military to rid the country of its corrupt political structure, as Ben Gbulie confirmed when interviewed.[8] Gbulie, also, argues in his book *Nigeria and the Five Majors* that:

> The truth of the matter, of course, was that the January coup was a coup of the progressive elements of the Nigerian Armed Forces - an intervention clearly necessitated by the breakdown of law and order in the country. It was therefore neither an 'Igbo affair' nor, for that matter the affair of any other ethnic group connected with it.[9]

The book confirms that the second coup was simply the North reasserting its power over the country. The chapter also considers the increasing tension between two military leaders. Gowon, who emerged as an acceptable military leader for the country, after the second coup and Ojukwu, who had been appointed by the previous military regime to administer the Eastern region. Ojukwu was unwilling to accept that Gowon had de facto control of the country.

Chapter 3 considers the events after the second coup, when the new military ruler, Gowon, found that his position was tenuous and precarious. Firstly because of the East's and its military governor's concern that Gowon was unable to stop the killings of Igbo people by Northerners, but secondly and most importantly the West's ambivalence to support the new regime. Initially the West led by Awolowo, the Yoruba's political leader and Adebayo, the West's newly appointed military ruler, sought compromise with the East. As Nolte explains in her book:

> By supporting the Gowon administration against Biafra, Awolowo disregarded, for the first time in his political career, popular opinion in his area of origin, Remo. After the clashes of 1965 and 1966, many Remo citizens were sceptical about the central government and thought that Yorubaland should secede from the federation, just like Biafra ... Throughout the Civil War, people in Remo housed and hid Igbo refugees who were in danger of being arrested for detention by central government.

She goes on to comment:

> One of the most important reasons for Awolowo's support of the military government was Gowon's determination to break up Nigeria's regions into twelve states, which closely reflected Awolowo's own views on Nigeria's political future.[10]

Ojukwu came to the Aburi meeting with an agenda confirming that the four regions within the federation should move apart and indeed that the federation should become more like a confederation. The other parties had no fixed agenda, treating the meeting more as a discussion to gain consensus on the way to keep Nigeria united. Ojukwu's carefully prepared plans convinced the other regional military leaders, including Gowon, of the soundness of his proposals. Sadly, as the chapter explains, Gowon reneged on the agreement.

The creation of many more states within the federation had always received support from Awolowo, and indeed had been considered during early colonial rule. Its focus was highlighted by Isaac Boro's ill-fated attempt to form an independent state in the Delta region. Although it had a very limited life, it did have the effect of determining the military regime to confirm the creation of more states.

The chapter looks at the state of readiness by both for war at the start of hostilities, the near defeat of Biafra at the start of the war and Biafra's attempt to defeat the Federal Government's forces by invading the West. It also discusses the lack of awareness of the conflict by the international community until newspapers and television were able to bring photographic evidence to the attention of their readers and viewers.

Chapter 4 discusses how Ojukwu made good use of pictorial press releases to convince the world of his cause. He was able to persuade most countries in the West that they should support Biafra, at least with humanitarian aid, if not recognition. He was also able to use, to good effect, his unrivalled intelligence network, some of whose Igbo members were prominent in Gowon's headquarters in Lagos. However as discussed his command and control of the region was often suspect particularly with regard to Biafra's army. There were many instances where he restricted the supply of arms and food to his troops, exposing them to unnecessary risk and hardship, and allowed his civil executive power and control over the army, both of which were detrimental to Biafra's success. This was in sharp contrast to Gowon's laissez-faire approach with his generals. He gave them so much independence that in some instances they were accused of running their own fiefdoms, having total responsibility for buying and supplying arms to their divisions.

This in turn often led to a detrimental effect on the federation army's ability to achieve its objectives, leading to a number of serious reverses.

Chapter 5 covers the intriguing ability of Biafra to suffer many reverses and defeats, and yet always to find resources which ensured her survival, which helped create the war's longevity. They ranged from attempts at settling the dispute through outside agencies, where Biafra would remain intransigent over its demands for sovereignty, to the use of propaganda through the excellent use of a foreign news agency, who became so authoritative in communicating its cause that even the British Cabinet would refer to it for confirmation of current events. It also considers the extensive use of Biafra's natural resources as well as its support and use of highly skilled and resourceful scientists who were able to devise many intriguing ways of helping Biafra to survive.

Chapter 6 considers the different styles, leadership and background of Gowon and Ojukwu, making extensive use of personal interviews not only with the two leaders but also with many people who had day to day contact with them, from their earliest days to the time throughout the war. It is an intriguing fact that neither men sought their positions of power. Both were appointed because of circumstance, therefore arguably neither had dictatorship ambitions to remain in power indefinitely. Indeed they gave the impression when interviewed that they both had had a job to do, that they exercised this to the best of their ability, but that their positions were subject to support of others, and if and when that support was removed they would resign.

CHAPTER 2

HISTORICAL BACKGROUND

History teaches that extremity of deception always produces extremity of dis-illusionment and reaction ... competition between the three majority ethnic groups in Nigeria brought about the civil war.

(Ken Saro-Wiwa, *On Darkling Plain*, p.11)

Arguably, there were six main historical reasons for the outbreak of the Nigerian Civil War in 1967, however in order to explain the background to the conflict it is necessary to understand the country's geographical variations, its divergent people, its religious interaction and the influence of outsiders, as well as post-colonial conditions, the two coups and finally two men with irreconcilable views. Firstly, it can be argued that the differences of the three main peoples involved in the conflict occurred because of the country's geography and its variable topography. This created regional hegemony but chronic divisiveness for the country as a whole. Secondly, the influence of religious diversity had a particular impact on the cause of the war because Islam, being a complete religion, encompassed all facets of life, not only loyalty to its faith but also to political unity, whereas Christianity made no political demands. This meant Northern Nigerians were more loyal to their political status quo and their religiously enshrined leadership, than the Southern Nigerians who felt under no such constraint and obligation. They were willing and intent on promoting their own political causes with no religious condi-tionality. Thirdly, rule over a subject people by the British was carried out in such a way as to ensure almost total financial control through a few narrow and easily manageable channels. This made it easy for the rulers of newly independent states to control their exchequers and dictate their uses.[11] The British style of administration, with regional rule, also meant that from Nigeria's inception its pre-colonial history of ethnic divisiveness was confirmed. Fourthly, post-colonial conditions were such that political power meant absolute power both legally and financially. Because of the population spread in Nigeria, the Westminster-style democratic system left by the British meant that one of the three main political power blocks would always be in opposition. This encouraged all parties to pursue ruthless and uncompromising methods either to attain power or to remain in power. Fifthly, there was inevitability about the two coups leading to the war, because of politicised tribalism and ethnicity and the army's naivety in meddling in politics, for which it was ill-prepared and ill-trained. Finally, the lack of understanding and the unwillingness to compromise, particularly by the two opposing military leaders, one refusing to acknowledge the other's position as de facto head of state, and the other being constrained by compromise in order to secure his precarious position, made an armed conflict inevitable.

Ethnicity

An underlying reason, which was to play a crucial role in the cause of the Nigerian civil war, was ethnicity. Its origins can be found in the country's topography and its very early history. Although it has a tropical climate throughout there are broadly two zones, savannah in the North and rainforest in the South. The southern belt of rainforest created an impenetrable barrier for invading armies. This, coupled with the tsetse fly which is endemic throughout the rainforests and indeed parts of the savannah, meant that survival of cattle and horses was impossible.[12] This was to have a dramatic effect on the ethnic development of modern-day Nigeria. Trade in the North was based on cattle and horses whilst in the South forestry and elementary farming was the norm.[13]

Knowledge of the early history of Nigeria is still a matter for conjecture, but it seems likely that from the seventh century empires and states flourished in the region. The Arab invasion at this time created trade and communication from the north to the south across the Sahara. Some of the earliest and most powerful of these states were the Kanem–Borno and Hausa states. It also seems likely that equally powerful states existed further south, namely Nupe and Kwarafa. The Hausa states developed into walled cities and engaged in trade and serviced the caravans that crossed the Sahara. Manufactured cloth and leather goods helped in the development and wealth of these city states. Indeed, the relationship between these states and the Mediterranean Arab rulers remained intertwined for many centuries and created much of Northern Nigeria's unity, but also its separateness from the rest of Nigeria.

Similarly, further south the Yoruba, Ife and Benin states flourished, but because of the topography there was little contact with these states by the North. Although, there are accounts in the sixteenth century of the Nupe state invading Yoruba land, by the fifteenth century the southern Benin Empire emerged as the region's most powerful state. The empire dominated the entire region including Yorubaland and spread as far east as Lagos and west as far as the lower Niger. The Oba (King) of Benin can date his line from 1170 to the present. It is also apparent that this empire developed far beyond subsistence farming. It developed not only its secular art, known today throughout the museums of the world, but also an elaborate system of rule and control. Ingeniously it established a chieftain system whereby chiefs were appointed to rule over various towns but scattered throughout the empire. This meant that no one chief could establish ascendant power which would challenge the Oba's rule. This probably accounts for the longevity of the empire. It is also likely that it traded with many other states, including northern ones which included the Hausa people. It was, for example, involved in slave trading with these northern states. There was ongoing demand for slaves in Northern Nigeria's Islamic societies because Muslims were not allowed to enslave other Muslims, only non-believers.[14] What is interesting about the Benin Empire was that it was not influenced by Islam and indeed Islamic influence over the Yoruba Empire was limited. It seems likely, therefore, that from a very early age, because of the Arab influence in the north of the country and its topography, there was an historic division between modern Southern and Northern Nigeria, causing much distrust between the two peoples and creating an underlying reason for the outbreak of the civil war.

The influence of Europeans from the fifteenth century also helped to confirm this divisiveness. The Portuguese arrived on the West Coast of Africa in the late fourteen-seventies looking for a sea passage to India. Having discovered the source of Arab gold and anxious to cut them out as the middle men in this trade, they started commercial activities in gold at Elmina in modern-day Ghana. They also traded in pepper at Benin. Indeed in 1483 King John II of Portugal had taken the title of Lord of Guinea. This initial European contact with the indigenous population on the south coast of West Africa permanently changed the axis of economic activity, especially in Nigeria. Up until this time all commercial activity outside each empire had been conducted in a northerly direction. From this time on the dynamics of trade in the south were focused firmly towards the sea. More importantly it had the effect of making the southern coastal peoples, of what was to become modern-day Nigeria, look to closer cooperation with Europeans rather than their Muslim neighbours in the North, thus compounding this divisiveness.

Religion

Islam came to Kanem in the eleventh century and it was introduced perhaps in the thirteenth century to Hausaland by Wangrawa from Mali. The camel was introduced into North Africa in AD 100[15] and gave immediate impetus to trans-Saharan trade. This trade had been in the hands of the Berbers, but after the Arab conquest of the Berbers this trade fell into Arab hands. As the Muslim states grew in prosperity so the demand for gold, ivory and leather increased. So did the demand for slaves. Negro slaves were in particular demand because as previously noted Muslims were not allowed to enslave other Muslims. Fulani nomads some of whom had been converted to Islam started to infiltrate into Northern Nigeria as early as the eleventh century. Some of their writers and administrators were employed in the Northern Nigerian Empires, bringing with them the Koran and the potential of literacy. However the spread of Islam in the north was patchy and sporadic, and many of these empires remained animist or adopted a mixture of animism with Islam. Over a period of time, these Fulani writers and administrators saw a decline in their influence over the courts throughout the northern areas along West Africa, and indeed the period also saw a decline in the influence of Islam. Because of this, the Muslim Fulani felt their only recourse to their pagan overlords was to revolt. A series of Jihads were instigated throughout the region. In Hausaland the Fulani had established themselves as important officials at the various courts and they had become openly critical of their masters. This criticism was to vent its focus through a famous Muslim scholar Usman dan Fodio. He justified his Jihad against the Hausa rulers by accusing them of professing to believe in Islam whilst at the same time mixing their beliefs with pagan traditions. By 1808 this Fulani Jihad had brought most of Hausaland under its control and it laid the foundation of the Sokoto Caliphate. By 1830 the Fulani were masters of modern-day Northern Nigeria. As far as later rivalries were concerned, particularly with regard to the Nigerian civil war, through controlling this vast area of the country and establishing a unified administrative and legal system, not to mention a singular religion, their hegemony was ensured in Northern Nigeria. This, however, was to the detriment of the region being able to integrate with the rest of the country on an equal basis once independence was achieved. The religious obligation demanded that 'our religion is a religion of obedience'.[16] That obedience effectively made the north unwilling to integrate with the rest of the country.

The census of 1952–53 showed that the proportion of Muslims in the country was 45%, the proportion of Christians 25%, and 30% were pagan. Christianity was introduced to the country with the arrival of Europeans. The Portuguese attempt to indoctrinate the country around Benin with Christianity, when they first arrived, met with little success. Indeed it is true to say that Christianity made little inroads into Nigeria until the slave trade was outlawed in 1807. The banning of this obnoxious trade was caused by a great evangelical resurgence in Britain and elsewhere within its expanding colonial empire. The spread of evangelical Christianity in Nigeria gathered momentum because these new missionary churches offered western-style education. People in Southern Nigeria took full advantage of this opportunity. However, due to later constraints on the part of the British administration, in order to gain the cooperation of compliant leaders, controls were put on Christian evangelical expansion into Northern Nigeria. This, coupled with the fact that followers of Islam were deeply suspicious of European religion as well as its education, meant that the North generally reacted negatively to these intrusions. Indeed by 1960, the year of independence, European-style education in the country was still hopelessly out of balance. The South had 842 secondary schools whilst the North could only muster 41.[17] This state of affairs had created two anomalies, both of which added to ethnic and tribal divisions, and can be seen as major causes of tribal friction, which was one of the important factors in the civil war. The first was that as the country drew closer to independence so more and more government jobs were Nigerianised, at the expense of the European community. Generally the only people competent and capable of fulfilling these roles were from the South, those indeed who had received a European-style education. Many of these Southerners increasingly took up professional careers in the North. Under equal conditions these jobs would have been taken by Northerners, but because of the lack of European-style education in the North they were simply not available. Indeed it is interesting to note that the North was reluctant to expunge its European workforce knowing that it would have to replace them with Nigerians from the South. The second anomaly, caused by the North's unwillingness to encompass European education, was one of simple jealous misunderstanding, leading many Northerners to fear the encroachment of Southerners into northern Nigeria, changing, usurping and taking over their lifestyles. This also affected the economic structure and the distribution of wealth in the North. By being better educated, Southerners assumed many of the professional and administrative opportunities at the expense of the less well-educated Northerners. This meant that Southerners, in these roles, tended to have higher remuneration than those Northerners in more menial forms of employment. These factors led to a series of unrests and uprisings culminating in the 1966 pogrom essentially against the Igbo Southerners from the east by educationally disadvantaged Northerners.

Colonial control

The European slave trade had begun in an unambitious way. In 1485 Pope John II gave the people of San Tomé the right to trade with the Benin Empire.[18] San Tomé, which proved difficult to settle, suffered from an acute labour shortage. However, Benin had an ample supply of labour and found it extremely profitable to supply people to San Tomé, thus fulfilling a simple economic need. It was then discovered that the gold merchants of Elmina were prepared to pay twice the price for slaves exported from Benin. This was the first step in the establishment of the export trade of people to the Americas, initially to the south, then to the Caribbean and finally to the north. It is estimated that during the next three hundred and fifty years some twenty-four million people suffered this ruthless trade which led to the tragic deaths of nine million people.[19]

For the Society for the Abolition of the Slave Trade, 1807 was a year to celebrate, but in southern Nigeria it gradually left the infrastructure of shipping fleets, agents and middle men without a commodity in which to trade. However, changing industrial and economic conditions in Britain and Europe meant increasing demand for soap as well as for vegetable oils, the best of which was palm oil.[20] The move from the slave trade to the palm oil trade in what became the Oil River States of southern Nigeria was fairly swift.

By 1860 this trade had expanded in the Delta region to £1,000,000 per annum,[21] leading to continuous friction between British traders and also to ongoing raids by the indigenous population. Furthermore, the French and Germans had started to take an active interest in trade on the Niger. Goldie Taubman, an ex-British Army officer, had been sent out to Nigeria by his family to manage a near bankrupt palm-oil trading company, called Holland and Jacques.[22] Holland and Jacques changed its name to the Central African Trading Company and by 1879 Goldie, who had conveniently dropped his German sounding surname, had amalgamated three competitive rivals into the United Africa Company. He had achieved this by convincing his competitors of two facts. Firstly, that they could sustain their production of palm oil and protect it from the vagaries of world market prices by joining forces and controlling the price they paid to the African producers and middlemen. The world price for vegetable oils had fallen as supplies from West Africa and other sources had increased. Secondly, he persuaded them that it was a way of countering increasing competition from French trading companies.

George Goldie was ambitious to expand his company's interest and keep control of trade in Nigeria. Goldie argued that 'with old established markets closing in our many factories, with India producing cotton fabrics not only for her own use but for export, it would be suicidal to abandon to our rival powers the only great remaining underdeveloped opening for British goods'.[23] His main fear was of competition from the French and he was concerned that the French government would annex the middle and lower Niger to give their traders a monopoly. Goldie's plan was that his company would take over the middle and lower Niger providing that the British government grant him a royal charter for his company. The company would then control this large territory as a monopoly and as a private colony. Goldie also had ambitions over the Sokoto Empire in Northern Nigeria, where he believed further rich trading opportunities were to be gained. His company already depended on trade in ivory and shea butter (a kind of margarine) from the Islamic kingdom of Nupe.

In 1886 Goldie had his request granted, and his renamed Niger Company gained its royal charter, which had been granted because of strong French colonial ambitions and also Germany's late volte-face with regard to colonies. In the meantime, although Sir George Goldie, as he became, had his charter company he was still vulnerable to French competition and the duplicitous indigenous rulers. Britain therefore agreed to fund a military force to protect the Royal Niger Company. The formation of the West African Frontier Force in 1898 was put under the command of Captain Frederick Lugard, a brave, diminutive, upper-class Englishman, who had found a degree of dubious fame in East Africa over his dealings with other competing colonial powers.[24]

In 1900, the British government took over responsibility for the Royal Niger Company's territories, and in the process formed the Protectorate of Northern Nigeria, the Niger Coast Protectorate and the Lagos Colony Protectorate territories. It is interesting to note that Goldie was well compensated for the loss of his company's charter status. The company was paid £450,000 plus a royalty on minerals from the company's former territory for a period of 99 years.[25] In view of the British Government's parsimoniousness, its changed attitude to its responsibilities was surprising, until one looks at the revenues that were being generated from all three areas. In the first six months of 1888 the palmoil trade was worth £1,172,840,[26] of which over half was in the hands of British traders, and much of the trade was going through Lagos, thus making the territory economically self-sustaining. However, more important at the time was the fact that France exercised direct colonial control, whereas Britain, in the interest of financial frugality, exercised indirect control, through Goldie's chartered company. It was this element of vulnerability which determined that Britain should exercise direct control over the West African Frontier Force and Sir George Goldie's independence, in order to counter French colonial ambitions.

In 1900 Sir Frederick Lugard, as he had now become, was appointed to the important post of high commissioner for the Protectorate of Northern Nigeria. His resources for subjugating this vast new territory were severely limited. This, and the parsimony of his political masters, determined the style of his rule over this territory. He interfered as little as possible with the social structure of his vast new territory and fostered a policy of indirect rule. For example, he allowed Muslim law to run alongside British law as a dual system. Also, in agreement with the Caliph of Sokoto, he excluded Christian missionaries so that there would be limited interference with the Muslim religion. Of course his resources in manpower and equipment may have been limited, but in the words of Hilaire Belloc:

Whatever happens we have got
The Maxim gun and they have not.[27]

Unfortunately the indirect rule approach, although laudable at the time, meant that in the future when Nigeria became independent it would help to foster the divisiveness which was to have such a devastating effect in the years leading up to the civil war. At the time, Lugard's prime objective was to create and protect trade, because the perceived wisdom was that colonial activity was only good if the new territory was financially viable and indeed could add value to Britain's commercial power. As it happened, Northern Nigeria was hopelessly insolvent commercially and had to rely on subsidies from the South to balance its books. Indeed when Lugard was appointed the country's first Governor General in 1912 he actually amalgamated the exchequers of both areas and he made the South contribute the North's deficit from alcohol duty.

Not only had Lugard's control of Northern Nigeria created the right atmosphere to induce divisiveness in the future, but it also fostered much hatred and distrust between the peoples. On his appointment as Governor General of the whole country he decided to keep the country split as two administrative zones, the North and the South. He refused to listen to the advice of others who proposed that the administration of Nigeria would be better served if it were split into more than two regions. One suggestion was for four areas: North, Central, West and East. The other was for five regions: the Hausa States, the Chad Territory, the Benue Provinces, the Western Provinces and the Eastern Provinces.[28] If he had heeded this advice it is much more likely that as indigenous political aspirations began to grow, although potentially regionalized, they would have had a greater national flavour and would not have been as enmeshed in ethnicity and religion as they became, with such disastrous results. It seems that Lugard was determined to administer the country simply as two units, firstly because he did not want to break up the rule in the North which he had so successfully instigated, but secondly because he planned his administration as a continuous one and did not want a break because of his absences when back in Britain.

Although there were many positive aspects to Lugard's rule, on balance he helped create and left behind a country which would be ill-prepared to cope with the rigours of self-government in the future. Not only had he refused to listen to the advice to have more than two administrative areas, which may well have paved the way for better government, but by curtailing the spread of missionary activity in Northern Nigeria, he hindered the spread of western-style education in the North. As the North had many fewer educated people than the South, and as Nigerians took over from Europeans, it was only natural that these vacancies were filled by those educated people who mainly came from the South. This meant that in the years before the civil war there were tens of thousands of Southern, mainly Eastern, Nigerians working in the North. Arguably this caused resentment and friction between the better paid Southerners and the less well-off Northerners who had had to accept much of the menial work.

Education also played its part in Lugard's efforts at indirect rule in the South. Missionaries had encouraged the growth of education in the South and had promoted further education in Britain for their brighter protégés; indeed the freed slave Samuel Crowther, who later became Bishop of the Niger, was an early example.[29] Lugard's attempts at indirect rule were somewhat thwarted by western-educated people who questioned Britain's presence in the country, such as Herbert Macaulay, the grandson of Bishop Crowther and founder of the first nationalist party in 1923.[30] Indeed in the East, where there had been no heritage of chieftain rule, there was a history of democracy emanating upwards from the villages, and indirect rule was found to be very difficult. Lugard appointed government chiefs, known as warrant chiefs, in the areas. These were anathema to the Igbo people, who conclusively rejected them.

1913 saw the amalgamation of Nigeria into three administrative areas: the crown colony of Lagos and the Protectorates of Northern and Southern Nigeria. Initially from this period, especially in the South, a gradual political consciousness and unity developed. Southerners were especially adept at absorbing western-style education, and this meant that a new professional class of people came into being, outside of tribalism. By being mainly excluded from the European administration, but indoctrinated with European ideals of political freedom, this class became politically aware in the new country, indeed questioning the very reason for European presence in their country. Embryo nationalism was created following protests in 1908 over the imposition of a general rate to fund new water schemes in Lagos.[31] The most outspoken critic of the British presence in Nigeria came from the aforementioned Herbert Macaulay who, on 24 June 1923, formed with his colleagues the Nigerian National Democratic Party (NNDP). Its initial aims sought municipal status and self-government for Lagos, together with plans for national compulsory primary education, as well as secondary education facilities and the Nigerianisation of the civil service. Opposition to Macaulay and his party mainly came from students at King's College Lagos, who formed the Lagos Youth Movement in 1934. This movement was strengthened three years later with the arrival of Dr Nnamdi Azikiwe, who had trained in America and had successfully run a newspaper in the Gold Coast for three years. However, these early political aspirations centred on gaining political power at town council level. It was not until 1944, when Britain and America signed the Atlantic Charter, which confirmed the right of self-determination by people for control of their homelands, that political awareness took on a greater national and nationalistic fervour. In 1946 under the terms of a new constitution, a national legislature, together with three regional assemblies, was brought into being. 1945 saw the first meeting of the National Council of Nigerians and Cameroons (NCNC), with Herbert Macaulay as president and Nnamdi Azikiwe as secretary. Interestingly Macaulay was a Yoruba and Azikiwe an Igbo. The NCNC was not a political party as such but represented all people who had an interest in Nigeria obtaining internal self-government within the British Empire.[32] However, tribal unity in the South was to be short-lived. The Yoruba elite increasingly felt that the party, the NCNC, was being dominated by Azikiwe and his Igbo supporters, and 1951 saw the formation of the Action Group Party dominated by Yorubas from Nigeria's Western region. At its inaugural meeting it sought to 'bring and organize within its fold all nationalists in the Western Region, so that they may work together as a united group, and submit themselves to party loyalty and discipline'.[33] In order to establish itself as a serious political party it was prepared to use all modern methods of political party discipline, but, and most importantly, it also enlisted the support and help of all the traditional Yoruba leaders. This effectively made it an ethnically dominated party. With the establishment of the Action Group led by Obafemi Awolowo, within the Yoruba-dominated Western Region, and the NCNC led by Nnamdi Azikiwe and mainly supported by Igbos from the East, Nigerian politics took on a distinctly regional and ethnic style. This was confirmed when the Northern leaders established the Northern Peoples' Congress (NPC) led by the Sardauna of Sokoto. Indeed following the agreement of the Macpherson Constitution,[34] which allowed for popular elections in all three regions, the establishment of Nigerian politics on ethnic lines was confirmed, with each mainly ethnic party being elected within each region. The North was to make its ethnicity even more divisive when Ahmadu Bello, the Sardauna of Sokoto, became premier of Northern Nigeria and promoted a 'Northernization Policy', whereby appointments to the Northern Nigerian Civil Service were to be given to qualified Northern Nigerians in preference to other Nigerians, and where there were none available then Europeans were to be employed.[35]

In the federal elections of 1954, it was therefore hardly surprising that the NPC won an overwhelming majority in the North, but, surprisingly, the increasingly Igbo-dominated NCNC won a majority in the West and the East. In the regional governments each dominant party continued in power with their leaders as regional premiers. With a scene increasingly set for ethnically divisive regional politics, the Nigerian constitution was revised to allow for greater internal self-government within the regions, and by 1959 all three regions enjoyed a large degree of internal autonomy, thus exacerbating divisive regional and ultimately national politics. The final federal elections in 1959, prior to independence, saw the NPC in the north win 142 seats out of 312, the NCNC from the east win 89 seats and the Action Group from the west win 73. Coalition government was to be the nature of Nigerian national politics. After much party manoeuvring the NCNC felt it would be able to control the Hausa North by cooperating with their predominant party, the NPC, rather than working with the Action Group from the West.

Post-independence

The post-independence period was dominated by the other two regions' fear of the power of the North, and also by the realisation that political power meant absolute power both legally and economically, by political wrangling within one of the major parties and finally by patronage and corruption. Furthermore, a rigged census did much to damage the integrity of the first administration. The break-up of the Action Group party, and its fragmenting into two parties due to ideological differences, and the jockeying for power, also undermined the electorate's confidence in their political masters. By independence the country was only a federation in name; in reality it was a country of semi-autonomous regions ruled by political parties who enjoyed enormous patronage and power. In the East and West the parties, with their power of patronage, secured absolute support, especially from the emerging middle-class professionals. Each region, which meant each regional government, had control over the regional banks and the marketing boards and many other economic activities; this meant that jobs, marketing board licences, loans and government contracts were given to party supporters, and to members of government ministers' extended families. Secession was never far from regional government thought, especially in the North. Minority interests were ignored and draconian methods were used to quell unrest. Elections were rigged; violence and anarchy were openly tolerated. Not atypical of the times was the man who appeared in court on a charge of intimidation and on being asked by the judge for his profession, replied: 'A daily paid thug, sir'.[36]

Under British rule, the loyalty of the elite members of the indigenous population had been rewarded with lucrative government contracts, but the bulk of commercial activity remained and was to remain under British and European control, even after independence. Also, prior to independence, there had been great discrepancy between the terms and conditions of employment for expatriate and local employees doing the same job. Post-independence, the indigenous employees, now finding they were in control, awarded themselves the same perquisites as had been taken for granted by the expatriate community. However, because much of the commercial power of the country remained firmly in British and European hands, most of these jobs were in the public domain, and as under the old colonial system, when they had been awarded to loyal elite indigenous servants, these were now awarded to the extended family and the party faithful who supported those politicians in power, but the 'national cake' had been seriously diminished. Therefore the power and patronage of the political parties and leaders took on a new significance. The British, being concerned for their commercial investment in the country (after all that was their raison d'être for being in the country in the first place), concerned themselves with ensuring that they left the country in a 'safe pair of hands'. Although they had had no control over the make-up of the country's population, it was seen to be to their great advantage that the North, being the most populated area, would have the largest presence in the federal assembly and therefore would be likely to control the first post-colonial government, albeit with coalition partners.[37] The North and its rulers were considered by the British to be more quiescent, amenable and supportive of Britain and her post-colonial role in Nigeria. Ever since Lugard's time, when he had instituted indirect rule, the British had relied on the support of the North's leaders in return for a large degree of autonomy. When Britain departed she left the country in the hands of the Northern-dominated NPC, with Sir Abubakar Tafawa Balewa as Prime Minister, but, because of the democratic rules, this was within a coalition with the NCNC and its leader Dr Nnamdi Azikiwe, who accepted the role of Governor General. The third national party, under the leadership of Chief Awolowo, found itself in opposition to the other two main parties, and took on the role of the official opposition. Awolowo led his party in parliament and delegated leadership of the western government to his deputy Chief Akintola, who took on the role of premier of the Western Region. This however created an imbalance as far as the Western Region was concerned. It was felt that the 'national cake' was unfairly in the hands of the two parties who were in government and that the official opposition was missing out on patronage. Indeed having gained power the two parties in government were keen to see that the status quo remained.

It was at this point that Chief Akintola as the Western Region's premier sought a political alliance with the ruling NPC.

As Eskor Toyo, the veteran trade union leader, so aptly put it, in a pamphlet entitled *Nigerian Soldier Peace and Future:*

> Here were two groups of Yoruba feudal and capitalist leaders. The first led by Akintola wanted the Action Group to join the Federal Government of Balewa in order that the Yoruba Chiefs and business-men might share in the Federal 'chop chop'. Why should that Federal 'chop chop' or the 'national cake' as the capitalists call it, be enjoyed only by the Ibos and the Hausas and Fulanis? Why should Awolowo allow this to happen?[38]
>
> The second group led by Awolowo did not want to join the Balewa Government merely to share in the Federal 'chop chop' but wanted to expand the Action Group in the other regions, build up its power among the people, use it to unseat the NPC-NCNC coalition gov-ernment and grab the whole of the Federal 'chop'. This line would need more patience; it would require fighting for more democracy so as to reach the people especially in the former Northern Region and carry them along. But in the end would yield more profit. Why, after all, must the capitalists of Nigeria and their professional and intellectual supporters and leaders with their more modern and pro-gressive outlook share power as minor partners with the conservative emirs, the conservative obas, and other 'elders' in the Yoruba land and elsewhere? Why should the capitalists, led by the Action Group, have all the power in their hands? So reasoned the Awolowo faction of the Action Group. Since the feudal emirs did not want to yield their power over the common people in the former Northern Region to the Action Group, and since the Ibo business wealth grabbers of the NCNC and their intellectual and professional allies similarly would not permit the far-sighted Yoruba business wealth grabbers and their professional and intellectual allies organized in the Action Group to capture their empire in the former Eastern Region from them, the NPC and the NCNC joined hands together and helped Akintola to split the Action Group and try to crush it, as it was impossible for him to capture it or to stay in it.[39]

The crisis came to a head in 1962 when Awolowo gained support from the executive of his party, the Action Group, and asked for the resignation of Akintola as premier of the Western Region government, and whom the party charged with maladministration, anti-party activities and gross indiscipline.[40] This followed Awolowo's attempt to steer the party in a socialist direction which Akintola and his conservative allies were set against. Also, Akintola wanted the party to be part of a national government, rather than, as Awolowo wanted, a party strong enough to determine its own destiny, and through popular and national appeal, form its own government. Unfortunately Akintola refused to resign his premiership; this resulted in physical uproar in the regional house of assembly, culminating in the Federal Government declaring a state of emergency in the West and replacing the Action Group government with its own administration. At the same time an enquiry was instigated into the mismanagement of public funds by the Action Group. Interestingly and surprisingly, although the Coker Commission found that indeed government money had been used for the benefit of the Action Group, Chief Akintola was exonerated from the misuse of public funds. However, the arrest of Awolowo along with other senior members of the party, who were charged with attempting to overthrow the Federal Government, was most damaging for Nigeria's fledgling democracy. The results were a distinct attempt by the coalition Federal Government, of the Northern and Eastern parties the NPC and the NCNC, to discredit Awolowo and to destroy the credibility of his Action Group party. Not only was Awolowo forced to defend himself, because his defence lawyer was not allowed into Nigeria, but the evidence produced by the prosecution was flimsy, dubious and full of contradictions.[41] Sadly Awolowo was found guilty and sentenced to ten years' imprisonment. Far from destroying his political career he became a martyr in the eyes of his Yoruba followers, who not unreasonably felt threatened by the seemingly unstoppable power of the North with its Eastern ally.

In the meantime, this turn of events allowed Akintola and his supporters from the Action Group to form their own breakaway party the Nigerian National Democratic Party (NNDP), and to begin overtures to the Northern NPC in order to achieve their policy of a national government. The 1962–63 census crisis culminated in Akintola and his new party being able to form a coalition with the ruling NPC. The census was of great importance to all political parties because population numbers from each region determined how many seats would be awarded to each region in the federal parliament. This was an extremely sensitive issue where Nigerian politics were concerned, given the ethnic divide of the country and its political divide on regional lines. The census showed a 200 percent rise in the population within a decade.[42] This figure was so obviously inflated that the Federal Prime Minister, Sir Abbakar Tafawa Balewa, ordered a recount. Sadly, the second count did not fare much better and more importantly the new figures showed that, if the NPC party were to gain the majority of allocated seats in the North, it could form a government in the federal parliament, without the support from one of the other political parties from the other two regions. This was totally insupportable as far as the government's Eastern Region partner, the NCNC, was concerned. However, Balewa declared, 'I am advised that my acceptance and publication of these figures is final'.[43] Being unacceptable to his coalition partners, it resulted in the break-up of the government alliance between the NPC and the NCNC.

The census debacle was quickly followed by federal elections in which the NPC sought a new and potentially compliant partner in the form of Akintola and his new NNDP. Not only had Awolowo's downfall enabled Akintola to form a new party but it had opened the way for him to achieve his ambition of forming a national government. Furthermore, the census results had created conditions where the North was prepared to make overtures to him, to the detriment of the East's NCNC. As the leader of the NPC, the Sardauna of Sokoto stated 'even if my party fails to get the required majority in the next federal elections, it will definitely not enter a coalition with the NCNC ... . The Igbos have never been friends of the North and never will be.'[44] The Nigerian National Alliance (NNA) was duly formed between the Sardauna's NPC and Akintola's NNDP. It is also interesting to note that at this point the new Nigerian National Alliance also attracted support from the Delta Region, in the East but outside of Igboland, in the form of the Niger Delta Congress and the Dynamic Party.[45] Not to be outdone over this new alignment in Nigerian politics, the NCNC formed an alliance with the Action Group to create another new party, the United Progressive Grand Alliance (UPGA). Opposition Northern and Middle Belt parties also joined this new Southern alliance.

The ensuing federal elections were fought in the most brutal manner. Each party used all and any means to ensure that they were victorious. Physical attacks were not uncommon, and the police were used regularly to intimidate opposition candidates. Tribalism and ethnicity entered the arena in a conclusive way. Not only had the Sardauna of Sokoto denigrated the Igbo people, but his party's election methods in the Northern region used trumped-up charges and arrested, and in some cases kid-napped, opposition candidates. Having control of the election machinery and feeling threatened that they, the UPGA, could potentially lose seats in the East, they refused to take part in the election. The result was a victory for the NNA, but the UPGA refused to admit defeat. So serious was the stalemate that the Igbo president of the federation, Dr Nnamdi Azikiwe, was prevailed upon to nullify the election. Indeed both sides considered taking members of the police and armed forces into their confidence in order to take control of the federation. There is evidence that Lt-Col. Odumegwu Ojukwu, the future leader of the breakaway state of Biafra, had approached Dr Azikiwe with a plan for the UPGA to take over the country with military support.[46] Finding, that as president of the federation, he did not have the authority to order the army to support him in nullifying the election, Dr Azikiwe asked the NNA to form a government. Interestingly, and probably by way of compromise, two NCNC elected members who were close to the new NNA government were brought in as ministers. However the election, in spite, or because, of the East failing to take part, had confirmed the ascendant and potential stranglehold position of the North in Nigerian politics. It also confirmed the divisive, tribalistic and uncompromising nature of the country's politics and showed how narrowly the country averted a total breakdown and reversion to regionalism and potential secession. Both sides had contemplated secession during the campaign.[47] These actions had also brought the military into the political arena for the first time.

No sooner had the acrimonious federal elections taken place than regional elections were due in the West. Akintola, who was now an important minister in the newly formed Federal Government, was determined that his national party and Federal Government party, which was a coalition of the North and his Western breakaway party from the West's Action Group, should win. Although Chief Awolowo, the former leader of the Action Group, was safely locked away, he remained extremely popular in the West, and many in that region felt that Akintola had sold out to the North, in order to pursue his own political ambitions. The election was violent, acrimonious and rigged, and resulted in a victory for Akintola and the NNDP. Within hours of Akintola being asked by the regional governor to form a government, violence erupted across the region by Action Group supporters who felt Akintola was a traitor to their party. It is also noteworthy that at this time Mr Eyo Esua, the Electoral Commission

Chairman, admitted that there had been serious malpractice during the regional election.

He said:

> It was a notorious fact that some electoral officers refused to accept nomination papers of certain candidates, or failed to report for duty. Some, in fact, after accepting nominations of the candidates of one particular party, thereafter deserted their posts before all other candidates in their constituency had a chance of filing their nomination papers.[48]
>
> The people of Western Nigeria now realized that they had lost their only opportunity under the constitution of getting a government of their choice in the region. They also knew that the Federal Government was most unlikely to shift its stand on the issue. The ultimate result was a serious outbreak of rioting and violence throughout the region which spread gradually towards Lagos.[49]

Mayhem ensued in the West. Between August 1965 and January 1966 it was estimated that two thousand people had been killed.[50] Many people felt embittered towards the federal alliance of Balewa and Akintola. Although asked to declare a state of emergency in the Western Region, the Federal Government did not react and indeed towards the end of 1966 ordered the withdrawal of troops from the streets of the West. Maybe it felt that the election irregularities had affected the troops' loyalty; many indeed had UPGA sympathies, with others supporting the NNA. However, the Federal Government appears to have been deeply concerned about the situation because it appears that, in a meeting, the Federal Prime Minister and his party leader the Sardauna of Sokoto proposed a military takeover of the Western region. First they sought the removal of the military commander General Ironsi by sending him on leave, and then they proposed the appointment of an NNA-supporting commander, Brigadier Sam Ademulegun , to lead the offensive. The ominous title of 'Operation no mercy' was to be used.[51] There were also indications that the Federal Government and the North were tiring of Akintola's inability to bring peace to his region.

According to the publication *The African Concord* of 9 October 1989, 'Records say that the Sardauna was embarrassed at Akintola's presence in Kaduna a day before he died but would not ward him off. Even the greater part of the authorities in Kaduna felt the Western Regional crisis and the Sardauna's romance with Akintola was in a mess.'[52]

The operation was due to take place on Monday 17 January 1966. Apparently being aware of it, the 'five majors' struck on 15 January 1966.

Instabilities in the post-colonial period and the two coups

There had been rumours of a coup in early 1966, with the Western Region in open revolt and the Eastern Regional government disaffected, but there had been little to warn the administration of a revolt by the army. Indeed in the constitutional crisis of December 1964 several, mainly Igbo, lieutenant-colonels, including Ojukwu, had talked of military intervention, but the plans were still-born.[53] The army of 8,000 members was small compared to the population size of Nigeria, and was generally regarded as loyal.[54] In 1965, in spite of there being senior officers with greater skill and potential, Johnson Aguyi-Ironsi, who was an Igbo, had been chosen as the first Nigerian officer to take over from the outgoing British commander. The Prime Minister could have chosen a Northern colleague to assume the role, but his trust in the loyalty of the army was such that the commander's job went to Ironsi. Undoubtedly the government was extremely unpopular with many in the country at the time especially Southerners. It had also gained an unenviable reputation for corruption and slavish loyalty to Britain.

This was reflected in an issue of *The Daily Times*; Peter Pan's section, entitled 'letter to a grandchild' said, 'Any school boy of ten would tell why our first experiment failed. The boy would invariably give two reasons. He would for the first reason say there was bribery and corruption and for the second, he would mention rigging of elections.'[55]

Other immediate reasons were the 1962 Action Group and parliamentary crisis, the 1962–3 census crisis, the 1964 Federal election crisis, and the 1965–66 Western region election crisis, all previously described: added to these were the Tiv minority riots in 1960–61 and 1964–65, both being ruthlessly suppressed, and the quota system in the army, favouring the recruitment of Northern Nigerians which allowed for political bias and patronage. These together with the underlying historic causes of ethnicity, religious diversity, British divisive rule and political instabilities after the colonial period, all added up to the potential for coups and revolution.

The coup, when it came, was seemingly well planned by a group of idealistic mainly Igbo army officers. In Kaduna and Ibadan it secured complete success, but in Lagos the coup was defeated. In Enugu, in the East, the plan failed, as it did in the Mid-West, where in fact no soldiers were stationed. It seems that the aim had been to take over the Mid-West once the East had been subdued. However the coup had succeeded in removing many of the leaders of government, including the Prime Minister, the Sardauna of Sokoto and Chief Akintola.

The leader of the coup declared:

> Our enemies are the political profiteers, the swindlers, the men in high places that seek bribes and demand ten percent, those that seek to keep the country divided permanently so that they remain in office as ministers and VIPs, the tribalists, the nepotists, those that make the country big for nothing before the international circle, those that have corrupted our society and put the Nigerian calendar backward.[56]

Major Nzeogwu, one of the coup's leaders, then went on to say:

> Like good soldiers, we are not promising you anything miraculous or spectacular. But what we do promise every law-abiding citizen is freedom from fear and all forms of oppression, freedom from general inefficiency and freedom to live and strive in every field of human endeavour, both nationally and internationally. We promise that you will no longer be ashamed to say that you are Nigerian.[57]

The coup, 'Operation Damissa', failed, but at its outset it was welcomed by most Nigerians, and if the words of its leader are to be believed it was laudable in its objectives. It was after all only expressing what most educated Nigerians had felt for very long time. It is interesting to note that the coup brought an almost immediate halt to civil disturbances. There were conflicting rumours that had the coup succeeded, the leaders were to release the Western Yoruba leader, Chief Awolowo, who had been imprisoned in 1962, and hand the reins of government to him. But the coup had failed, and although it had been declared in the name of the Nigerian army, it had left its forces extremely divided. In the event, however, it was the army which took power.

Ironsi, the officer commanding the army, had escaped the coup, and was able to assume control. There were in fact conflicting reports that he had been due to be eliminated, but he subsequently came to be associated with the members of the coup, and became implicated in it. His position, however, was extremely precarious, and although the rebels had failed in their attempt, Ironsi was careful to take account of the rebels' demands. He interned them when captured, but made very slow moves to prosecute them. The fact was that the coup's popularity made it very difficult for Ironsi to know which policy to pursue to secure the country's future. His policies proved to be not dissimilar from the aims and objectives of the coup leaders, but his big weakness was his maladroitness in exercising them. Nzeogwu stated just after the coup, 'after all we have now got to get experts to do the job rather than profiteers';[58] Ironsi followed a similar policy of keeping politicians out of government and of creating an administrative rather than a political government. Both men were part of a small and rapidly depleted group, because of the coup, who were less well-educated and certainly less experienced at running large organisations than their civilian peers, and were therefore wary of power-sharing with other groups. Ironsi was a very ordinary and loyal soldier of average ability and he was certainly no politician. He had had a limited education, and during the Second World War he had been an ordnance clerk. His experiences had not instilled in him much political tact, a weakness which was probably to be his undoing over enacting decree number 34, at the end of his tenure.[59] He had a reputation for hard drinking and intrigue, but being an ex-ranker he was able to identify with the common soldier. These attributes probably saved his life when the coup leaders struck, and enabled him to secure the loyalty of troops in most parts of the army. Interestingly Major Hassan Katsina, who was to become governor of the Northern region during Ironsi's regime, initially sided with the rebels. When Major Nzeogwu, the coup leader arrived at his house, armed, he was asked, 'Which side are you on? Are you with me or are you with them?' Hassan Katsina replied, 'Don't bother I'm on your side.'[60]

Lt.-Colonel Ojukwu who was to lead the secessionist government, and was stationed in the North, sided with Ironsi at the time of the first coup. With Nzeogwu failing to gain the vital support of Ojukwu, his position became more isolated and precarious. Ironsi, having secured the loyalty of much of the army especially in the South, in Lagos, was able to gain Nzeogwu's surrender, but only after guaranteeing the safety of all coup participants, as well as guarantees of immunity from legal proceedings against them, and most importantly an affirmation that those people removed from power would not be reinstated. Although the coup leaders were not prosecuted, the dilemma for the Ironsi regime was what to do with them. This was to become an increasingly important issue during Ironsi's rule. The coup leaders were very popular in the South, but in the North feelings about the coup were varied and potentially volatile. It was widely felt in the North, as time went on, that this had been an Igbo-inspired coup; six of the seven coup leaders were Igbo or of Igbo origin, only one was Yoruba,[61] and the Ironsi regime's lack of political will to bring the plotters to trial was to be one of the causes of the North's counter-coup. Ironsi's next move was to call a meeting of the remaining members of the government in order to validate his army orders. The challenge for Ironsi was that he could not ensure the ongoing loyalty of his officers unless he took control of the country.

Unquestionably the coup had wiped away the old order. The Sardauna of Sokoto, the feudalistic and autocratic leader of the North, was dead, as was his subordinate, the Federal Prime Minister, Tawafa Balewa. Chief Akintola was also killed; he had been accused of vote rigging, not only in federal elections but also in the Western regional elections, and had been seen by many Yoruba as a traitor to his people. Chief Okotie-Eboh, who had been seen as portraying the worst side of political power, with excessive shows of luxury, greed and corruption, had also been eliminated, as well as many others who had displayed the excesses of the first republic.

On 27 January 1966, the *Nigerian Morning Post* ran the caption 'Bribe? E Done Die. Chop-Chop-E No Dey' ('Bribery is dead. Corruption is not there').[62]

There are conflicting accounts as to whether Ironsi was invited to take over the government or whether he simply demanded that he take control. He allocated political responsibility to only six of his senior officers, having formed a Supreme Military Council, together with a Federal Executive Council. Both councils consisted of military personnel together with the Inspector General of Police and the Attorney General. Advice from civil servants was sought on an ad hoc basis at the federal level, but in the regions civil servants sat on the executive councils and took part in the decision-making process, and the former civilian governors were appointed to advise the new military rulers. The two appointments which were later to have dramatic consequences were Lt-Colonels Gowon and Ojukwu. Ojukwu was appointed military governor of the Eastern Region, based in Enugu in Igboland, and Gowon was appointed Chief of Staff to the army based in Lagos.

Initially Ironsi's regime started on a high note. The old corrupt order had gone, he had promised to consult with the people on the country's future style of government and he resolved to dismantle his military regime as soon as possible. He also allowed the effective civil service to carry on its work unhindered by corrupt politicians. The police force, although fully stretched during the first coup, was allowed to carry on policing the country without military interference. All political appointees were removed from public office and investigations into politicians' probity were instituted. So what went wrong? Within seven months Ironsi was dead and his regime had been superseded by another military regime.

There appear to have been two strands of political pressure during Ironsi's rule.

There were those radically inspired people, mainly from the South, but also including some Northern intellectuals, who were keen to see a centralised and unitary form of government. Others, and these predominated in the North, wished for a looser federation with a high degree of regional autonomy. There was a further smaller group who represented the minority tribes, who felt that some local autonomy was necessary together with control from the centre, in order that their position be protected from the more powerful regions. These minority tribes were from the Middle Belt and from the Eastern Region, including the River States.

Unfortunately, as soon as Ironsi took over, his administration began to move towards a unitary form of government. Arguably, this was only natural coming from a man who had spent his whole working life in a rigid and firmly hierarchical organisation. In fact he knew no other way to operate and probably felt that the only way to run the country was very much the way he ran the army. Indeed he treated the military regional governors as junior officers.[63] A naïve instinct, although a natural one, when one appreciates that they were very much his juniors not only within the army's structure but also in age and experience.

The catalyst that set in motion the series of events which led to the second coup can probably be attributed to two factors. First was Ironsi's intent to establish a unitary government. He initiated this by appointing another Igbo, Francis Nwokedi, to a one-man commission of enquiry to look into 'the establishment of administrative machinery for a united Nigeria, and the unification of the five public services and judicial services in Nigeria'.[64] Although a second Igbo was appointed to the commission, which satisfied nobody, the enquiry posed serious issues which, if implemented, could undermine the autonomy of the regions. There was no suggestion that this was a consultative commission, and the inference was that its findings could be implemented without further consultation or approval. At the same time a Commission on Constitutional Reform was set up. In this case its findings and implementation were due to be approved by a referendum. Ironsi then introduced his financial budget at the end of March 1966 and in it he spoke of his conviction that most people wanted a unitary government. Secondly, Ironsi did nothing to placate the Northern soldiers over their loss of colleagues in the first coup. The perpetrators, although incarcerated, were not brought to justice and were not investigated over their actions in January 1966. On top of this they continued to receive their army pay. These actions hardly reassured the conservative Northerners, including the Northern soldiers who made up seventy percent of the army's strength and those from the middle classes in the North who formed the regional civil service.

Sulemanu Takuma, a Northerner, made some telling comments in a letter to the press in April 1966:

with regards to the constitution, much has been written on the dangers and disasters brought on us by Federalism, and the few who have the privilege to write to the papers have even gone to the extent of forcing 'Unitary' Government on us without ascertaining the wishes of the people .... One sad fact which these journalists as well as some of the Military top advisers refuse to admit is that a Nigerian unitary government does not necessarily unite the people of Nigeria ... I say bluntly that nothing short of 'Federalism' is good for Nigeria.

He also commented on the coup of 15 January 1966, writing 'those who subsequently assumed power have so far failed to do anything to the mutineers and possibly, the alleged civilian brains behind such a mutiny'.[65]

On 24 May 1966 Ironsi broadcast to the nation and introduced his infamous decree number 34. He declared 'the former regions are abolished, and Nigeria grouped into a number of territorial areas called provinces. ... Nigeria ceases to be what has been described as a federation. It now becomes simply the Republic of Nigeria.'[66] The North, feeling threatened by the potential of further Southern and essentially Igbo incursion into their sovereignty, instigated severe and violent civil unrest, centred on attacks on the Igbo population. Although Ironsi attempted to placate the North by embarking on a tour of Northern cities, culminating in

an address he was to make to a Natural Rulers Conference in Ibadan
on 28 July 1966, a Northern military mutiny broke out on the evening
of 28 July 1966. Ironsi and his host Lt-Col. Fajuyi were arrested at
Government Lodge in Ibadan. Their whereabouts and their subsequent
deaths were not to be officially acknowledged for another six months.
The counter-coup appeared to be Northern led, and quickly spread to
Kano and Kaduna. The remaining senior officer, Brigadier Ogundipe,
attempted to negotiate with the rebels, but when his efforts failed he
handed his command to Lt-Col. Gowon, the army's chief of staff, who
also attempted to bring the rebellion under control. After fierce discussion with a rather hot-headed and unpredictable Northern officer,
Murtala Mohammed, it was accepted that Gowon should take charge
and attempt to bring a semblance of stability back to the country's anarchic and lawless state.

The two military leaders

Lt-Col. Yakubu Gowon, a Northerner, but a Christian, and thus acceptable to most soldiers, became de facto leader of Nigeria in tumultuous
and potentially anarchic conditions. Not only was the North considering
secession, but the West, under the political leadership of Chief Awolowo,
who had been released from prison by the previous military regime, was
also considering its position. Added to this, the East was feeling increasingly vulnerable to Northern attack because of increasing anti-Igbo sentiment shown in the second coup and by subsequent physical attacks in
Hausaland. This was to lead to the mass exodus of most Igbo people from
the North, many of whom had lived there for many generations. Added
to this, Lt-Col. Ojukwu, the military governor of the Eastern Region,
who had been appointed by the previous military regime, not only had
military control of the region but his political position in the region was
on the ascendant, and he was not prepared to accept Lt-Col. Gowon as
supreme commander of the army, let alone head of state. As he stated,
'Militarily Gowon is not my superior and the question of acknowledging
him does not arise'.[67] Ojukwu's unwillingness to accept Gowon's de facto
position and their deteriorating relationship was to be an important factor
which led to the outbreak of the civil war. Consequently Gowon's position was tenuous and extremely precarious. Gowon also made a somewhat
ambivalent announcement to the nation, when he told the country what

had happened when announcing that he had taken control:

> As a result of the recent event and the other previous similar ones, I
> have come to strongly believe that we cannot honestly and sincerely
> continue in this wise, as the basis for trust and confidence in our
> unitary system of government has been unable to stand the test of
> time. Suffice to say that putting all considerations to the test, polit-
> ical, economic as well as social, the base for unity was not there, or
> is badly rocked not only once but several times.[68]

Did this mean that the federation was no longer a feasible option or did
he simply mean that unitary government was not the way forward? His
speech was to lead to much speculation. Finally Gowon found the postur-
ing of his highly volatile Northern colleague Lt-Col. Murtala Mohammed,
who was intent on mounting an immediate invasion of the East, very difficult to contain.

By mid-September 1966 Gowon had brought the army under sufficient
control to feel that his position was less vulnerable, and to be in a position
to call an 'Ad Hoc Constitutional Conference' in Lagos. He offered the conference four options for the country's future government: a federal system
with a strong central government, a federal system with a weak centre, a
confederation, or an entirely new unproposed system. Interestingly no region
suggested secession, but a confederation was proposed by the North and the
East. Shortly afterwards the North reversed its proposal for confederation and
came down firmly on the side of federation. It would seem that the Middle
Belters, including the Tiv minority group and the army Northerners, felt
that confederation would lead to dominance once again by the traditional
Hausa-Fulani Northern rulers, and they were anxious to avoid this at all
costs. These deliberations were hastily abandoned in the light of serious
troop rioting in the North, leading once again to the slaughter of Igbos and
looting and burning of their property. This latest pogrom led to the mass
evacuation of most Igbo people from the North, during which time the
Northern government did little or nothing to contain attacks on the Igbos.

An example of the mayhem which ensued came from a fireman at
Kano, who stated that he was on duty when eight armed soldiers arrived
at the station:

> A sergeant ordered that all Easterners should raise their hands ...
> The sergeant asked us whether we could remember what happened
> on January 15th when the Prime Minister (Balewa) and the premier

of the North (the Sardauna of Sokoto) lost their lives and the Ibos were all very happy. We said, 'No, Sergeant.' Paying no heed to that he asked us to give our names and addresses and send any messages we have for our people because we were going to die. ... They drove us five miles away to the Katsina road, brought us down and started shooting us. I felt my leg shattered and fell down ... . I managed to crawl into a bush.[69]

The massacres continued throughout September and October, and Ojukwu, the East's military leader, made much play then and throughout the ensuing war about the numbers of people killed during the pogrom. Although accurate figures are impossible to obtain, accounts indicate that several thousands of Igbos lost their lives, and the idea of secession as a protective mechanism for the survival of the Igbo people took hold. In fact it is reasonable to comment that from that time onwards a confrontation between the federalists and the East was not a question of 'if' but 'when'. Indeed Ojukwu himself felt threatened, and refused to attend any more meetings of the Supreme Council. These were critical days for Nigeria's future as a nation. Its survival hung very much in the balance; not only was the East in a state of extreme insecurity but the West was feeling vulnerable to incursion by the North. At the heart of the problem was the North's reluctance to withdraw its soldiers from the Western Region. However this seems to have been eased by Gowon when he invited Chief Awolowo to be his deputy in the country's new government. This move effectively brought the Western Region firmly on to the Federal Government's side. This, together with robust support from the North's and Mid-West's military governors, meant that the Federal Government's power was in the ascendant, and Ojukwu and the East were increasingly isolated. It was not Gowon's intention to ostracize the East. Indeed he went out of his way to ensure that all Igbo civil servants who were forced out of their jobs in the North and fled to the East continued to receive their civil service pay. However matters were clearly now deteriorating towards a clash between the East's regional government and the rest of the Federation, particularly when it was discovered that a crashed plane destined for Port Harcourt in the East contained a supply of arms destined for Ojukwu's government. Gowon stated, 'If circumstances compel me to preserve the integrity of Nigeria by force, I will do my duty.'[70]

Was there an inevitability about this war? Undoubtedly from the earliest days of its inception Nigerian religious diversity created the ingredients for confrontation. This indeed was exacerbated by the first ruling Governor General's unwillingness to administer the country other than as two autonomous regions. Perhaps if he had listened to other advice, to run the country as a number of regions to cater for the needs of ethnic minorities, nationalism may have become a stronger political force and therefore ethnic politics would not have created such division within the country. It is also arguable that the Westminster style of government was inappropriate for a country with such ethnic and cultural diversity. Furthermore, the British did not help the economic development of the country except in areas which directly benefited British commercial strength and power. This meant that by the time independence arrived there was insufficient inward investment to help in the development of infrastructure. Perhaps the biggest indictment of British rule was the way it acted as 'gateman'[71] to the economic well-being of the country; this meant that whoever was in power after independence not only controlled the exchequer but all movement of funds and trade in and out of the country, much in the style of Britain's rule. This in itself led to an appalling abuse of power, which indisputably created the right atmosphere for the first coup. It was also the chronic fear of the Western and Eastern Regions of being taken over by the North which made these regions continually try to control the power of the North. Ultimately though it was the intransigence of two men, unwilling to compromise and see the other side's point of view, that led to this horrific and tragic war.

Lugard was put under enormous strain to control the country, not only because he had to subjugate the North, his job in the South having been done for him to a large extent by the Royal Niger Company and the crown colony of Lagos, but also because of financial constraints. An option to rule indirectly, through compliant rulers in the North, seemed an extremely attractive alternative to direct rule. This however came at a cost. The cost was to leave the North hopelessly behind the South educationally. This was to have a devastating effect when the time came to Nigerianise government institutions. There simply were not enough western-educated Northern Nigerians to fill the vacant posts in line with the North's population. It was therefore inevitable that rivalry and jealousy of the most appalling kind should break out in the North following the first coup. Even before that time there were incidents in the North of ethnic conflict, hardly surprising when the opportunities for advancement were seen to go to the North's ethnic rivals from the South. Not only did they grasp the government institutional jobs but they were also seen to be creating the best entrepreneurial opportunities as well as filling many of the professions. Could this have been avoided if Lugard had challenged the Northern rulers' determination to keep the region unsullied by Christianity? Logically the answer must be in the affirmative. Islamic-style education, although meritorious in its own right, was hardly a match for Western education, in view of the fact that British and by inference Nigerian institutional government was based on European traditions and its style of democracy. Questionably, Lugard's other failing was not to listen to more experienced advice, which had recommended the country be divided into a series of regions to take account of ethnic minorities. This might have allowed for a stronger voice for political nationalism, which might then have triumphed over tribalism. This argument could well have been strengthened if the North had embraced western education. The initial efforts by Herbert Macaulay and Nnamdi Azikewe were still-born after Awolowo became intent on creating a party which demanded support from the West and the Yoruba people, and showed no favour to other tribal and ethnic groups. Inevitably this led to politics taking on a distinctly ethnic and regional flavour.

Britain's reason for colonizing Nigeria had been for trade, and to stem the interference and competition from other European powers. Having developed and capitalized on this trade it was anxious to protect it, especially as independence approached. It was therefore important that it left the country in the hands of a compliant and friendly government. Having instituted the Westminster style of government she was able to hand over control to the one people through whom she had ruled the country in the North, the Hausa-Fulani. This was based simply on the fact that the North, being the most populated, had produced the most votes and therefore the most members of parliament, and thus the majority in a coalition government. However, real power was still vested in Northern rulers, especially the Sardauna of Sokoto. As *The Times* reported, after the first coup, and following the Sardauna's assassination: 'he ran his party autocratically and his administration as his personal court. To the emirs he was British interference carried to extremes ... for the emirs it meant that colonial control instituted by Lord Lugard was at last ended.'[72]

Rule by a sycophantic friendly North was very satisfactory for the British, but it hardly matched the expectations of the educated members of the population, especially from the South, who sought greater democracy for the federation. The weakness of this style of government was further compounded by the ease with which the new rulers found that they could control and spend the county's wealth. They realised early on that their interest was best served by 'the same strategy of gatekeeping that had served the colonial state'.[73] To say that they treated the excheq- uer as their own funds is no understatement; the outward ostentation and corruption of some government ministers and the abuse of power led many Nigerians to question the desirability of the first republic, and made them determined to replace it.

A further factor that must be taken into account was the physical dominance that the North exercised over the rest of the country. Not only did it cover the largest geographical area, it was the most populous, which, under the Westminster-style constitution, gave it the greatest political power, but it was also the favoured inheritor of sovereign power from Britain. Fear of crushing domination by the North encouraged both the West and the East to court her cooperation for political power. When this failed to satisfy the country's intellectual elite and growing educated middle class, and when the North's corruption and corrupt practices seemed to invade all aspects of Nigerian life, the only option was rebellion.

Undoubtedly Ironsi's decree 34, ordering the unification of the civil service and the confirmation of greater centralised government, hastened the demise of his short-lived regime and made the North determined to bring the rest of the country back under its control. Indeed, following the second coup, it was with the greatest difficulty that the newly appointed de facto head of state had restrained his Northern brother officers from overrunning and crushing the power of the East. Fear of such an invasion by the North only exacerbated the East's desire to break free from the Federation and the oppression of the North. The West also felt oppres- sion from the North, firstly because of a reluctance to withdraw Northern troops stationed in the West and secondly because of her vulnerability and isolation should the East secede from the confederation. As late as May 1967 Chief Awolowo, the Western region Yoruba leader, declared in a speech to the Western opinion-formers:

> Only a peaceful solution must be found to arrest the present wors- ening stalemate and restore normalcy. The Eastern Region must be encouraged to remain part of the Federation. If the Eastern Region is allowed by acts of omission or commission to secede from or opt

out of Nigeria, then the Western Region and Lagos must also stay out of the Federation.[74]

Finally it was the intransigence and irreconcilable differences between Gowon, the de facto leader of the Federation, and Ojukwu, the Eastern Regional governor, appointed by Ironsi, the former leader, that determined an inexorable slide towards civil war. When he assumed power Gowon's position was extremely precarious. He was only acceptable to the North because he was a Northerner, albeit a Middle Belter, and to the South because he was Christian. One of his first moves on taking power was to rescind Ironsi's decree 34, thus immediately placating the North. However his position remained tenuous, particularly in his relations with Awolowo and the West, although he did placate him by bringing him into his administration as his deputy. But it was his relationship with Ojukwu that proved intractable. For his part Ojukwu never accepted Gowon's position and refused to serve under him. He would only compromise by serving the Federation as Gowon's equal, an impossible state of affairs for controlling and running such a large and diverse country as Nigeria.

CHAPTER 3

THE PATH TO WAR AND ITS BEGINNING

Let us learn our lessons. Never, never, never believe any war will be smooth and easy, or that anyone who embarks on the strange voyage can measure the tides and hurricanes he will encounter. Once the signal is given, the statesman is no longer master of policy but the slave of the unforeseeable and uncontrollable events – all take their seats at the Council Board on the morrow of a declaration of war. Always remember, however sure that you can easily win, there would not be a war if the other man did not think he also had a chance.

Churchill, *My Early Life* (1958)

One of the effects of the second coup were the uncontrolled racial attacks on the Igbo people, which created paranoid fear, leading to a determination that the East's destiny was secession from the Federation. However it was the different interpretations by Gowon and Ojukwu of the Aburi Agreement, which engendered a breakdown in communications by both sides. The effect of Isaac Boro's declaration for independence of his people helped lead Gowon and his senior civil servants to propose and then initiate the formation of twelve separate states within the Federation. This action effectively led the Eastern Region unanimously to declare a state of secession from Nigeria. Biafra's declaration led Nigeria to declare a 'police action'[75] or 'Operation Unicord'[76] against the recalcitrant region, because many within the Federation, including the British High Commissioner, thought that Biafra would be quickly defeated and her people brought back into the Nigerian fold.[77] At the outset the Federal Government little

realised the determination of the East to defend its independence, especially against the all-invasive power of the North, and that it would fight
until recognition by the wider world would confirm its independence. The
opening stages of the conflict proved disastrous for Biafra but its brilliant
counter invasion of the Mid-West Region dramatically altered the Federal
Government's thinking on its conduct of the war. Following the result
of this invasion and its ultimate failure the war then settled into a finely
balanced contest between both sides. It was not until June 1968, that the
outside world suddenly became aware of the conflict, through the medium
of the press with its graphic pictures of 'pot-bellied' black children.

The effects of the second coup

The killing of the military Head of State, Major-General John Ironsi,
left a power vacuum within the military junta and the army hierarchy. Indeed for some days following the second coup the country was
without a government. The struggle for control of the country centred
on the army barracks at Ikeja in Lagos; here the troops were in no
mood to take orders from Northern officers, who had ostensibly instigated the second coup and the killing of Ironsi. Brigadier Ogundipe,
the most senior surviving officer within the army hierarchy, finding
he had no rank-and-file support, had gone into hiding, and Colonel
Robert Adebayo, the next most senior officer, said:

> I realised, as a Yoruba, that my people only accounted for 600 men
> within the army of 10,000, and I accepted that I would not receive
> popular army support. Conditions were extremely volatile at the
> time and the army's rank and file were in no mood to support a sen-
> ior army officer who was a Westerner. I realised how serious it was
> for the Yoruba people that so few of our people had favoured making
> the army their career, so I set about making it my business to ensure
> that many more Westerners were encouraged to come forward and
> join the army.[78]

For several days it seemed that the country would be taken over by Captain
Martin Adamu, who commanded the largest number of troops in Lagos.[79]
However, the struggle for power centred not only on this man, who had
some popular rank-and-file support but also Major Murtala Mohammed,
who sought de facto control with support from the Northern Emirs and

their politicians, as well as some Northern soldiers.[80] Neither side could agree on a power-sharing formula, and consequently a compromise candidate was sought. Lt-Col. Jack Gowon was proposed because, although he was a Northerner, he was a Christian and a member of the minority Angas people.[81] He was proposed by Colonel Robert Adebayo as a compromise candidate.[82] However, during these eventful days in Lagos, the Military Governor of the Eastern Region, Lt-Col. Emeka Ojukwu, who had been appointed by General Ironsi, was in Enugu and took no part in the activities at Ikeja barracks, and significantly had no influence in choosing a successor to the murdered former military head of state, General Ironsi, once rank-and-file military support for Ogundipe proved to be nonexistent. Gowon, the most senior Northern army officer, received support from Lt-Col. Hassan Katsina, military governor of the North, and Lt-Col. David Ejoor, military governor of the Mid-West. Gowon's support in the Western Region was precarious because the very popular military governor, Lt-Col. Fajuyi, it was assumed, had been killed accidentally in the second coup. As Kaye Whitman commented: 'At that stage nobody was admitting to Ironsi's position; it was to take six months before the Gowon administration issued statements confirming the death of Ironsi.'[83]

However, that changed when Colonel Adebayo took over that role, with the support of the Yoruba leader Chief Awolowo, who had recently been released from prison.[84]

> The Gowon government hoped to benefit from Awolowo's popularity in two ways, namely by legitimising its own policies in the Western Region and by consolidating the tentative unity of its Yoruba communities which had emerged after Awolowo's imprisonment in order to prevent further political factionalisation and conflict. Colonel Adeyinka Adebayo, the Western Region's military administrator, facilitated this process by inviting a large number of former politicians and other opinion leaders from Yoruba communities throughout the Western Region. Appealing to them to overcome past divisions, he suggested that it might be to the benefit of all if the Yoruba spoke with one voice and enjoined those present to elect a leader.[85]

It was from this point that Ojukwu's own misgivings about the unity of Nigeria took shape; in his opinion Gowon may have become de facto head of the Nigerian State, but in law he had no legal basis for that position, there being other more senior people, including himself, who should have been elected to power. Not only, as he said, did he refute Gowon's position from the legal point of view, but also the practical point of his inability to put a stop to the methodical killings of officers and men which were taking place at the Ikeja barracks three days after Gowon had been elected as supreme commander. Indeed at one point he managed to telephone Murtala Mohammed to ask him to put a stop to the killings.[86] 'When people have been subjected to a degree of inhuman violation for which there is no other word but genocide, they have a right to seek an identity apart from their aggressors.'[87]

In September 1966, after Gowon had abolished Ironsi's unification decree and reinstated the federal system which had existed before May 1966, Ojukwu made plain to the Consultative Committee of the Eastern Region his conclusion that the basis of unity no longer existed and the East should manage its own resources and its affairs, including foreign policy. Indeed the Consultative Committee gave Ojukwu the authority and the necessary measures to protect the integrity of Eastern Nigeria.[88] As Ojukwu commented:

> It was the uncertainty of Ironsi's fate that gave weight to my thoughts that the North through Gowon's concurrence was simply re-establishing its ascendency over the country and this was simply uacceptable for the people of the East, especially in view of the unabated killings of Igbo people taking place in the North at the time.[89]

Even Danjuma, the officer heavily implicated in the second coup, throws doubt on Ironsi's fate. He claims that he took no part in the killing of Ironsi and Fajuyi:

> I was detailed to go to the governor's house where Ironsi was staying and to take him into protective custody. When I reached the residence with my troops, both Ironsi and Fajuyi refused to come out of the building. My Northern troops were very agitated and were nearly out of control. They wanted to enter the building and shoot Ironsi. With the aid of a primed hand grenade I persuaded them against this, but they still manged to get inside the building and man-handled Ironsi and Fajuyi out of the building. Fajuyi was very protective of Ironsi and refused to leave him. My soldiers then insisted on stripping both men of their clothes, because they

wanted to ensure that no hidden 'Ju Ju' would protect them. I then ordered my men to put Ironsi and Fajuyi into one of our trucks and take them to a nearby jail for their safety and protection. While this was happening I could hear a 'phone ringing in the guest quarters, and I went and answered it. I am convinced that the man on the 'phone was Gowon. I think Gowon thought I was somebody else because he said that he did not want to hear about any more killings. My men then took Ironsi and Fajuyi out of the compound. I can confirm to you something I have never told anybody, that I had no hand in their killing, indeed it was my order and wish that these men should be protected.

At this point in the interview Danjuma became very emotional and it took him some time to compose himself.[90] It was to take six months after Ironsi's disappearance for the Gowon administration to confirm his death.[91]

Once Gowon had been chosen, and deemed acceptable to the majority of the army with Northern and Western affiliations, he sought help in restoring a semblance of government and control over the state. The one man he felt he could trust and to whom he could lay bare his misgivings over his momentous task was the British High Commissioner, Cumming-Bruce.[92] Appealing to him for help, he admitted that he was 'only a simple soldier' and had no experience of affairs of state, let alone taking charge of a country as diverse and fragmented as Nigeria.[93] The immediate problem facing Gowon was the total disintegration of Nigeria, initiated by the North. The North was intent on secession. It was only through the support of Cumming-Bruce and his close friendship with the Northern Emirs that Gowon was able to exert authority over the North. Cumming-Bruce was able to persuade the Emirs that secession would have been an economic disaster. As Cumming-Bruce stated:

> But it wasn't on the face of it easy to get them to change, but I managed to do it overnight. I drafted letters to the (British) Prime Minister, to send to Gowon as Nigerian Head of State, and for my Secretary of State (Michael Stewart) to send letters to each of the Emirs. I wrote an accompanying letter to each of them because I knew them personally. I drafted all these and they all came back to me duly authorised to push on at once. The whole thing was done overnight and it did the trick of stopping them dividing Nigeria up.[94]

He continued:

> Britain had no formulated policy in view of the events of the second coup and that as Britain's representative I should decide on policy as I saw fit, being the man on the spot; hence my action with the emirs. I had particularly cordial relations with the emirs because we all shared a love of polo and of course because of that we met socially and my position also meant that we met on more formal occasions. However, I had been totally unaware of an impending coup, my security people had heard of no rumours to unseat the Ironsi regime. However my relationshuip with Ironsi had always been somewhat distant, I always felt that he didn't entirely trust me, perhaps because of my personal relationship with the emirs and sultans of the North, so that was probably the reason the second coup caught me by surprise.

Of course such unilateral action, with no consultation with the other interested parties, especially Ojukwu and the East, was to have dire consequences, especially after the Aburi meeting. Such action also encouraged Gowon and his administration to accept that a federal state with strong control from the centre was the way to keep Nigeria united. It was this mindset that persuaded Gowon's senior civil servants to insist that the Aburi agreement was unworkable. Furthermore this unilateral action was to determine British, and by agreement, America's policy towards Nigeria throughout the conflict and to lead the British Government into increasingly acrimonious difficulties with its own supporters and indeed with many members of the Western European and American public. Indeed it could be argued that Cumming-Bruce's action, although laudable from where he stood at the time, in the light of future circumstances was, to say the least foolhardy, especially with regard to the longevity of the war. It could be argued that if Cumming-Bruce had not interfered, Nigeria would have fragmented into separate states, possibly as a confederation, in the style proposed by Ojukwu, and most importantly war would have been avoided. However, Cumming-Bruce was only extending British policy which had been formulated during the run-up to the country's independence: that Britain's investments[95] would be best protected if the country was left to run 'in a safe pair of hands', those of the Northern rulers.[96] The volte-face by the North confirmed for the Gowon administration that the only way of keeping Nigeria united was with strong control from the centre. By this time also, the North had appreciated that by seceding it would lose its political stranglehold over the country, a position which it had held since independence, and a position that, once secession had lost its appeal, it was determined to hold on to for the future. Such has been its determination that it still holds this position to the present day.[97] On a second meeting with Cumming-Bruce he greeted me with the comment: 'I sometimes wonder whether I did the right thing in keeping Nigeria together.'[98]

In the light of further riots in the North against the Igbo population living there, and the many killings and damage to property, which Gowon's new regime seemed powerless to stop, relations between the North and the East deteriorated. This made the Eastern ruling elite champion secession. Indeed Dr Ukpabi Asika, an Igbo from Onitsha, who was to become the Federal Government's administrator for one of Gowon's promulgated twelve states, East Central, has claimed that as early as April 1966 his Igbo colleagues were planning secession, on the grounds that unity was non-existent.[99] 'The nation teetered on the edge of disintegration .... At campus encounters, open-air bars and other informal gatherings, at which the secret service made no pretence at disguising their presence, we railed at the government's lukewarm concern for the plight of the Igbo.'[100]

Ojukwu also complained to Gowon about his inability to contain the pogroms in the North against the Igbo people living there.[101] The killings seemed systematic and organised:

> Then the killings began again, with renewed vigour, between 18 and 24 September, while the ad hoc constitutional conference was sitting in Lagos. The outbreaks began within days, sometimes hours of each other, at Makurdi, Minna, Gboko, Gombe, Jos, Sokoto and Kaduna. They quickly spread to Kano, Zaria, Oturkpo, Bauchi, Zungeru and elsewhere .... Again, rented buses were seen speeding across the North, bringing armed agitators to fresh towns and villages. In each case the message was the same; kill the Easterners .... In the main centres hideous massacres took place as mobs, sometimes led by army men and native police officers, raged through the Sabon Garis hacking, spearing, cutting, chopping and shooting any Easterners they came across.[102]

However, Gowon's own position was extremely tenuous and he was forced to compromise in order to hold on to power. He admitted that at that stage he was unable to control the killings.[103] Indeed, in view of the disturbances, he suspended the conference, which had been set up to find a way forward to govern the country. It could be argued that the constitutional conference was adjourned because delegates from the East felt their lives were in danger, since Northern troops, contrary to agreement, were still stationed in the West, and were instituting random killings of Easterners.[104]

> On the evening of September 11th all the Eastern delegates were united in Enugu, ready for the morning take-off for Lagos. During the afternoon reports began to come in of an outbreak of killings of Easterners in the North. The delegates with the events of May and July/August fresh in their minds [when there had been similar attacks on Igbos, in the North] promptly lost their nerve and refused to fly to Lagos the next day. Emeka ... spent hours trying to persuade them to attend the conference ... . They refused. Emeka ... told his father, Sir Odumegwu, what had happened ... . he went from house to house cajoling the men to change their minds. At midnight he returned to State House triumphant. He had persuaded them; they would fly the next morning.[105]

Sadly for Ojukwu, his father was to die that same night.

Gowon has conceded that it was over a year before he felt secure in his position as Military Head of State, when he felt he had the support of the majority of the Military Ruling Council.[106] The rioting and indiscriminate killing of innocent Igbo people living in the North reached its highest intensity between July and September 1966. These killings and maimings of innocent Igbos was to have a chronically emotive effect on Easterners themselves before and throughout the civil war. Ojukwu and his colleagues used it unashamedly as a propaganda tool, referring to it as genocide, and exaggerating the numbers of those killed, from a conservative 5,000 as noted by the British High Commission to 15,000.[107] Both figures are a matter of conjecture, but Hunt, as the British High Commissioner at the time, offers the following opinion:

> In January 1967, i.e. over three months after the massacre, Ojukwu gave an interview to the Italian Ambassador, who gave me a full account. Speaking in a manner which made it plain that he was consciously exaggerating Ojukwu said that the number killed, in

September and the previous May, was as high as 7,000. Plainly,
therefore, the man who was likely to know best and had an interest in putting the figure as high as possible, thought that about
5,000 had been killed (if the true figure had been 'between 10,000
and 15,000' he would have told the Italian Ambassador 25,000).
Calculations made in the North, on adding up the figures from
various different localities, also produce a figure of about 5,000. I
quote this fact for what it is worth; the calculations were carefully
made though the basic figures are a little shaky in many cases. But
Ojukwu's statement is sufficient evidence that the true figure cannot be higher.[108]

However the visual effects of attacks on Igbo people by Northerners were
real enough.[109] Not only did the new military government seem powerless to stem the flow of violence in the North, but she offered very little
support for the huge influx of refugees returning to the East from the
North.

In his report on the war Hunt, the British High Commissioner, makes
the following comment with regard to the number of refugees returning
from the North to the East:

> The Eastern Regional Government called on all refugees to register at
> special offices set up throughout the region; these offices were under
> the control of a British civil servant, a Mr. Savile, who told Mr Parker
> [the British Assistant High Commissioner based in Enugu] that the
> total registered was 150,000. This is the only solid and official figure
> in existence. According to Mr. Parker the Eastern Region authorities
> manipulated it in the following way. First they doubled it 'because
> only about half the people who could have registered did so' (though it
> could be argued that some people who were not refugees registered in
> the hope of benefit); then, finding 300,000 an insufficiently impres-
> sive figure, they assumed, falsely, that all those on the register were
> men, made the assumption that all these men were married and had
> an average of three children, multiplied by six and produced the figire
> of 1.8 million. This of course was always rounded upwards: I remem-
> ber with amusement Ojukwu saying to me at our interview in March
> 'and then we have two million refugees – no I must not exaggerate,
> 1.8 million.' Two million became the classical figure, and then over
> two million . . . . You may find me inconsistent if I say that the official

figure always struck me as probably rather low: I used to say a quarter of a million.[110]

Ojukwu in his propaganda speeches homed in on an arbitrary number of two million. Sadly this number seems to have been used in countless accounts of the disturbances during this period, and what were highly questionable figures seem now to have become fact.

Aburi

The Federal Government exacerbated the situation by subjecting the East to an economic blockade.[111] It was because of the ongoing racial conflict in the North, and the seeming helplessness of Gowon's regime to bring this under control, as well as the blockade and the lack of help by Gowon's regime for the returning refugees to the East, that a meeting between the four regional governors and members of the ruling Military Council was proposed. Cumming-Bruce states that it was Malcolm MacDonald's idea, because of his close relationship with the military ruler of Ghana, Lt-General Ankrah:

> I invited Malcolm MacDonald over to Lagos, in the guise of a holi-
> day, but of course in reality he acted as my emissary, keeping the
> doors open, in an attempt at trying to stop hostilities breaking out
> between the opposing parties. He travelled extensively between
> Lagos, Enugu and Kaduna. Of course the whole idea was to uphold
> the unity of Nigeria. The idea was for him to visit me as a friend
> and not in any official capacity so that way he was free to visit as
> many of the interested parties as possible, but not as my authorised
> representative.[112]

MacDonald seems to have enjoyed a degree of success, or so he thought. After Aburi he told Hunt, the new incoming British High Commissioner: 'It's simple, that's its merit: the constitution is to be further amended to give each region almost total autonomy and in return the East acknowl-edges the unity of Nigeria and recognises the Federal Military Government with Gowon as its head.'[113]

The tragedy of Aburi was the 'backpedalling' by Gowon's Military Government in its aftermath. The meeting was agreed with good intentions, but the two sides led by Gowon and Ojukwu had totally different agendas.

Cumming-Bruce said: 'I didn't attend the meeting but I saw Gowon just before he left for Ghana, and I felt he was in no fit state to take part in the meeting because he appeared to have an extremely debilitating fever.'[114]

Gowon's plan was to have an open and frank discussion with his military colleagues in a relaxed and informal manner with no fixed agenda, in an attempt to resolve the various differences and to plan a way forward which would ensure the unity and security of Nigeria.

Ojukwu had other ideas. He came to the meeting with very clear-cut objectives, fully briefed by his senior advisors who were determined to achieve an agreement which would give the East a high degree of independence. Furthermore, he insisted on the meetings being recorded so that there would be no misunderstanding for the future. In retrospect it would seem that Gowon and his colleagues took an unusually naïve stance on their negotiations at Aburi. One possible explanation is that they had very little real understanding of the anguish and fear which the Northern riots had engendered in the Igbo people. Lagos, where most of the Federal Government was still centred, was very distant and remote from the rioting areas and from the East. It was perhaps this remoteness that fostered a degree of relaxed compromise.[115] Furthermore, the other delegates had limited fear of racial attacks; the Igbos were the race under attack and all Igbos had reason to be concerned for their safety, especially in the North. Even Ojukwu feared for his personal safety, as Adebayo, the newly appointed Western Regional Governor, said during an interview: 'Both Ojukwu and I were concerned for our personal safety in the West because of the presence of large numbers of Northern troops, whose loyalty to the new government was questionable, and Ojukwu made no further trips to the West.'[116]

The fact remained that Ojukwu's approach was very business-like with clear-cut objectives, whilst the other side had no particular agenda. A further fact was that all delegates insisted on returning to their respective regions at the end of each day, allowing for no relaxed social intercourse. Under these circumstances it is not surprising that Ojukwu's demands and persuasive arguments gained support from the other members of the meeting. The delegates agreed on a much looser confederation and much greater autonomy for the regions.[117]

At Aburi Gowon's position was also one of intermediary; in all his negotiations he had to ensure that he carried the North and the West with him, and his position as military head of state was still precarious. His other intention was to ensure that Ojukwu agreed to respect the new military command structure. Indeed it can be argued that Gowon's main objective was to restore the reputation of the army and to reintegrate it into the country as a whole. He felt that if this was achieved the regional and federal senior civil servants could work out the detail.[118] He simply failed to understand Ojukwu's essentially intractable position. Ojukwu had no constraints in convincing other parties of his objectives. The Consultative Committee in the East had given him a mandate to negotiate on their behalf. The intention was that the regions would gain a high degree of independence within a Nigerian confederation, strong regions with a weak centre.

At Aburi it was also agreed that all parties would renounce force to achieve their objectives and finally that 'any decision affecting the whole country must be determined by the Supreme Military Council, which it was agreed would effectively be a collegiate leadership. Where such a meeting was not possible such a matter must be referred to the Military Governors for comment and concurrence.' [119]Effectively this meant that if one regional governor did not agree with a proposal that would be the end of the affair. Such a power of veto was going to make governing Nigeria very difficult indeed, but Gowon and his supporters seemed blissfully unaware of such constraints. Two other details from Aburi were to have future and near future resonance. Firstly, there was an agreement that there would be a concerted effort to recruit Yorubas into the army, to address the regional imbalance of ethnic recruits. The effect of this was eventually to help to keep the West firmly in the Federal and, by implication, in the North's camp. Secondly, there was an agreement to pay Igbo civil servants, especially those on lower grades and those paid hourly, who were now suffering degrees of hardship and who had fled back their homeland, until March 1967. Demands for more support for the East went unheeded and this was to become contentious as the days progressed towards war. However, Ojukwu had achieved his objective and he was to promote the slogan 'By Aburi we stand' to the world.

Tragically, Gowon reneged on the Aburi Agreement after pressure from some Northern emirs and his senior civil servants. Indeed the civil servants pointed out to him that his position was untenable if he kept to the Aburi Agreement, because it granted almost complete autonomy to the regions, leaving very little absolute power at the centre. A further factor had also come into play: the majority of these civil servants came from minority peoples across Nigeria, and they were in no mood to accept the ongoing domination of the three main ethnic groups within the country. Indeed it was pointed out to Gowon that if the country accepted the Aburi Agreement his own tiny ethnic group, the Angas people, would be under threat. The minority groups represented some forty percent of the population and such people were opposed to confederation.[120] This was echoed by an official memorandum submitted by the Acting Secretary of the Federal Military Government to members of the Supreme Military Council, rejecting several of the Aburi decisions on the grounds that they were incompatible with maintenance of effective control over essential matters. There were two major issues. First was the concern for the respective powers of the centre and the regions, and second the power of veto by any regional governor over proceedings of the Supreme Military Council. These issues had been raised by law officers when they met in January 1967.[121] From Gowon's and his supporters' points of view agreement in these areas meant that the provision of the 1963 Constitution, whereby the Federal Military Government retained the authority to declare that a Regional Military Governor was abusing his powers, was essential if the federal status of the country was to be retained.[122] From Ojukwu's standpoint of confederalism this was totally unacceptable. As far as Ojukwu was concerned, the Aburi Agreement had confirmed confederalism, and any movement away from the Agreement would be rejected by the East.[123]

In an attempt to placate the East, a meeting of the Supreme Military Council was called, to be held on 10 March 1967 in the Mid-West Region, in Benin. Ojukwu did not attend. At the meeting the Federal Government promulgated decree 8, which confirmed the extent to which the Supreme Military Council would go to meet Ojukwu in his demands for a confederation, as agreed at Aburi. Although it allowed for extensive internal self-government, it made the point that federal law was superior to regional law. It also stated that if 'the democratic institutions of Nigeria are threatened by subversion and it is necessary to declare a state of emergency' this could be sanctioned by the head of the Military Government supported by at least three of the Military Governors.[124] Ojukwu rejected the decree, as did his colleagues in the East, and they confirmed their policy of secession. However Ojukwu did make some effort to keep the Western and Mid-Western regions on his side, through meetings with their respective governors, Colonel Adebayo and Lt-Col. Ejoor, as they in turn attempted to keep the East within Nigeria.

> There is no doubt that Awolowo, Ejoor and myself made every effort to agree to Ojukwu's demands. It was also apparent to us that both Gowon and Ojukwu were potentially prepared to compromise, but they were both being pressured by forces which were in no mood

to be conciliary. The East felt increasingly vulnerable and were pushing for a separate existence, and the North, through Northern politicians and rulers, were unwilling to compromise, both.'[125]

Military action was increasingly seen as the only way to bring the Igbo people back into the Federation. Gowon was egged on not only by his Northern colleagues, particularly Col. Hassan Katsina, but also the newly appointed British High Commissioner, David Hunt. Both felt that the Nigerian Army could bring the recalcitrant Igbos into line within two weeks.[126] British policy had always favoured the North, so the High Commissioner's sentiments were simply following a tradition. Cumming-Bruce said: 'David Hunt, my successor, who had also been my deputy in Lagos, was very dismissive of the military prowess of the Igbo people. I myself thought they were too clever by half.'[127]

However, Gowon's position was still extremely precarious and con-strained. It was not until he received confirmed support from his former military superior, now the West's military governor, and Chief Awolowo, whom he appointed as his finance minister and his deputy, that he felt secure enough to counter secession by the East and to hold the Nigerian state together as a single entity. An alliance with Awolowo took time to achieve. Having been released from prison, Gowon was keen to have his support for his new regime. Without it, and in spite of Adebayo's cor-roboration, it is likely that Gowon's regime would not have gained the backing of the Western region and its necessary financial support. One of Awolowo's misgivings was that Northern troops remained stationed in the west. On 7 November 1966 Awolowo led a delegation to Gowon, appealing to the Federal Government to remove Northern troops from Lagos and the West. He stated: 'The consensus of opinion among the majority of people in Western Nigeria and Lagos is that northern troops in the two territories constitute an army of occupation, and their non-removal has virtually reduced the said territories to the status of a "Protectorate".'[128]

Indeed even as late as May 1967 Awolowo was still seen to be support-ing neither the Federal Government nor the Eastern Region as the crisis deteriorated. In his speech 'The Four Imperatives', his third comment was the most controversial:

[If the] Eastern Region is allowed by acts of omission or commission to secede or opt out of Nigeria, the Western Region and Lagos must

also stay out of the Federation ... . Before the Western delegates
went to Lagos to attend to the meetings of the Ad Hoc Committee,
they were given a clear mandate that if any region should opt out
of the federation of Nigeria, then the federation must be considered
at an end; and then the western Region and Lagos should opt out
of it. It should then be open to Western Nigeria and Lagos as an
independent sovereign state to enter into association with any of the
Nigerian units of its own choosing, and on terms mutually acceptable to them.[129]

Awolowo's confirmed support for Gowon and the Federation's continu-
ity finally occurred when the Northern emirs and leaders of thought
committed to the creation of more states in the country, and urged
Gowon to set this in motion. Awolowo had always been a keen advo-
cate of the creation of additional states. Furthermore, he was treated
very shabbily by Ojukwu in May 1967, when he and a delegation held
talks with him to avert the crisis. Comments at the time suggested that
Ojukwu treated Awolowo cavalierly and that he made rude remarks
to him.[130]

The Gowon government hoped to benefit from Awolowo's popularity in two ways, namely by legitimising its own politics in the Western
Region and by consolidating the tentative unity of its Yoruba communities which had emerged after Awolowo's imprisonment in order to prevent
further political factionalisation and conflict. Colonel Adeyinka Adebayo,
the Western Region's military administrator, facilitated this process by
inviting a large number of former politicians and other opinion leaders
from Yoruba communities throughout the Western Region. Appealing
to them to overcome past divisions, he suggested that it might be to
the benefit of all if the Yoruba spoke with one voice and enjoined those
present to elect a leader.

Proposed by an old supporter and seconded by a former NNDP
[Nigerian National Democratic Party] member, Awolowo was chosen as
the Asiwaju Yoruba, or vanguard leader of the Yorubas.[131]

With Awolowo's decision to put his considerable popular support
behind the Federation, Gowon's position was substantially strengthened.
Not only did Adebayo, as the West's military governor, promise substantial financial help, which meant that most armaments were paid for in
hard currency, but this support continued throughout the war, in some
cases to Adebayo's detriment.[132]

Less interested in the idea of progress through ethnic nationalism than Awolowo, Gowon's main ambition was to use state
creation, controlled by a more centralised national government,
in order to undermine the Biafran project by appealing to non-
Igbo citizens of the Eastern Region who wanted administrative
independence. Despte these differences, the shared commitment
to federalism by Awolowo and Gowon created a political alliance in which Nigeria's future was decided, to the detriment of
Biafra.[133]

However, a new and somewhat unexpected development occurred.
Having been encouraged by both the American Ambassador and
the British High Commissioner, when he came to power, to hold the
state together, Gowon's position was undermined by both countries'
attitude to the East's proposed secession. Both Britain and America
hoped Nigeria would remain united, but they would offer no positive guarantees to support the Federal Government should the East
secede, indeed America stated it would remain neutral.[134] Gowon was
extremely frustrated by both countries' reaction. Paraphrasing John
F. Kennedy, he said 'governments have no friends or enemies – only
interests'.[135] Britain's position was coloured by the outbreak of the Six
Day Arab–Israeli war, which closed the Suez Canal and thus potentially limited her supply of oil. Pragmatic over its vested interests, it
was probably a sensible policy to offer more ambivalent support to the
Federal Government, in view of the East potentially taking control of
Nigeria's oil. The reality was that oil revenues went to Lagos, and as
the war progressed, although oil supplies were very limited and the
East made attempts, which failed, to hold Shell to ransom over oil revenues, most oil produced reached the Federal Government, and limited
exports went to Britain.

Ojukwu suffered no constraints: not only did he have the support of
the East's ruling elite but he also had popular support throughout the
region, because he was seen to be the person who could protect the people from their paranoid fear of genocide by the North. Furthermore, as a
people Easterners felt rejected by the rest of the country. Having spread
throughout the country through many generations utilising their skills
not only for personal benefit but also for the good of the communities in
which they settled, they now felt ostracized for little justifiable reason.
They also mistrusted Gowon's Lagos administration, which had been

unable to control the Igbo killings and destruction of their property in the North. Ojukwu was able to declare on secession, 'There is no power in this country or in black Africa to subdue us by force',[136] and:

> Gowon will hum and haw for sometime. The North will be impatient and start to hare down here with a ramshackle army. Once they cross into Biafra we'll take the war to them. I have the wherewithal to ensure that what is a large part of the North is completely destroyed and put under the control of Biafra.[137]

Although this statement was propagandist, arrogant and boastful, to a point his comments bore substance. In his previous role in the Nigerian army he had had complete knowledge of its structure, its strengths and weaknesses, and he had the benefit that most Nigerian army officers with technical skills were of Igbo origin and had fled to the East. Also, of the fifty-seven officers commissioned before independence, only five were available to Gowon, while Ojukwu had access to seventeen.[138] Gowon's lack of trained officers was to cause him and his subordinates unending problems and constraints throughout the campaign, and can be seen as one of the reasons why it took him so long to secure an armistice.

Boro and Gowon's twelve-state decree

The concept of regional independence, within the Nigerian state, was not new. When Lord Lugard was given charge of the country, discussions centred round creating between eight and twelve regions within the country. Chief Awolowo, as leader of the Yoruba people, felt that the country would be better served with a number of regional states.

> Awolowo had reflected on the role of the regions' political machines in his own political marginalisation in his book 'Thoughts on the Nigerian Constitution' (1966), written during his time in prison, and argued for the creation of eighteen states based on Nigeria's larger ethnic and linguistic groupings to further the development and emergence of Nigeria's ethnic nations. Beyond such immediate concerns, Awolowo also anticipated that the creation of six states out of the former Northern Nigeria would give progressive politicians, like himself, the chance to undermine the monolithic

politics that had characterised the Northern Region under Ahmadu Bello's leadership.[139]

At the London Conference, 4 August 1953, a joint memorandum, on central-regional powers under a new constitution, issued by the NCNC (National Council for Nigeria and the Cameroons, changed in 1962 to National Council for Nigerian Citizens) and AG (Action Group) stated:

1. Nigeria should have a constitution which is Federal in character;
2. The Federation should have three Regions as at present; (but it is believed that in a self-governing Nigeria the Federation should consist of more than three Regions to be determined by a Constituent Assembly).[140]

In 1958 the Willink Commission[141] had recommended that the Niger Delta be given special attention for separate development.[142] Indeed in 1960 the Niger Delta Development Board was established, but it failed to help development in the area. Isaac Adaka Boro became a political activist whilst a student at Nsukka University, and formed a group with like-minded students from the Niger Delta region; all were Ijaws. They were frustrated by the lack of development in the Delta region. With the help of Samuel Owonaru and Nottingham Dick, they created an organisation called the Niger Delta Volunteer Service, whose objective was to disassociate itself from the recently formed Nigerian military government under Ironsi.[143] With the objective of creating a separate state within the Delta region, the Delta Volunteer Service succeeded in taking over parts of the region and proclaiming an independent state. It lasted for twelve days. Boro and his associates were arrested, tried and condemned to death for treason. Whilst they were in prison the second coup occurred, bringing Gowon to power. Rather than carrying out the court ruling, Gowon commuted Boro's sentence; indeed he pardoned him and offered him the opportunity to fight for the Federal Government against the East. Boro, who had long felt that his people were subjugated by the Eastern Igbos, accepted the opportunity and joined the Nigerian army with the rank of major. Boro's action had the effect of making Gowon and his senior advisors decide on a policy for the formation of twelve states within the country. Two of those new states were within the area where Boro and his followers had campaigned for independence, Rivers and Cross Rivers States.

Colonel Achuzia says:

> The idea for creating twelve states first came to the Gowon regime's mind following Boro's failed attempt at creating an independent Delta region, his subsequent trial and conviction and then release by Gowon. I feel this was a masterstoke by Gowon affecting the future course of the war, and it addressed two of his objectives, one that it would undermine the East's power base and two that it would help his administration's power base by giving support to more minorities within the country. [144]

However the formation of twelve states and the Federal Government's declaration of a state of emergency on 27 June 1967 were followed by the Eastern region declaring itself the Republic of Biafra, and seceding from the Federation on 3 June 1967.

Military strengths and weaknesses

This was a war fought with modern armaments and technology, and controlled and led on both sides by Sandhurst- and Mons-trained men, who had all been comrades in a very close-knit community, the Nigerian Army. They had been taught all aspects of conducting military campaigns as learnt and perceived by European and Western societies. However the war was also contested by ill-educated and generally illiterate people who had little understanding of the modern independent state of Nigeria, let alone a war fought in European style with fairly up-to-date equipment, and who were still living a traditional way of life, often as subsistence farmers living in obscure communities, as they had done for generations. They were suddenly awoken into the harsh reality of a modern and ruthless war for which they had little understanding and for which they were totally unprepared. This fact was to have a strong bearing on Biafra's invasive success through the extensive use of 'attack markets'.[145]

James Eneje, who was a member of the Biafran Organisation of Freedom Fighters (BOFF), says:

> Attack markets were very popular with Igbo people because they gave us the opportunity to conduct cross-border trade in goods which were becoming increasingly scarce in Biafra. The other point to make is that both sides found such markets useful and therefore

they could carry out their business relatively immune from military attacks from either side.[146]

However, with a people still largely bound to a traditional way of life, it also meant that rumour-mongering to create fear and foster superstition was rife. The emotive word 'saboteur' was to have a morally undermining effect on Biafra's willingness to win the war. Coupled with this was the fact that the East consisted of a heterogeneous population: Biafra comprised about twelve million people, of whom seven million were Igbo. Five million were from other ethnic groups such as Efiks and Ibibios. As the idea of secession began to gather acceptance with the people of the East, it culminated in a meeting of the consultative assembly, a representative body of all peoples from the Eastern Region, giving the Igbo elite a fully supportive mandate to declare the sovereign state of Biafra.[147] However in view of the Federal Government's declaration of twelve states, Biafra's other ethnic groups were always going to have the potential to undermine her power base. Indeed this became apparent in the early stages of the campaign when the federal forces overran the Mid-West and attacks were made on Calabar and the Delta area. The peoples of these areas became ambivalent in their support for Biafra as a nation. In spite of surviving for nearly three years, the minority ethnic support was virtually to disappear and it was left to the indigenous Igbo people to hold the battered nation together. By the end the only area left of Biafra was a depleted Igboland.

The armies of both sides had to undergo a rapid programme of recruitment and training. Often these recruits came from people who were more accustomed to a traditional and rural life than a life imbued with all the trappings of modern western technology. The Nigerian army was a British invention, created as a defensive and ceremonial force. It was not an offensive armed force. Admittedly some 30,000 Nigerians had volunteered for British Crown service during the Second World War, but by the time of the Nigerian Civil War most of these men had retired, and although some volunteered to serve again, on both sides, during the conflict and were a valuable asset to both armies, most of them were beyond serving age and were not combat troops. Because of the two coups virtually the whole senior army corps had been killed. In fact there were only two senior officers left, a brigadier and a full colonel. Ogundipe, the brigadier, was to serve as Nigeria's High Commissioner in London and Adebayo, the colonel, was appointed as military regional governor of the West, so neither took an active part in the war on either side. The remaining officer corps consisted of very inexperienced young lieutenant-colonels, a few of whom had witnessed live operations as part of the United Nations peace-keeping mission to the Congo, but they still had had no combat experience. The remainder, ranked major and below, had never seen active service. Some were lucky enough to have received their officer training either at Sandhurst or Mons. 'Mons focused on turning out platoon commanders, whilst Sandhurst interested itself with the attitributes required of generals.'[148] This was to have a bearing on both sides' ability to win the war.

> Most Biafran officers from the original Nigerian Army were Sandhurst-trained who focused on being generals. They were pleased to accept the kudos of successful attacks but were nowhere to be seen in the event of failure or reverses. They would indeed make hasty retreat back to their headquarters.[149]

A very few had attended staff college in Britain, India or Canada. Many of the officer corps, especially those with a technical background, were Igbos who had made their way back to the East to offer their services to the Biafran army.

In total the Nigerian army consisted of just under 10,000 men, made up of six battalions, of which one was stationed in the East. There was also an artillery regiment, and support staff to run the army. It was notionally of divisional strength. Of the officer corps Nigeria could count on one hundred and thirty-eight officers, and Biafra ninety-three.[150] The Federal Government planned to wage the war against Biafra in four phases. It was to be over within one month. The capture of Nsukka and Enugu was seen as the priority, followed by Ogoja and then Abakaliki. The first area command, consisting mainly of Northern troops from Kaduna, was to be the fighting force, and was to start its attack on Biafra's northern borders around Nsukka, and the second area command, based in Ibadan, was earmarked for the defence of the Mid-West. The Lagos garrison, a mainly ceremonial force, was for the defence of Lagos. This was the state of the Nigerian army and of its plans to bring the 'police action' to a quick conclusive victory at the start of the war. On top of this the Nigerian navy was detailed to blockade the East from the sea, in order to stop the importation of goods, armaments and food to the breakaway region. Lagos also sanctioned an embargo on all international flights to the East without her permission, doing her best to discredit the secessionist territory in the eyes of the international community. However in order to curry favour with its overseas allies the Federal Government continued to participate in efforts at finding a peaceful solution. Arguably this was one of the constraints, which hindered Nigeria from conclusively defeating Biafra in purely military terms. The peace process continued unabated throughout the war. Indeed as one former Nigerian army officer pointed out, throughout the war the army always knew when an attempted peace process was being negotiated because the supply of arms would be severely restricted: 'We always knew when peace negotiations were in progress because there would be a severe shortage and rationing of arms and ammunition.'[151]

Biafra's military position was arguably even more disorganised and precarious. Notionally its army consisted of one battalion, stationed at Enugu. Even before the start of hostilities Ojukwu, in agreement with Gowon, had arranged that all Northern soldiers stationed in the East be repatriated to their homes. In order to protect themselves they were allowed to retain their rifles and their ammunition, on the understanding that these would be returned once they reached their homeland; this never happened. This situation left the Biafran army depleted of men and arms. However it did have the nucleus of a trained officer corps, although they were mainly technically qualified, but it was very short of infantry-trained officers. Although its one battalion had been denuded of arms she did have a limited stock of armaments. There is evidence that it had sent emissaries abroad before the start of hostilities to buy arms. However these efforts had had limited success; indeed one aircraft supposedly carrying arms for Biafra crashed over Cameroonian air space, much to the embarrassment of the East's administration. The East denied that the arms were destined for Enugu.

Efforts were made before the war to secure arms from overseas. With some colleagues we travelled to Europe to buy arms and were reasonably successful in achieving this. When the war started Ojukwu took charge of the stocks of arms, but he had a habit in being so restrictive in their supply that often the lack of arms had dire consequences on our ability to sustain attacks, and led to some notable failures. However as the war progressed arms became much more available, partly because we became much better at capturing the enemy's arms. During attack they would often up sticks and run away leaving their arms and ammunition behind. The other thing was that as the war continued so we seemed to get much more support from France for arms.[152]

I think it would be worthwhile recording that the first large-scale arms delivery to the East arrived in October 1966 [nine months before the start of hostilities]. It was of Czech small arms and light machine guns, shipped from Szeczyn, in Poland. These were the arms with which the Biafran army was fitted out .... by October 1966 Ojukwu already entertained the idea of secession. The communist countries originally favoured or were prepared to support Ojukwu, and didn't change their minds until 1967, probably in June or July when the Federals approached Russia.[153]

By May 1967 further arms had been imported into Biafra, and she was able to form two new battalions, the 9th and the 14th, consisting of university and secondary school students. There is now further evidence to show that even before the start of the war the East had set up a militia force, based round Port Harcourt, although initially it did not receive the support of Ojukwu, who felt that it would have too strong political connotations. The business community around Port Harcourt had instigated it in order to protect the area against an aggressor. With the assistance of Lt-Col. Ogbugo Kalu, a regular Sandhurst-trained officer from the Nigerian army, a force numbering some 5,000 men was recruited and thoroughly trained in infantry warfare. Added to this was the fact that a major electrical component manufacturer, run by Joe Achuzia, in Port Harcourt, was ordered by the East's military government to turn its expertise over to arms production.

Achuzia had an extremely colourful and successful career. He originally trained in Manchester, as an electrical engineer. Finding himself in Britain at an age when he was obliged to do National Service, he joined an infantry battalion, only to find himself, after training, posted to Korea; this was at the height of the Korean War. He appears to have acquitted himself extremely well. According to him he received a field commission, and became expert in infantry warefare.[154]

Army archives show no record of a 2nd Lt. J. Achuzia, but according to Major-Gen. Thompson, Achuzia's commission was possible though unlikely. Whatever the truth, the fact was that this experience was to prove invaluable for Biafra, and arguably was the reason for him becoming a war hero during the Biafran War. At the end of the Korean War Achuzia found himself in captivity in North Korea. When he finally returned to England, he and some English colleagues went to Port Harcourt, in Eastern Nigeria, and set up an electrical component manufacturing company. The company prospered, and according to Achuzia's English wife, Josephine, the family lived in style in Port Harcourt. Achuzia was held in some regard by Ojukwu; not only was he asked by him to turn his factory over to manufacturing arms, but Ojukwu asked him to supply timed bombs to be driven to Lagos and detonated. Achuzia duly supplied the bombs, and drivers were detailed to take them to Lagos. Unfortunately, when the drivers reached Lagos with their destructive cargo, they abandoned their vehicles and one bomb detonated outside a cinema, in Yaba, Lagos, killing many people, including Igbos. A further plan to send a boat loaded with timed bombs and sail it into Lagos harbour was abandoned when it was pointed out to Ojukwu that such a move would probably flood large areas of Lagos. Through his father Ojukwu had large property holdings in Lagos. However, these cavalier attacks on Lagos made Gowon realise how vulnerable Lagos was to amphibious attack.[155]

Gowon said:

I heard about rumours of an amphibious attack, and they prompted me to carry out an aerial reconnaissance to look for a more secure capital for the Federal Government. I chanced on the small community of Abuja, positioned fairly centrally in the country, and well away from the coast and thus not subject to sea-borne attacks.[156]

Although the infantry-trained militia were regarded dismissively by members of Biafra's regular army officer corps, once the war started, and Biafra realised it was in need of all the armed help it could get, the militia was eventually integrated into the regular army. Interestingly, once Port Harcourt had set up a militia, other towns in the East started to follow suit. It is evident, therefore, that Biafra was able to organise a defensive army fairly quickly, albeit with limited arms.[157]

Biafra also quickly formed 'directorates' for the consistent and controlled flow of supplies. There were directorates of food, petroleum, transport, clothing, housing, propaganda and many others. This put Biafra on a planned and organised war footing which was to prove, especially in the early days, far superior to that of the Federal Government, whose position, although in theory far superior to its adversary, in practice was constrained. It was severely short of trained officers, and the men under their command had no combat experience. Its army also had severe logistics and communications problem. Although it had a reasonable supply of arms, its soldiers were extremely wasteful in the consumption of ammunition, believing that shooting aerial foliage would cause noise and alarm and therefore defeat for its enemy.[158] As noted above, as the war progressed Gowon also had the very unnerving habit of ordering restriction on arms supply during peace negotiations, of which there were many, all abortive.

The opening stages of the conflict proved disastrous for Biafra. In the early hours of the first day, in Nsukka province, Nigeria's northern sector, 1st Division successfully attacked Okpo and Igbo Eze districts and overran the area. By 12 July they were within twelve miles of Enugu. 'I was second-in-command of a freshly formed infantry battalion, 7th, which was under the command of Lt-Col. Adigbo, who came from Brass. Adigbo had no working knowledge of Igbo, and this made it extremely difficult for him to communicate with his troops.'[159] Biafra, being short of arms, retaliated with smoke bombs. Colonel Madiebo commented: 'My view at the time was that if Enugu fell the war was virtually over and lost, and having started fighting the people of Biafra did not want an abrupt end'.[160]

A counterattack under the leadership of Lt-Col. Madiebo was eventually launched, which succeeded in stalling the enemy at Obollo Eke. Nigerian troops, having exhausted their ammunition within thirty minutes of the counterattack, were stunned into confusion when attacked by very limited Biafran mortar fire.[161]

The commander of the Biafran army, Brig. Njoku felt incredibly frustrated because of his failure to convince Ojukwu of the need for additional arms to help stem the onslaught.[162] The lack of faith and trust between senior Biafran officers was to be an ongoing feature of the war. Deep suspicion was also engendered between the military and the civilian directorates. One of the issues was that Ojukwu was the only military person on his advisory council; this meant that his civilian advisors were often out of touch with the needs of the army. They were more intent on securing their own positions than helping Biafra to achieve a victory.[163] This led to ongoing shortages of all the army's needs throughout the war, from food and clothing supplies to arms and fuel supplies. These short-ages were to occur at crucially important times of the campaign and can be seen as one of the reasons why Biafra eventually sued for peace.[164]

Biafra's invasion of the Mid-West

On 9 August 1967 Biafra launched a surprise attack on the Mid-West Region. The Federal Government was taken totally by surprise by this unprovoked foray into neutral territory. Col. Victor Banjo, a close friend and colleague of Ojukwu, led the attack. He was briefed that his objectives were Ibadan and Lagos. He came very close to achieving these. When reaching Lagos he was to make contact with sympathetic people particularly in the Nigerian military. There is some evidence that the prime source of contact was to be through the writer Wole Soyinka, who was due to put Banjo in touch with the military, including Obasanjo.

> When I made a visit to Biafra, and met Ojukwu I also met Banjo, who gave me a message for Obasanjo which said: 'Let them understand in the West that I am not leading a Biafran Army but an army of liberation, made up not only of Biafrans but of other ethnic groups. Make the governor of the West and other Western leaders understand this. Urge them not to be taken in by any propaganda by the Federal Government about a Biafran plan to subjugate the rest of the nation, especially the West.'[165]

Shortly after this episode Soyinka was detained, and remained in detention for the duration of the war. Victor Banjo was not Ojukwu's first choice to lead the Biafran attack into the Mid-West. Unfortunately the man he had chosen to command the invading force, Major Nzeogwu, one of the leaders of the first coup in 1966, had been killed at the start of hostilities. There is evidence that other people had been considered, including Lt-Col. Kalu.[166] The attack that Banjo led was extremely successful. Admittedly he had very little opposition, as many people in the Mid-West were closely related to Easterners and welcomed the invaders. However when he reached Ore he stalled. He was only one hundred and fifty miles from Lagos and there was little to oppose him except Gowon's small group of five hundred troops, based in Lagos, who were largely used for ceremonial functions rather than armed combat. Accounts confirm that the bridge at Ore and indeed all bridges leading to Lagos had been destroyed. 'As military governor of the Western Region I instructed that all bridges approaching Lagos should be blown. As a consequence of this I believe that this was the final reason why Banjo's invasion failed, and why we were able to successfully counterattack.'[167]

Although a destroyed bridge did make it difficult for the Biafran troops to cross the river, and caused delay, it was not sufficient reason for a complete halt to the Biafran attack. With the attack losing its momentum at Ore, the Federal Government was given the chance to move troops from Nsukka, thus weakening the Nsukka front and stalling the attack on Enugu, to the West. At the same time a new division was formed under the command of Lt-Col. Murtala Mohammed, Gowon's rival for power and a radical, intent on the destruction of Igbos. This hastily formed 2nd Division was created from some members of the First Division from the Nsukka front and students and prison inmates.[168] This was not the best material for creating an infantry division, and their inexperience and aggressive tendencies were to show themselves throughout the rest of the campaign, especially in unwarranted killings as they counterattacked through the Mid-West, particularly at Asaba.

From most of the evidence available it would seem that, in spite of Adebayo's comments, Banjo's agenda differed from the invasion instructions given him by Ojukwu. Because Banjo was Yoruba and a fairly senior officer in the Nigerian army, he felt he could make contact with some of his army colleagues, including Obasanjo, and arrange a new power structure in Nigeria.[169] This is conjecture, but he could well have had in mind a new order, amalgamating support from the West for the East, including the Mid-West, against the North.

Soyinka comments:

I called Obasanjo over a secret telephone. We agreed to meet unaccompanied and unarmed at a petrol station on the road between non-commercial Jericho and Mokola sections of Ibadan. I was to tell him in very bald terms that Victor [Banjo] wanted unimpeded passage to Lagos, that he wished to avoid battle in Western Nigeria – finis! This was the exact message I delivered ... Banjo did not act to promote Biafran secession or aid an Ojukwu takeover of power in Lagos. If anything, Banjo felt that he should take over power. I have no doubt whatsoever that Banjo represented the most viable corrective.

Obasanjo's response, that I would later transmit to Victor Banjo, was this. 'Well, tell him I have taken an oath of loyalty to Lagos. There are other routes to Lagos – by water through Ukitipupa for instance. If he makes it to Lagos and takes over, well, my oath of loyalty is to Lagos, and I'll stand by that. But to let him pass through my Western Command, that would be betraying my oath of loyalty. Whoever is in power in Lagos – that's the person to whom I owe my allegiance.'

After my fateful meeting with Obasanjo concluded, I took up residence in the hidden bungalow. It was from this bungalow that I telephoned Obasanjo's reply to Banjo in Benin, verbatim. I kept up communication with him and his increasingly impatient collaborators in the West. I would 'phone and exchange notes also with Banjo's sister, Mrs Ogunseye, then lecturer, Institute of Librarianship at the University Ibadan, in an attempt to assess this warrior's likely, real intentions, to understand why he remained in Benin playing governor or kingmaker, instead of moving straight to Lagos and dislodging Yakubu Gowon's government. Banjo had organised cadres of people committed to the 'Third Force' standing by ready to support Banjo once he had crossed over into Lagos. The links were widespread and were run by politicians since the West had begun its protests against Federal military presence in the West, decrying it as an army of occupation, and demanding its removal.[170]

Certainly at this stage the Federal Government had only instituted 'police action' against Biafra's secession and not an all-out war. However it seems that Banjo was too late to put his plans into action, political conditions having changed in Lagos, with Lt-Col. Murtala Mohammed successfully pressuring Gowon to adopt a more belligerent approach to Ojukwu and the people of Biafra. Mohammed boasted that he could defeat Biafra 'in a matter of weeks'.[171] Certainly by then Adebayo, with Awolowo, having failed to convince Ojukwu that secession was not his best option, were prepared to ensure that the necessary revenue was available for the Federal Government to declare an all-out war on Biafra. As Adebayo explained:

The North was always hopelessly insolvent, and in no position to embark on an expensive war against Biafra. In spite of her military and political aims of defeating and subjugating the Biafran people, without the West's financial support the Federal

Government would not have been financially capable of fighting a successful war.[172]

From Biafra's position the tragedy of the Mid-West invasion was that her senior army officer corps, including the army commander, had been totally excluded from the planning.[173] The invasion, a daring plan, executed with limited troops but little opposition, was a resounding success, and if Banjo had continued the attack there is little doubt that they would have reached Lagos with little opposition. There were few troops in Lagos and the remaining combat forces were engaged in the drive on Enugu. Banjo took Benin without the loss of a single life; indeed the inhabitants gave the invading troops a jubilant welcome. Once in Benin, Banjo decided to stay there, and would not countenance any contact with his army headquarters in Enugu. He even refused to communicate with Ojukwu. He spent time arguing with Enugu as to who should be the new military governor of the Mid-West. By this time he had also antagonised his field commanders, to the point where he had one of them, Colonel Igboda, arrested. This officer remained in prison until the invading Nigerian force arrived and released him, when he was promptly beheaded.[174] As a consequence of Banjo's ambivalence over his orders to defeat the Federal Government, Biafra's fate was sealed. Having reached Ore, the Biafran troops had been in a position to reach Ibadan and then Lagos; it seems likely that Biafra would have succeeded in overrunning the federal administration. Banjo's dithering stalled the invasion, and once he had been recalled by Ojukwu to Enugu to answer Ojukwu's accusations that he had sabotaged the operation, the Biafran attack petered out and turned into a rout. Her troops were forced on the defensive, allowing the federal troops to launch an aggressive assault which gave them passage to Asaba and the river Niger.

Ojukwu's bold plan to invade the Mid-West had obvious merit. Success would have meant control of an important region for Biafra, and would have given him control over the oilfields, as well as creating a buffer from the West and the North. Added to this was the fact that Biafra could count on sizeable support from people of the region. It was, as events showed, that the military stationed in the Mid-West had divided loyalties. In the event Colonels Nwawo, Nwaji and Trimnel and Lt-Col. Nzelli went to Enugu under suspicion and were held in custody until their loyalty was confirmed and they were absorbed into the Biafran army. Strangely, even the military governor of the Mid-West, Brigadier Ejoor, was allowed to remain at

the offices of the British High Commission, in Benin, without interference from the invading Biafran force. He eventually effected his escape
and had an adventurous trip on a bicycle to Lagos. Without Banjo plotting to make contact with the West there is little doubt that the Biafrans
would have overrun Ibadan and Lagos, ensuring a negotiated settlement,
which would have ended the war.[175] Banjo, with plans based on personal
ambition, undermined the invasion and ensured its failure. Forsyth comments that Banjo caused the ruin of Biafra.[176] Ojukwu felt that if he had
taken charge of the Biafran force when Banjo purposely delayed at Benin,
he could have reached Lagos and forced Gowon to resign, and brought
Adebayo and Awolowo, with the West, on to his side.[177] However, Biafra's
defeat in the Mid-West determined, first, that it would never again be able
to mount a serious invasive attack on the Federal Government and second,
arguably, the outcome of the war. Interestingly, the Mid-West invasion
had enhanced Ojukwu's and Biafra's standing in the eyes of the international community, because it put her in a stronger position to propose a
ceasefire and a negotiated settlement. Two other factors emerged: first the
international community's concern that Biafra's secession might encourage
similar movements in other parts of the world. Secondly, because Biafra
had managed to buy two, albeit old, B-26 bombers from Europe, which
posed a threat to the federal side, Gowon made earnest attempts to persuade Britain and America to sell him planes to counter the threat. Both
firmly declined. However, Gowon was determined to resolve this issue and
turned for support to Russia, who had no concerns about supporting the
federal cause and indeed welcomed their involvement.[178] This second factor
put Gowon in a much stronger position when negotiating arms supplies
from Britain. In spite of the British Prime Minister Harold Wilson's weak
political position in Parliament, he and his government were to remain the
Federal Government's main arms supplier throughout the campaign.

As Gowon stated:

> When I met Harold Wilson at Ikeja airport, at the start of his
> visit to us, I accompanied him into Lagos, and was able to have
> an off-the-record conversation. He was keen to point out that
> he was very committed to his government continuing to supply
> arms to my government, but that it was very important that this
> should not be made common knowledge, especially at the forth-
> coming press conference, and not to be mentioned in any official
> communiqués which either of us might make.[179]

Ascendant and descendant positions

Arguably there were two strategic errors made by Gowon over the confrontation between the East and the North. The first was the inability, or indeed unwillingness, of the Federal Government to reassure the Igbo people that their rights as Nigerian citizens would be upheld and protected; indeed it could be argued that this position was further undermined with the economic blockade and the lack of positive support for the East over help for the refugee problem from the North.

> One of the serious blunders of the Nigeria–Biafra conflict was made with regards to the conflict spiral which emerged after the pogroms of 1966. Unlike the leaders in January 1966 who attempted to placate the North, which suffered most from the coup, the federal military regime rendered no apology, took no concrete steps to reassure the Easterners of their security and rights within Nigeria, and gave no meaningful assistance to the massive refugee problem .... Nigeria at the time seemed morally anaesthetized.[180]

Whilst finding the above comments somewhat biased, they are subjectively correct. The author's comments totally ignore the fact that Gowon's position on taking power was extremely precarious, and in those early days his role simply did not allow him to be more supportive and conciliatory to the East. He was after all a compromise candidate, and pressures on him from people such as Murtala Mohammed who could challenge his authority were too great.[181] The options at that stage were for him to resign or be deposed, and it is likely that those taking over, probably from the North, would have ensured immediate aggressive action against the Igbos. Secondly, the Aburi Agreement was a grave mistake and led Gowon, under pressure from his advisors and detractors, to renege on it, failing totally to understand that without honouring it a conflict was inevitable between the East and the Federal Government. Of course it could be argued that Ojukwu should have been more placatory and understanding of the sensitivities of the Northern rulers, and should have been willing to compromise. He had had, after all, very close relationships with the North's ruling elite, many of whom were his friends. This situation stemmed not only from his formative years, because of his father's national standing and connections, but also from his time in the North as commanding officer of the 5th Battalion of the

Nigerian Army, based in Kaduna. There is also the important consideration that during the first coup Ojukwu had proved his allegiance to the Federal Government, and by inference the North. Such was the strength of these relationships that Ojukwu was to have his mother repatriated to Biafra during the war:

> Ojukwu's mother ran a very successful restaurant in Kaduna. It was a great favourite with all army officers and she was very popular. After the war started she was left somewhat stranded in the North, and Ojukwu was concerned for her safety. He therefore contacted his friend, the North's military ruler, Lt-Col. Hassan Katsina, to arrange for his mother to return to the East. To hasten her return Katsina laid on transport for her by way of a helicopter.[182]

However by then pressure was put on him by the Igbo people, especially the Consultative Committee of the Eastern Region for self-determination.[183]

The opening stages of the war had seen the Federal forces in the ascendancy, during Gowon's so-called 'police action' period. Not only had they been able to overrun Biafra's northern borders and capture the university town of Nsukka, but they had come close to threatening Enugu. Indeed it is fair to say that during this initial phase there was nothing to stop them overrunning Enugu.[184] However, it has also been pointed out that Enugu was easily in the grasp of the Federal forces, except that the troops were severely restricted in the supplies of ammunition for their offensive, and it seems that this was the reason the attack on Enugu stalled, giving Biafran troops time to regroup. As far as Gowon was concerned, this was not all-out war but simply a 'police action'. Gowon felt he could achieve his objective with limited arms supplies and the minimum of loss of life.[185] However, it is fair to comment that at this juncture both sides were testing each other's strengths and weaknesses. They were embarking on an exercise in which at best only a few officers, from both sides, had classroom experience, from their Mons and Sandhurst days. Even their limited experience in the Congo as part of a peacekeeping force had not prepared them for a belligerent confrontation. A further consideration was that both sides' equipment for launching a campaign was also limited. It is true that the Federal army was better equipped and that Ojukwu, having been in charge of arms procurement in the Nigerian army before the war, knew the exact armament strength of the opposition. He had also trained some of the newly appointed Federal army divisional commanders and was aware of their strengths and weaknesses. However, the Federal army's timely pause in the attack on Enugu enabled Biafra to launch a surprise initiative in the Mid-West. Its success until it stalled at Ore meant that Ojukwu found himself and the Biafran army in the ascendancy, and he found that his cause had growing sympathy from the international community. It began to take serious note of Biafra for two reasons. Firstly there were concerns that Nigeria would degenerate into another Congo and that secessionist movements in other parts of the world might receive inspiration. From America's point of view this was especially true in relation to her concerns in Vietnam. Secondly was the west's and Africa's concern over Russia's support for the Federal cause.[186] However, as Gowon pointed, out he needed an air force to counter Biafra's ageing B-26 bombers. Ideological influences did not enter his thinking; it was simply that Russia was willing to supply the necessary fighter planes. As events were to prove, Russia's influence was at best very limited. Her ideologies were of limited interest to Gowon, although the west did not know that at the time, and this new development gave Gowon and his administration greater negotiating power over the supply of British arms.[187] However Ojukwu's ascendant position was undermined by Banjo's treachery, allowing Gowon to take the initiative and force Biafra on the defensive.

International awareness

The war at this stage did not exactly hold huge significance for the international community. Indeed it can be argued that it was regarded as simply another skirmish between opposing forces in yet another unstable, recently independent African country. The *Daily Telegraph* in Britain commented in August 1967 that it was surprised that neither the Commonwealth nor the British Government had treated the conflict particularly seriously or with any degree of urgency. It compared Britain's attitude to Rhodesia where it 'sabre rattled', yet did nothing to Nigeria.[188] It was to take an initiative by Ojukwu to motivate the international community to put pressure on both sides to negotiate a peaceful settlement and to take the war with any degree of importance or seriousness. However, it could be argued that in taking this initiative he calculated that the effect would strengthen his position and put him into the ascendant, so that he could assert his county's independence and gain international recognition for the state of Biafra. He invited the British newspapers *The Sun* and the *Daily Sketch*, as well as television crews, to visit the war in Biafra and to report back to their readers and viewers the status of his country at that time. The first pictures to arrive in newspapers in the west were of small 'pot-bellied' children, with headlines like 'Children wait to die',[189] 'The land of no hope',[190] 'The scandal of Biafra',[191] 'Children need milk Britain sends bullets'.[192] These emotive headlines were based on reports by Michael Leapman of *The Sun*, and Brian Dixon of the *Daily Sketch*.

> Michael Nicholson of Independent Television News had told us about a nearby hospital, in Biafra, which looked after sick children. So we visited the hospital looking for a story and possible pictures. With the help of some of the nurses we were able to photograph sick children suffering from degenerative diseases, particularly kwashiorkor. I admit that some of the pictures were posed, which added to the emotive issues, but which also strengthened our case for the serious issue of starving children in this little-promoted African war. Because of the way reports and photographs were sent for publication in those days we were able to get our story and photographs into our newspapers before similar television accounts appeared.[193]

Added to this Leslie Kirkley, director of Oxfam had visited Biafra on a fact-finding mission in June 1968. He reported that unless food relief came to Biafra in six weeks, up to 400,000 children would die of kwashiorkor.[194] Finally film crews weighed in with newsreels of the brutality and human cost of this war, for public consumption in the west. The international community did not seek confirmation of any facts and images. Imagery was sufficient to confirm in the American and western public's mind that this must be stopped and an end put to this savagery and human misery. Unfortunately these reports were a major contributory factor in helping maintain the war for a further eighteen months, and arguably why it proved impossible for either side to find a peaceful solution to the conflict.

CHAPTER 4

THE SECOND PART
OF THE WAR

From Mid-1968 to January 1970

When you have finished,
And done up my stitches,
Wake me near the altar,
And this poem will be finished.
              (*Limits,* Christopher Okigbo, Biafran poet, killed in
                          action on the Nsukka front in July 1967)

The Biafran War falls into two distinct time frames. The second period is from the middle of 1968 until Biafra's collapse in January 1970. The characteristics of the second period were an ebb and flow of battles and skirmishes, which saw both sides on the ascendant and on the descendant. At times it appeared, especially to the outside world, that Biafra would succeed in her attempts at self-determination, and at others that Federal forces would subjugate her enemy and achieve victory. However it included a number of features which made it difficult for either side to assume that it would achieve its objective.

The first was Ojukwu's campaign to market Biafra's cause effectively to the outside world. His unashamed use of the foreign press to report on his country's privations, especially starving and malnourished children, undoubtedly gave Biafra an ascendant position over the Federal Government and arguably gave it moral superiority. Added to this was

Biafra's innate ability to infiltrate into the Federal army through recruiting young men, for 'attack markets' and her extensive intelligence network. Ojkwu's style of exercising power, and the control and influence the civil executive had over the army, led to excessive and unecessry shortages. This was also true with regard to Gowon's lax style and control over his generals. Arms supplies also proved problematic for both sides. Topography and the climate also became a factor which constrained the Federal forces to achieve ascendancy over Biafra. Finally, January 1970 saw the end of the war which, circumstantial evidence shows, occurred in conditions of reluctant resignation. There is, also, evidence to show that by the end of 1969, not only had Biafra lost much of her territory but many ethnic groups who made up the territory of Eastern Nigeria had long given up support for an independent Biafra; indeed it is debatable whether many of these people had really supported the breakaway state in the first place. It is probable that they had simply gone along with the initial general euphoria that an independent Eastern state would free them from Northern oppression, especially in the light of corroborated reports of genocide. There is some unsubstantiated evidence to support this view. However the fact remained that by January 1970 only a determined few in authority were prepared to continue the war. With Ojukwu and his entourage effecting their escape, in the guise of seeking a peaceful compromise, and with limited territory under its control, Biafra as a state had become unsustainable.

Propaganda and the international press

With the fall of Enugu and only three months into the war, Biafra had effectively lost two thirds of her territory and Gowon was determined: 'I am resolved this crisis won't continue for long … and end it by 31 March 1968',[195] raising false hopes for the Federal Government and the people of Nigeria.

> It is certainly true that there is much merriment about the perpetual announcement of an imminent finale. 'We were finished forty-eight hours after the war started', said one captain, 'Then it was three weeks, three months, six months, a year, July, August, September. By October first, Gowon was supposed to be drinking palm wine in Umuahia.'[196]

Such was the confidence in Federal circles that it was only a matter of time before the rebels were defeated, that as early as October 1967 Dr Ukpabi Asika, an Igbo lecturer at Ibadan University, who had elected to stay at his post and not flee to the East, was appointed as civilian administrator for Enugu and the recaptured areas of East-Central State. However, despite Gowon's prediction, by the middle of 1968 the war had reached a stalemate, neither side having given or lost ground since the success of the Federal forces in the initial stages following Biafra's retreat from the Mid-West region. After Biafra had failed in sustaining its invasion of the Mid-West, due to Banjo's ignominious behaviour at Benin, it had endured an ignoble retreat east across the river Niger to Onitsha. His perfidiousness resulted in the loss of determined military leadership, and led to Biafran troops making their own disorganised way back to the river Niger, not because they were pursued by Nigerian forces, but because they were following rather chaotic orders to retreat.[197] It never attempted to mount such an opportunistic offensive operation again, and its military policy from then on was one of defence, together with small-scale offensive attacks. Ojukwu argued that it was much better to utilise limited national resources in defending its boundaries and seeking international recognition for its status as an independent nation, than to launch strident offensive operations against Federal forces even if it had been in a position so to do.[198] It might be argued that this was Biafra's way of saying that it recognised the ultimate superior forces of the Federal Government, and its only hope for independence was the support of the international community.[199] However, although the Federal army was gaining in strength and had overrun the Biafran capital, Enugu, and was on the ascendant and many in the breakaway state felt that it was only a matter of time before Biafra collapsed, the Federal forces had chronic logistic and manpower problems.[200] These factors led to a lull in the fighting, giving both sides the opportunity to regroup, rearm, and recruit and train more people for their armies.[201] Although from this time Biafra's army became a defensive force, it arguably placed it in the much stronger position of defending its territory rather than launching dubious military adventures to win allies or to subjugate the rest of the country. Biafra's prime objective was to create a sustainable independent and sovereign state, and it is interesting to note that from this period on this indeed became its focus. The promotion of the Biafran state to the outside world became a priority, to persuade other nations to recognise its sovereignty and to convince them that Biafra had the right to an independent existence. By appointing Markpress, a

Geneva-based publicity company, Biafra was able to show the outside world its condition and her determination to remain an independent country.

> This was one of the first wars to be sold by public relations companies on both sides. William Berhardt, who had been involved with Biafra from 1967, through his Geneva-based company Markpress, started to send his press releases from Biafra in February 1968. He later explained that when he was first approached by Biafra he thought it a kind of toothpaste. Under his banner of Markpress he projected the world's conscience and exerted a powerful force in keeping the world aware of Biafra throughout the war. At the height of the agency's effectiveness it was distributing communiqués to five major news agencies as well as briefing Britain's parliament and America's congress. Even Harold Wilson, the British Prime Minister, was impressed with Markpress's reports and they were regularly featured in cabinet meetings.[202]

Ojukwu however was also intent on showing the world how indiscriminate the Federal army was in its efforts to overrun Biafra by its uncontrolled bombing of hospitals, schools and markets, which was leading to the deaths and maiming of innocent civilians, especially children.

He was also intent on showing the world how the effects of the Federal forces surrounding Biafra were creating conditions of extreme hardship, leading to starvation and malnutrition. As described at the end of Chapter 3, British correspondents and cameramen intent on obtaining sensational headlines inadvertently promoted this position. They had been invited by Biafra to tour the front lines and report back to their readers a true appraisal of conditions in Biafra. One of the newsmen and his team was invited to report and film conditions in a front-line hospital. When they arrived at the hospital conditions were not as critical as they had been led to believe and they had to look round the hospital for examples of maimed and desperately ill people. Finding a child who was obviously suffering from kwashiorkor, a disease caused by malnutrition which is endemic on the west coast of Africa, they arranged for him to pose looking pathetic and desperate. Because of the way press photography was processed round the world in the 1960s, it took some days for the report and pictures to be published in the international communities' national newspapers.

Gowon. From Cronje, S., *The World and Nigeria*.
(London: Sidgwick & Jackson, 1972)

Ojukwu. From Cronje, S., *The World and Nigeria*.
(London: Sidgwick & Jackson, 1972)

Ojukwu's father with his daughter (left) and the wife of Costain's managing director (centre). From the private collection of Julia Burrows.

The Sauduna's residence on the morning following the first coup. From the private collection of, and taken by, Simon Watson, manager, Bank of British West Africa, Kaduna.

Biafran currency. Britain-Biafra Association, Rhodes House.

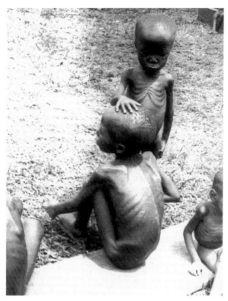

Malnourished Biafran children. Britain-Biafra Association, Rhodes House.

Ojukwu inspecting a guard of honour. Britain-Biafra Association, Rhodes House.

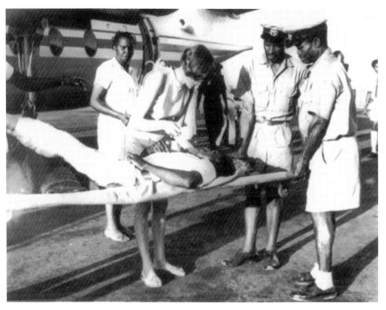

Treatment of Igbo wounded at Enugu airport, following racial disturbances in the north, July to September 1966. Britain-Biafra Association, Rhodes House.

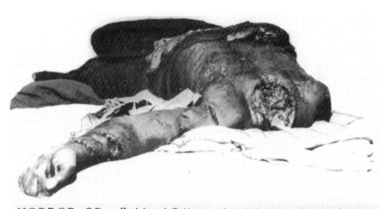

HORROR OF SAVAGERY Head chopped off with an axe. Stomach ripped open and intestines flowing out. Six-foot Onwuanaibe Anyaegbu was travelling by train from Pankshin, near Jos and met his tragic end at the Oturkpo Railway Station in Northern Nigeria where he was beheaded by Northern savages and his body put back in the train travelling to Enugu in the East. Many more men, women and children were beheaded in other Northern towns. The picture summarizes the grief of Eastern Nigeria.

Photograph of an atrocity committed during the northern racial disturbances, July to September 1966. Britain-Biafra Association, Rhodes House.

Protest march in London to stop the Nigerian civil war. Britain-Biafra Association, Rhodes House.

BIAFRA
The third year of war

Nigeria

0 ___100___ miles

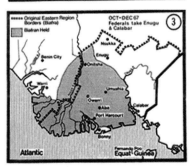 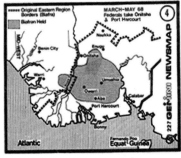

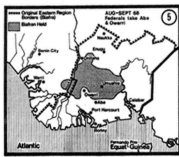 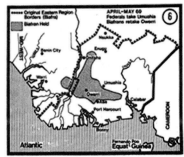

Maps showing the geographical reduction of Biafra from August 1967 to May 1969. FCO 51/169, Public Records Office Kew.

Lt-Col. Benjamin Adekunle (The Black Scorpion), who commanded the 3rd Commando Division of the Nigerian Army.

Lt-Col. Achuzia (left), Adekunle's opposite number in the Biafran Army, and Lt-Col. Morah (right), whom Achuzia threatened to shoot, after Morah had apparently absconded with two million pounds. Achuzia was ordered not to shoot Morah, but to send him back to Enugu, where he was promptly promoted.

When Gowon was asked about supposed indiscriminate bombing by Federal planes he said:

I personally ordered all pilots to avoid bombing civilians, markets, churches, schools and hospitals and any other areas where civilians might assemble. But we had a major problem in so far as the Nigerian Air Force was a young and inexperienced organisation and it was hamstrung by its inability to attract trained pilots from overseas and its limited ability to train Nigerian pilots. This all happened at the time when we thought Biafra was able to build an air force. The problem for us was that Britain had refused to even contemplate supplying us with planes and so we found ourselves looking around for willing suppliers. The Russians came to our resue, not that we even considered the international political implications, and offered to supply fighter aircraft, but refused to offer pilots. We eventually found that we could recruit Egytian pilots, but they were a mixed blessing because many of them did not know how to fly the Russian planes. We also found that they had no loyalty to the Federal cause and were only interested in earning their large fees. We found that these pilots' tendencies were to fly into the war zone and drop their bombs from great heights, where they had no control over bombing intended targets, and with no contact with enemy aircraft. I feel that it was because of this type of indiscriminate bombing which led to tragic consequences of some civilian areas being struck. However I want to to put on record that nobody on the Federal side ordered that civilian sites should be attacked, but it is to my lasting regret that I did not ban all indiscrimate bombing.[203]

In his interview Michael Leapman was disparaging about the excessive claims made by Biafra at the time.

I felt that both sides used the international press to promote their causes in extremely manipulative ways. At the time we were all young ambitious reporters anxious to find dramatic stories and get them back to our editors and to the attention of our readership. One example of this was my colleague Michael Nicholson, of Independent Television News, who was invited to witness and film the execution of a young Nigerian Army lieutenant. Michael insisted on holding up the execution until his cameraman and his equipment had arrived, in order for the whole grisly business to be filmed, and so that Michael could record the affair in detail for his viewers' consumption.

Arguably the Federal Authorities allowed this for international consumption to show the world that Federal forces were not above the law and that justice should be seen to be done. The soldier concerned had been accused and convicted of shooting an unarmed Biafran prisoner of war at Port Harcourt in September 1968.[204]

Its appearance caused an immediate sensation in Britain, Europe and America. These accounts were quickly followed by televised reports of the same incident, which in turn were followed by further examples of atrocities supposedly carried out by the Federal forces. The effect of these reports was to create awareness in the homes of western society, especially the middle classes, of a devastating and barbaric war in a remote part of a little-known country on the west coast of Africa. 'A terrible bloody war is going on. Why do we hear little or nothing about it in the press or on the radio? ... But the need must be known. The strange silence in Britain about this war must be broken.'[205]

Until this time the war had progressed with little awareness by the public of western democracies. The Vietnam War was in progress and its atrocities had been proclaimed by the press, creating an international awareness. Suddenly the world was confronted with the horrors of another war. Because of this, there were mass efforts to help, primarily through large donations of cash to the international aid agencies. The British Foreign and Commonwealth official report states:

> Partly because of the encouragement given by the rebels to western television teams, the most obvious immediate effect of the propaganda campaign was to focus international attention on the civilian Biafran victims of the civil war. Starving babies seen repeatedly on television came to symbolise the Nigerian conflict for millions of people in Britain, Western Europe and North America. Because the communications media, prone in any case to sensationalism and superficiality, had more than their fair share of Biafran sympathisers, much press and television reporting was partial, slanted and even mendacious. But even without rebel propaganda and television

or press bias the sharp television images of human distress would almost certainly have been enough to arouse an irresistible demand for remedial action. As it was, humanitarian concern for the victims of the war in Biafra often became hopelessly intertwined with political partisanship on behalf of the rebels; and the pressure of public opinion in almost all western countries forced governments into active intervention in relief matters as the price for holding aloof from political involvement with one side or the other. The symbol of this urge to intervene was Joint Church Aid.[206]

As Tim Brierly, Oxfam's director in Nigeria at the time, pointed out: 'The allocation of funds under my jurisdiction for Nigeria and Biafra, from June 1968, expanded at a disproportionate rate.'[207]

Not only did mass communication create awareness and support for Biafra's maimed, ill and starving children but it also moved governments' positions on arms supply. By May 1968, Czechoslovakia put an embargo on arms sales to Nigeria. It was quickly followed by Holland, Italy, France and Belgium.[208] By its unashamed use of the media Biafra gained a certain moral superiority over the Federal Government in the eyes of the world's communities. And it could be argued that it led Gowon to counter what in his opinion was Biafra's false moral stance[209] by appointing a team of independent international observers to counter allegations of indiscriminate killing and genocidal attacks on Biafran civilians.[210] The observers spent a considerable amount of time ascertaining the truth of Biafra's claims and eventually, even after exhaustive research, could find very little evidence to support Biafra's charges. It should however be said that that the observer team was restricted in its access to certain areas and was severely constrained in its efforts to uncover evidence of atrocities to civilians within Biafran territory. So although it did much to disabuse Biafra's claims, the perception remained with the public in the west that Federal troops were intent on killing innocent civilians.

Two unfortunate incidents which gave substance to this perception were the unlawful killings of civilians by Federal troops when they reached Benin and Asaba, in the light of Biafra's retreat through the Mid-West:

Witnesses were able to testify that, in the Mid-Western region, where there was a big concentration of Biafrans residing, mass exterminations took took place in the towns of Benin and Asaba.

In Asaba I was informed that all males of Biafran origin were told to gather together in the market-place to welcome the advancing Federal troops. What resulted was that all these people were razed to the ground by machine-gun fire. The witness who gave this statement was in the Mid-Western region at the time of the incident, and he states that about 700 people were killed on this day of ceremonial welcome. The witness referred me to the *Observer* newspaper of 21st January, 1968, where this incident was reported.

In Benin, the Federal capital of the Mid-West, evidence was given that all Biafran residents in this town were called out into the open where they were also exterminated.[211]

However Ojukwu's moral superiority was severely tested in the eyes of the international community when a group of Italian oilmen were ambushed, captured and killed by Biafran troops, under the leadership of Colonel Achuzia. Not only did the international community condemn the killings, but extreme pressure was brought to bear on Ojukwu to release the survivors. The western press had reported that the survivors were to be put on trial for espionage and if found guilty were to be shot. As Ojukwu wryly put it: 'The world was up in arms over the fate of a few white Europeans. The deaths of a few million Africans paled into insignificance.'[212]

Even the Pope became involved in the affair, writing to Ojukwu, who is a Roman Catholic, and reminding him of his Christian responsibilities. The truth of the story, which perhaps has more credibility, is that Biafra's army was accustomed to carrying out incursive raids in the Mid-West region, ever since it had so reluctantly retreated from Ore to Onitsha. One of these incursions involved attempts to gain access to the oil-producing area at Kwale, or at least to prevent the Federal authorities benefiting from it. At the time this oil supply was being funded by Shell and being accessed by a group of Europeans including Italians. In the ensuing ambush by Biafran troops, some of the oilmen were shot and killed, and the remainder taken prisoner. As Achuzia said:

> Biafra was particularly annoyed by Shell's activities in the region because at the start of hostilities Shell's representatives in the East had been repatriated on the understanding that the company, or at least their representatives, would not involve themselves in oil extraction for either side whilst the conflict ensued. Ojukwu felt

very let down by Shell over its breaking their, albeit, gentleman's agreement.[213]

Ojukwu said:

A total of eleven charges were preferred against them. Of these they were acquitted on nine and found guilty on two. The two counts on which they were convicted carried, in accordance with our law, the death penalty. They were accordingly condemned. In response to the direct appeal by His Holiness the Pope and the intercession of our friends, I two days ago on June 4 1969, exercised my prerogative of mercy and granted the men a reprieve. We meet today on this solemn occasion, to witness their release. . . .

There is a significant side-line to the events connected with the release of these men – a situation from which all Africa should draw a healthy and wise lesson. For the lives of eighteen individuals, the entire white population of the world – from east to west, north to south – have risen in impressive solidarity. Even those who for two years of war have actively supported Nigeria in the slaughter of thousands and thousands of black lives in Biafra, have raised passionate voices and made desperate moves. I am not a racist. Far from it. But it is impossible to avoid the need to point these facts and to make appropriate deductions.

He then went on to propose that friends of both parties get together to facilitate ways of bringing this 'futile' conflict to an end.[214]

The Biafran authorities had secured their objective and had blocked this oil access to the Federal regime. Biafra declared that the Italian oilmen had been taken into custody. In reality, according to Achuzia, he entertained them in his officer's mess and accorded them every facility, including making arrangements for them to attend mass at a nearby Roman Catholic church.[215] The fact was, as Ojukwu said, 'Rather than wanting to use these captives as scapegoats, they had become more of an embarrassment to us. We had achieved our objective of securing the oil source, and we were keen to see these men repatriated as soon as possible.'[216]

The incident gives a good example of the international community's ignorance of Africa and particularly of Nigeria at the time. The perception generated by an avaricious western press intent on generating a salacious story, in order to sell their newspapers, was that savage behaviour over the capture of these oilmen was the norm in this underdeveloped backwater in this unknown and perceived inhuman continent, especially in the light of the Congo conflict. The reality was so different. As Ojukwu commented, in order not to lose face Biafra was obliged to be seen to follow a due process of law, but it had no intention of carrying out any sentences handed down by the courts.[217] Added to which, as Gbulie commented, 'The Biafran judiciary, a very British-based institution, ensured that the oilmen had received a fair and open trial.'[218]

However, pragmatic as ever, the safe return of the Italian oilmen was important to Ojukwu, because at the time the incident had done much to undermine his moral superiority in the eyes of the international community.[219]

As the *Daily Telegraph* pointed out:

A hideous mistake is probably the best explanation for the now discovered killing of 11 foreign oil prospectors by Biafran troops. But even that seems hard to accept when 13 others are awarded the death sentence. The Biafran leader has warned foreigners employed in the Federal Nigerian economy that they are there at their own risk. He has accused the 18 oil men, who like the massacred prospectors are mostly Italians, of 'fighting side by side with the Nigerians.' His reticence about the massacre at the Okpai caravan site and the speed of the announcement of death sentences imply that much less than justice is being done. The Biafran leaders seem, inexplicably, to be running amok.

In every respect Col. Ojukwu is blundering. A lengthy report has just been published on cases of genocide suffered by the Biafran people. The caravan site massacre shows that both sides have massacred in the heat of victory. He is deeply offending world opinion which has been largely instrumental in aid reaching him when European governments failed to recognise him.... Panic and derangement seem to be his motives. Moreover, as Col. Ojukwu bases all his military hopes on reaching Port Harcourt and controlling Nigeria's oil supplies again, a policy of frightfulness to those oil operatives whom he captures must defeat his own aims. Initially the Italian and German Governments are seeing what can be done by intercession. Let us hope it succeeds.[220]

The murder, and then the passing of death sentences on the survivors, of the Italian oil drilling team by Biafra had some far-reaching implications, even though the condemned men have now been reprieved.[221]

Ojukwu's use of propaganda throughout the campaign was, generally, promoted to good effect and to Biafra's advantage, as will be seen in Chapter 5 on Biafra's longevity. His public relations organisation successfully used accusations of Federal genocide together with peace initiatives and aid support, whenever they could be focused to put Biafra in a favourable position in the eyes of the international community. Gowon's attitude to publicity was in marked contrast. He believed in his cause, and therefore as he said being in the right, as he saw it, he would achieve his objective without the need for promotional activity. It was only later in the war that he began to realise the importance of public relations.[222]

Biafran infiltration and intelligence

The people of eastern Nigeria are great market traders and the war opened opportunities for such traders to exploit business opportunities on both sides of ever-changing and flexible borders throughout the war. 'Attack markets' proved a great way of moving goods from Federal to Biafran territory. Although the Federal Government had made a determined effort to undermine the fiscal strength of the Biafran economy by changing her currency in January 1968, rendering useless some £2 million taken from the Mid-West's central bank back to Biafra during its retreat from Benin, this had little effect on Biafra's ability to continue cross-border trading through 'attack markets'. These markets were able to satisfy the demands of people and soldiers from both sides by providing goods and indeed services. Such was the nature of this war that Federal troops especially were disinclined to continue fighting outside of traditional working hours. Fighting would end by dusk and would usually not resume until first light.[223] Indeed as dusk approached both sides would lay down their arms, a local market would be set up and trading for locally produced food and drink for both sides would take place.[224] These 'attack markets' were endemic throughout the war and throughout Biafra's borders, satisfying Federal troops' demands for food, drink and local women and creating income which helped sustain the Biafran economy.

The federal soldier presents an easy target as, with his rifle slung carelessly at his side, he climbs a mound of red earth and bellows across the Aba River where it separates the two Nigerias:

' My brother!'

A hundred yards away on the far bank, a small group of ragged Biafrans appear under a clump of palm trees and answer his call. Federal officers and men amble up to join their comrade as he begins his 30 minute dialogue with the 'enemy'. Then the Biafrans drift back into the jungle, having agreed to return later with home-made gin, or 'hot drink' to exchange for beer, cigarettes and food. The Federals return to their trenches where they suck oranges to the serenade of Biafran drums.[225]

At the end of the first batch which was sold faster than we had expected, we made so much profit that I realized why many people went over to what we called in those days 'Ahia Attack' [attack markets], to survive the war. Bold people disguised themselves and went close to the frontiers between Nigerian and Biafran lines to buy such commodities that were not found in our own enclaves and these were the people who made money. The disadvantage was that many lost their lives or their virtues in that attempt.[226]

Cross-border infiltration to the Federal camps by young Biafrans was also commonplace. Ojukwu had instigated the setting up of the Biafran Organisation of Freedom Fighters (BOFF).[227] Within this organisation young boys were encouraged to take part in military training and form an effective boys' guerrilla movement working behind enemy lines. Ben Okafor, who has recently written a play about the war called *Child of Biafra*, stated:

I was 13 in 1966 when the war came and was at school. Indiscriminate bombing started soon after the war began, which caused all schools to be shut in the East. We left Onitsha when the Federal army attacked the town, in the family car (Dad was a recently retired assistant commissioner of police) and so were considered fairly well off in those days. We took very few possessions with us and went to my maternal grandmother's home at Ogbunike, mid-way between Onitsha and Awka, on the road to Port Harcourt. We were there for over a year and all lived together as one large extended family. We all had our jobs to do, such as gathering wood, collecting water and going to the nearby market for food on a regular basis. After Enugu fell we found life more difficult, and my Mum helped our position by cooking for government people who lived nearby. She also went back to Onitsha and collected her few possessions including jewellery, which she proceeded to sell piece by piece to enable her to buy food for the family.

The bombing encroached on our home at Ogbunike, making my dad fearful for our safety. This annoyed me and encouraged me to get involved. So I joined the army. Every day unknown to my parents I would walk to a nearby army camp for training, having joined a boys' company. The training consisted of learning how to use small arms, disarming people and what information to collect once behind enemy lines. This action had been going on for some time, it was easy for us young boys to go behind enemy lines and allow ourselves to be captured. We would then be taken on by the enemy as houseboys, doing all the menial tasks. All the time our job was to gather sensitive information about the troops we were working for. As soon as we felt sufficient or important information had been collected we would simply disappear and return to our home base.

By the end of my training I had been promoted to 2nd/Lt. Shortly after my company was told it would be shipped out to infiltrate the enemy and gather information. My rendezvous with my company was set for midday the following day. I went home to tell my parents. They were very upset, as was most of my community who had all gathered in the village square when they heard the news. Eventually my dad said I could go and gave me a £5 note to help me if I needed to get back home. The next morning as I'm about to leave to meet up with my company, my mum implores me not to go. The effect of this was to delay my departure so by the time I got to the rendezvous the others had already left and I was told to report back next day. The following morning my sister and I heard that my company with other companies had been rounded up by Nigerian troops, they had had their eyes gouged out and were then sent back to Biafra.'

He then recounted how, at the end of the war, he was witness to mass rape by Federal soldiers: 'The Federal soldiers took over the town where I was living, with my sister, and proceeded to round up all the women. I saw women being abused in a most horrible fashion. My sister was lucky to escape.' He also stated:

> When the war was over I walked back to my home town of Onitsha. When I got there I asked about some boyhood friends, and was told about one boy in particular, who, in a group, had been rounded up by Federal troops, and taken to Fege, a suburb of Onitsha. Here the older and taller boys were singled out and shot.[228]

As de St Jorre states:

> Discipline, was always on a razor's edge in the Second Division, weakened and looting and wanton destruction followed another inexcusable atrocity. The soldiers massacred 300 or so of the few inhabitants who had dared to stay, including several local leaders and a number of woman and children, in Onitsha cathedral where they had gathered to pray. This was as senseless and brutal as the Asaba killings.

These killings had been carried out by the Second Division at Asaba during their advance across the Mid-West region to the River Niger.[229]

The Biafran Organisation of Freedom Fighters (BOFF) was established as independent groups surrounding Biafra's borders; at any one time there would be twenty to thirty of these groups acting independently from each other but from a central command. The boy soldiers, up to the age of 16, having received their military training joined detachments within the BOFF movement. Each unit had boy non-commissioned and commissioned officers and worked behind enemy lines. They would infiltrate Federal army units and be recruited by the Federal soldiers as boy workers within the unit. They would spend several days, in some cases weeks, within the enemy camp gathering intelligence. They were welcomed by the Federal troops, not suspecting in the war's early days that they were spies and infiltrators, because the troops had constant demand for menial help, whether helping in the kitchens preparing food, acting as general factotums for officers or indeed in some cases waiting at table at company and battalion dinners. It is likely that many Federal soldiers were aware that many of these boys were from the East or indeed the Mid-West. Initially, it is unlikely that the troops appreciated the significance of this infiltration. To Federal troops these boys were simply useful recruits who helped them to make life more bearable. However these boy recruits were able to gather intelligence with regard to troop movements and troop positions on a large scale, and the Federal authorities became increasingly aware that the enemy was continually able to predetermine their movements. Suspicion centred on the influx of an ever-changing group of young local boys. The Federal forces were determined to put a stop to their ability to secure confidential information, and there are several recorded incidents of atrocities carried out on these boys to curtail stolen intelligence. Some of them were interrogated by Federal troops and then had their mouths cut open and were returned to the Biafran side as a deterrent for other boy recruits. Eventually, on orders from Ojukwu, the recruitment of boy soldiers and their infiltration into enemy territory was discontinued.[230] BOFF, however, proved to be an effective guerrilla force for Biafra, as James Eneje commented in an interview:

> We operated in small groups which were virtually independent of each other and fairly self-sufficient. I feel that by the end of the war there were between 20 and 30 of these groups surrounding Biafra. At the end of the war none of us in our group could understand why the war was brought to a sudden end. As far as we were concerned we had been very successful in infiltrating enemy territory and had caused much disruption and had been successful in pinning down large numbers of Federal troops.[231]

The promotion of 'attack markets' and cross-border trade was to remain a feature of the war and did much to help sustain the Biafran population, helping to foster the belief that eventually Biafra would achieve its objective. Integration was undoubtedly aided by the fact that the war was fought in the East and confusion as to which side people were on was endemic, borders and boundaries remained fluid throughout the war and because of the East's topography people simply carried on their daily lives, in the countryside, often under conditions of great hardship and duress, whoever notionally had the upper hand militarily in their area. Arguably this had advantages as well as disadvantages. On the one hand it created a source of essential supplies and intelligence gathering, which worked positively to support Biafra. On the other hand the fact that people could cross the ever-changing border with relative ease meant that the war turned against Biafra through loss of territory and resources, and also meant that Biafran people could give up the fight for independence and integrate into Federal-held territory. Achuzia gives a good example of infiltration when he spoke of needing some intelligence on Federal troop dispositions. 'I simply donned the insignia of a lieutenant-colonel in the Nigerian army and visited a company of Nigerian troops.' The troops accorded him respect as a senior officer, gave him details of their situation and attack plans. He then made his way back to his own lines and altered his plans accordingly.[232]

Ojukwu: control and supply

One of Biafra's main weaknesses, which arguably did more to undermine her right to self-determination, was the lack of co-ordination and communication within the state through all the functions of government, filtering across all strata of Biafran society. It resulted in a lack of trust between government, the people and the army. The seeds of this distrust probably stemmed firstly from the fact that as the war progressed there was suspicion that people from minority ethnic tribes within the East were ambivalent about their support for Biafra, and secondly from the fact that Eastern Nigerians and the Igbo people in particular are the most egalitarian and democratically-inclined people to be found anywhere.[233] The perception by Biafra's people of the army after its apparent defeat at Ore and subsequent retreat through the Mid-West, established the notion, which was to become endemic throughout Biafra, that the country was infiltrated by saboteurs. Therefore local towns and villages took it on themselves to institute teams of vigilantes, under the guise of a local militia, to secure road crossings and other strategic points. This led to many unfortunate incidents where Biafrans challenged Biafrans under the guise of protecting national security. Ojukwu as leader seems to have done little to disabuse this sentiment and it led to many incidents which damaged the unity of Biafra, and had an undermining effect on her ability to prosecute the war successfully. This caused mortal damage to Biafra's survival, and the very body whose job it was to defend the survival of the fledgling state, the army, was constantly undermined. Not only did the army have to defend Biafra against encroaching Federal troops, but it had to counter a civilian population who were suspicious of it, especially its officer corps. It was felt to be a breeding ground for saboteurs, in the light of Banjo and his colleagues' treachery. There was suspicion that officers trained in the pre-war Nigerian army had divided loyalties. It could be argued that if the civil administration had given greater support and cooperation to the army the outcome for Biafra could have been very different.

Biafra's ruling executive council consisted of civilian commissioners holding and being responsible for a wide range of portfolios. In theory this meant the equal and fair distribution of limited resources. However, because of two fundamental weaknesses this created chronic shortfalls of necessary arms, equipment and food supplies for the army. The first weakness was that the appointed directorates were responsible for distribution of all limited supplies not only to the military but also to the civilian population, and the directorates were controlled and staffed by civilians who had little appreciation or understanding of military needs. Secondly, the strict hierarchical nature and accountability of civilian servants in each directorate, led to people in positions of power within the directorates protecting and enhancing their own personal positions. Two examples show how damaging this system of distribution was to the well-being of the Biafran army. The first concerned the distribution of food to the army, which found itself crippled for supplies as a result of the Food Directorate's inefficiency. The army tried to bypass the Food Directorate and suggested that the army's supply and transport force take responsibility for the army's food distribution. Not only did Ojukwu, as the army's commander-in-chief, renege on his decision-making responsibilities, but he passed this request to the chairman of the directorates for a decision. However, the chairman of the directorates proposed that if the army should be allowed to distribute its own food this might have an adverse effect on food distribution and supply to the civilian population. The implication was that some army commanders might stockpile food supplies, which might lead to some army units, as well as civilians, suffering food shortages. The directorate's chairman then went on to suggest that the army's supply and transport companies should be disbanded and their places taken by the relevant directorates, and that the food directorate should have sole responsibility for food distribution to the army. He even went so far as to suggest that members of the food directorate should be given local military ranks and put into army uniform. This suggestion was not confirmed, and consequently both the food directorate and the army's food distribution arm continued to procure and supply food, continually leading to serious food shortages within the army and in some cases outbreaks of kwashiorkor within the military. The other example was over fuel distribution. At the start of the war Biafra had access to large supplies of oil, but as the war progressed it lost many of the oil-production areas. However it remained adept at refining its own oil, but its distribution to the army was continually under constraint, leading to the unnecessary abandonment of military vehicles. In one instance, a military unit had been able to build up some reserves, but by August 1969 an indent for 800 gallons by the unit only produced 10 gallons from the fuel directorate. The officials within the directorate blamed the lack of supply on scarcity. The reality was that the black market within the confines of the fuel directorate's depot was able to supply 100 gallons at a market rate of £5–£8 per gallon; the official rate at the time was £1.[234]

The sole military representative was Ojukwu himself who, whilst titular head of the army, having been promoted general of the army by the Consultative Committee, and also head of state, was not strictly speaking an active member of Biafra's military hierarchy and was therefore unable to assess the day-to-day needs of the army. His focus tended not to be on the army but on other pressing matters, such as structural control of the state and active involvement in peace negotiations and obtaining international recognition for Biafra. He was therefore hardly in a position to have an accurate assessment of the day-to-day needs of his army. If he felt that there was a weakness in one of the army's positions he had a habit of bypassing the army command structure and dealing with the local commander directly, or indeed appointing somebody else to take responsibility without reference to the army's structural command.

There are countless instances of Biafran troops fighting with limited armaments, no transportation and limited or non-existent fuel supplies, as well as having no food and no uniforms. So acute did these shortfalls become that Biafran soldiers became adept at overrunning enemy positions and capturing any and all equipment in order to ensure physical survival and being then in a position to carry out further attacks on the enemy. At one stage it was estimated that forty percent of Biafra's fighting force was equipped with captured Nigerian equipment, which included a number of armoured cars, taken when their Nigerian crews simply ran away.[235] Njoku, who was the first commander of Biafra's army, recounts how in the opening stages of the campaign at Nsukka, he had no arms to supply his frontline troops, and although he indented for supplies they were simply not forthcoming. His situation was made even more precarious because 'My troops were always running short of arms and ammunition. The governor [Ojukwu] would not let me know the quantity and quality of weaponry available in the Armoury to help me plan for either offensive or defensive.'[236]

Ben Gbulie makes a similar comment about the Nsukka front, as does Joe Achuzia, both going into action with very limited arms and ammunition.[237] There was also the extraordinary case of Biafra's Captain Ujam, who when interviewed said that throughout the war he had retained his battalion's position, but because of a lack of all kinds of supplies had had to rely on the local people for food and the Federal opposition for armaments. Whenever his battalion was short of ammunition, short aggressive assaults into enemy territory became necessary. Each time his men were successful in gaining fresh supplies of arms. Captain Ujam remained with his battalion of nearly 1,000 men in the same geographic area throughout the campaign's thirty months.[238]

The Biafran state civil service, under the direction and overall sanction of state commissioners, controlled the distribution and supply of limited resources. All state commissioners were civilians with no understanding of the armed forces' constant demand and need for an inexhaustible supply of resources, ranging from arms to clothing and food supplies to medical support. There is evidence that civil servants were in the habit of stockpiling supplies in order to protect their own positions, and there is evidence to prove that in some circumstances a healthy black market developed in the supply and procurement of limited resources. The Eastern Nigerian's innate temptation to trade was never far from the minds of many Biafran civil servants. These nefarious activities led to chronic shortages of supply for the hard-pressed troops fighting for the very survival of Biafra. It seems strange that military demands to put an end to such practices went unheeded by the Biafran establishment. Only on occasions when Ojukwu himself became involved in a military operation did the supply of necessary arms and equipment, and basic needs, fulfil the needs of an engagement. It seems that civil servants, with the support of the Biafran government, were intent on preserving limited supplies to the detriment of successful military actions.

By the middle of 1969 the Army was getting not more than 10 percent of all food available to the Directorate, and this amounted to a meal in four days to each soldier. Among the anomalies I identified with the Directorate was the fact that they worked daily from 0800 hours to 1500 hours and did not work at all on Sundays. Their services or assistance were therefore not available over weekends .... The sum total of the ugly food situation was that a good number of soldiers in the front lines either moved back in search of food or stayed on and fraternised with the enemy in the hope of getting presents of food and cigarettes from him.[239]

In the long term this was to have a debilitating effect on Biafra's soldiers, and many instances show that some troops were resigned to failure and were more than happy to surrender to Federal troops. It was to take draconian measures on the part of a small number of the officer corps to ensure that troops remained loyal and supportive to the Biafran cause. When questioned on these comments, Ojukwu did admit to such shortcomings during the war, but commented on the lack of trust between the military, the civilian administration and the Biafran population. He admitted that his own lack of trust and his doubts about loyalty within the military stemmed from the time when he had put much faith in Lt-Col. Victor Banjo and Biafra's invasion of the Mid-West. Indeed not only did Banjo's treachery undermine Ojukwu's faith in his armed forces but it also started the rumours of saboteurs.[240]

The rumours and counter-rumours of saboteurs were to become a disabling link in the defence of Biafra, and arguably a contribution to its eventual collapse. The aftermath of the Banjo affair was to have reverberations throughout the remainder of the war. There is little doubt that in the eyes of many Biafran civilians the army had let Biafra down badly through its failure to keep control of the Mid-West. Sabotage, rumour and counter-rumour were to become features of the war in Biafra. It was reported that even in the early stages of the campaign accusations of sabotage abounded, as in the case of Biafra's ill-fated 54 Brigade, who were regularly attacked thirty minutes before their own attack on a particular front. The aforementioned Lt-Colonel Banjo and his assistant Major Alele accused the army commander, Colonel Njoku, of sabotage. Major Alele, a civilian political commissar, with the honorary rank of major, broadcast to the nation that there were saboteurs among top-ranking Biafrans. Tragically, without substantive confirmation, the people tended to believe him. Although in the broadcast he made no mention of names, he hinted that the blame lay with the army, and the effect of this was to undermine the army commander's authority, leading to his eventual replacement.

Both Banjo and Alele were executed following accusations of plotting to overthrow the Biafran state after the disastrous incursion into the Mid-West.[241] However, it was the effect of Biafra's failed attempt to take over the Mid-West and the execution of the supposed coup plotters that sealed the fate of the army in the eyes of the civilian population until the end of the war. The population regarded every senior military officer as a saboteur. Indeed the early defeats to the Biafran army were blamed on saboteurs, much to the consternation of Madiebo who had replaced Njoku as army commander.

Arms

When the war started, both sides were ill-prepared for a conflict of any duration, and immediate efforts had to be made to rectify shortages and shortcomings. The Nigerian army had never been designed to fight an internal war, let alone a civil war. Both sides found themselves encountering new experiences and new challenges. It is interesting to note how each side resolved the problem, but in totally different ways. Recruitment into the Nigerian army had always been problematic, because it was not generally seen as a desirable career option. It was obliged therefore to look for recruitment for the expanding army in other areas. Recruitment of students, prison officers and indeed ex-prisoners became popular.

> I was given the task of recruiting what amounted to a whole new division. I looked for my recruits mainly in Lagos where I selected men from all walks of life, but found that some of my best soldiers, after training, came from the dregs of society. Many of my men had formerly been in prison, and were released to serve in my division. The 3rd Marine Commando Division was created from scratch by me from such dubious sources as street thugs, outlaws and renegades, mainly from Yoruba ethnic groups. I then had the task of moulding them into a credible fighting unit.[242]

In the early days of the war Biafra had no such constraints. Defence of Biafra became a popular sentiment, and the authorities found themselves oversubscribed with applicants to the army. It was only later in the war, when Biafra's cause had lost support from the minority peoples of the East, that recruitment to the army became problematic and the authorities were obliged to introduce conscription, which had mixed results on the army's efficiency. It led to some farcical incidents, as happened when a recruiting team raided a dance hall in Umuahia in December 1968. The dance was held to raise funds 'for the successful prosecution of the war'. Not only were two lieutenant-colonels recruited on that evening but many women were obliged to return home without their menfolk. Such a forced style of recruitment eventually became an embarrassment, and public conscription was stopped, its place taken by an equally unpopular quota system.[243]

It is, therefore, unsurprising that throughout the campaign both armies maintained their methods of operation and their traditions as though this was still the Nigerian army of pre-independence days. The strict hierarchical nature and divisions of class were endemic within the army and were to remain so on both sides throughout the thirty months of the campaign. As Colonel Achuzia commented after he had trained a militia of 5,000 men in Port Harcourt, there was determined resistance by the Biafran army to allowing any men from his militia to taint the army. Indeed for a long period of the war, the various militias in Biafra were not integrated into the regular army.[244] An interesting observation was made by one former Sandhurst-trained serving officer about Achuzia, to the effect that he was not a proper trained soldier at all and had had to persuade Ojukwu to grant him a commission, which was awarded much to the distaste of many senior officers in the Biafran army.[245] It was said at the time about the military:

> in fact, it was the code of Kipling that influenced the conduct of the war on both sides. Until the very end Effiong [Biafra's chief of staff] looked like a British staff general – polished Sam Browne belt, a sword for ceremonial occasions and a chauffeur-driven, khaki-coloured English Humber car bearing a general's flag. His officers were similarly indoctrinated – moustaches, swagger sticks, batmen, officers' mess.[246]

The effect of this tradition and rigid hierarchy was to make both sides adopt inflexible attitudes, which made for slow limited advances by the Federal army and entrenched positions by Biafran troops. At the start of the campaign the average Northern Federal soldier had little respect for the fighting qualities of Biafran soldiers, and expected only token resistance. However the fighting prowess of many Eastern soldiers was to change this opinion. The Welsh South African Major Taffy Williams, who fought for Biafra for twelve months of the war stated:

> I've seen a lot of Africans at war, but there's nobody to touch these people. Give me 10,000 Biafrans for six months, and we'll build an army that will be invincible on this continent. I've seen men die in this war who would have won the Victoria Cross in another contest. My God some of them are very good scrappers.[247]

A further comment was made as the war progressed:

> At the start of the conflict the general impression among the federal troops was that the Ibos would display only token resistance. It appeared, however, that the fortitude of the Ibos stemmed from their fear of annihilation and their leaders' belief that, if they held out, the world would rally to their cause.
>
> The military tactics of the Biafrans were to place a series of defended posts, usually well sited, but not mutually supporting, across the line of federal advance. In their main defensive positions, particularly those in the north facing the federal first division, the Biafran soldiers showed great endurance.[248]

Furthermore the Easterners fighting on their own territory and over ever-changing boundaries found it easy and highly advantageous to infiltrate the other side. They were able to gather intelligence on enemy movements and this, coupled with the fact that they had details of the Federal army's communication codes and had Biafran supporters placed at the army operations centre in Lagos, meant that they were often able to pre-empt the enemy's movements.[249] This is borne out by the fact that within hours of the British High Commission military attaché's assessment of the war being completed, Ojukwu had a copy of it. The report gave the breakdown and order of battle of the 'final big push, being enacted towards the end of 1969, each division's offensive capability, their tasks, and dispositions'.[250] The Biafrans had access to most Federal troop movements throughout the war.[251]

> The strongest point of the Biafrans was their highly efficient intelligence network. They had their agents living amongst the Ibo population in Lagos and appeared to have access to both supreme

and army headquarters. They even operated their own radio network from Lagos to Ojukwu's headquarters.[252]

Being constantly aware of the Federal army's movements meant that Biafran soldiers could always harass enemy positions; it also meant that Federal troops would only attack after making overzealous preparations and as they attacked expending inordinate amounts of ammunition.[253] However due often to lack of equipment and ammunition on most occasions Biafran troops tended not to stand and fight but simply disappeared into inaccessible parts of a friendly and supportive countryside.

As the war progressed both sides did attempt to break the traditional mould. Ojukwu made extensive use of Achuzia and his unorthodox methods, as well as instructing Major Steiner, the German ex-Foreign Legion sergeant, to form a commando force of some 3,000 men, divided into six small battalions. Steiner, together with the Welshman Williams, formed the Biafran Fourth Commando Brigade.

'Steiner selected the sector on the Enugu to Onitsha road, an area which was to remain in Biafran control until the end of the war.'[254] He did have limited success in stalling the advance of the Federal Second Division. The Second Division's commander, Colonel Haruna, admitted that Steiner's actions along the Onitsha to Enugu road had stopped him joining Nigeria's two other divisions in their attempt at the final subjugation of Biafra.[255] Steiner also achieved notable success with his commandos at Amansee, Uku and Amieni. Achuzia succeeded in stalling Mohammed's First Division crossing of the river Niger from Asaba to Onitsha. Achuzia stalled Mohammed three times, and it was not until Mohammed realised the inadequacy of his position that he took his division north, crossing the river clear of Achuzia's division, and was able to force his way south to Onitsha. Although Federal troops eventually took control of this important Biafran trading town, laying waste to the largest covered market in Africa at that time, with considerable loss of civilian life, the Biafran forces continued to battle with the enemy, and Onitsha was never fully under the control of Federal troops until the end of the war.

Ojukwu commented on the Federal army's attempt to cross the Niger, following Biafra's retreat from the Mid-West:

I had been an instructor on the staff at Teshi, in Ghana, lecturing on infantry tactics in 1959, and one of my students was Second

Lieutenant Murtala Mohammed. One of the questions I set my students was how to attack Onitsha from the west of the River Niger. I recalled Mohammed's response so knew what sort of approach he would take and was able to forestall his attack.[256]

Indeed such was the tenacity of Biafran troops that the Federal forces were never able to control the entire road from Enugu to Onitsha. The Biafrans kept control of a section of the road of some six to twelve miles until the end of the war. This was to cause Federal forces continual frustration and arguably, because of the number of troops pinned down and deployed at this point added to the longevity of the war. One of the most spectacular ambushes of the war occurred in this area. A large supply column containing munitions and petrol, escorted by two armoured cars, had been sent from Enugu to support Murtala Mohammed's division at Onitsha. At Abagana it ran into an ambush set up by Colonel Achuzia, who witnessed it, and said the results were spectacular:

A lucky shot hit the leading petrol tanker and the ensuing flames spread back throughout the column, destroying everthing in its path. All the enemy's supplies were lost, including all their vehicles and many of their troops. It had a remarkable effect on Biafra's morale and indeed the remains of the attack were left for visiting journalists to inspect and photograph for the reminder of the war.[257]

An eyewitness account of the state of the Biafran army in late 1968 is given by Stephen Lewis, a Canadian journalist who visited Colonel Kalu,[258] the commander of the important Owerri sector, with headquarters at Oguta:

The key town of Oguta, just north-west of Owerri a few miles from the strategic Uli airport, and three weeks ago in Federal hands, has been retaken ... the Biafrans are in command of every inch; in fact, Oguta serves as Brigade headquarters.

The Colonel, like his head of state, is, ironically, a product of the best British military colleges. He is soft spoken, contemplative, self-critical, and balanced. In fact, I find the apparent moderation of Biafran leadership quite unsettling; it violates all my pre-conceived prejudices about the nature of the military mind.

He runs a tight fighting force. This is no rag, bob-tail outfit. Commando units move in and out by jeep with startling precision – armed to the teeth .... . At the administrative centre, paper-work is simply and effectively organized. The atmosphere is tough, but not oppressive. Despite the still critical shortages of vehicles, gas, and weapons, morale couldn't be higher. You can't help but marvel at the spirit against such formidable odds; the Nigerians do have an inex-haustible armoured military machine.

Colonel Kalu acknowledges an upswing in Biafran prospects over the last few weeks .... . He attributes a large part of it to the slight but steady increase in arms; but feels that the halting of the Federal advance is the overwhelming morale factor.

The account goes on to record an extremely important comment relat-ing to Biafra's survival and the optimism shown by many people when interviewed, that Biafran desire for self-determination would finally be successful.

When you pore over maps with a man like Kalu, the mystery of Biafran resistance is gradually clarified.

One gross misconception has been put abroad from the start of the war. It is assumed that when a provincial capital falls – like Port Harcourt. Or Aba, or Owerri, or Umuahia – the province falls with it. Nothing could be further from the truth. What was indicative of traditional Europeans patterns of war cannot be superimposed on Biafra.

In this country, control of a provincial capital usually means control of that capital and not one inch more. Biafrans just move their administrative headquarters a few miles away, with minimal interruption of the war effort.

To talk, therefore, of a tightening net, based on the capture of certain main centres, is simply to talk nonsense. Much of the hin-terland is firmly in Biafran control. It is difficult to talk of identi-fiable 'fronts'. The front is incredibly fluid; it changes materially every day. The Biafrans are not squeezed into some ever-dimin-ishing pocket one-tenth its former size (as I was wont to believe not so long ago). You can travel scores of miles in every direction from Umuahia, and get no sense whatsoever of an 'enemy'.

It is possible to cross back and forth through federal 'lines' with impunity, because 'lines' don't always exist. Even in those provinces where Nigerian troops control the Capital, Biafran admistrators collect taxes, organise the local population and report regularly to Colonel Ojukwu.

And everywhere there is stepped-up, sophisticated guerrilla resistance. In fact, that's the kind of struggle Biafra really wants to fight, and is now prepared to fight – an unconventional war. Sharp guerrilla thrust by night; swift commando action and retreat; cutting off vulnerable Nigeria supply lines – these are the very heart of Biafran tactics.[259]

Adekunle's Federal Third Commando Division made strides to break conformist traditions, but had rather less success than the opposition. His success can mainly be attributed to his abusive and draconian control over his officers and men.

As he commented, he demanded absolute obedience from his officers and men and gained a reputation as an austere, remote and fearsome divisional commander. As he said by 30 I was a hero in the eyes of the Nigerian people and was known as the 'Black Scorpion'. He said that he had an absolute love for his training at Sandhurst, and regards his defining moment during training in England when he was introduced to Queen Elizabeth the Queen Mother, and was invited to stay at Sandringham. The invitation was never confirmed but the thought by her made a lasting impression on him. In spite of his success as divisional commander he was modest about his achievements. However he is bitter about his dismissal as a divisional commander, to be replaced by Colonel Obasanjo, who he feels enjoyed all the success without enduring any of the the hardships along the way.

Soyinka comments on Obasanjo:

but [he] is, basically, a fortunate recipient of the largesse of fate. After all, how many soldiers, after the bulk of a civil war had been fought and won by others, find themselves positioned to receive the articles of surrender from the enemy, thus appropriating the mantle of the architect of victory?[260]

He commented that his dismissal was because he refused to even to consider conversion to Islam, which he says was a condition for him to retain his command. There is little evidence to support this, but there is evidence to support the fact that the Federal Army headquarters were concerned that their divisional commanders were exercising too much independence,[261] were potentially becoming too popular with the population and in the interests of security for the regime, and its attempts to achieve victory, changes were necessary.[262]

As he admitted when he was given the task of recruiting, staffing and training this Third Commando Division, he invited prison officers and ex-prisoners to form the basis of his force – not the best people to turn into a competent fighting force.[263] During the early stages of his campaign he enjoyed a considerable number of successful advances, after he overran Calabar. In May 1968 his division finally overran the strategic town of Port Harcourt, after his capture of Abakaliki. By September he had taken Aba and in mid-September Owerri. It seemed that his advance was unstoppable. 'He runs an area the size of Scotland with the authoritarian and arbitrary hand of a medieval king.'[264]

Gowon announced a further 'final offensive' to bring the war to an end. The reality was, however, that the war was not in fact running in Lagos's favour. In April 1968 Biafran troops overran Federal troops at Onne, Arochukwu and Aletu and then proceeded to take back Ikot-Ekpene, Oguta and Enugu-Aku. In October there was a decisive battle at the strategic town of Umuahia, when Adekunle's Third Commando Division lost two-thirds of its force. By November his lines of communication to Owerri were threatened. The recapture of Owerri was probably the most successful action of the campaign by Biafran troops. Throughout the war, once Biafra had been put into a defensive position, she enjoyed certain strategic advantages. Not only did she know her own topography, she had the support of the local population. Federal troops tended to advance only on main roads and did little to secure surrounding territory during their advance.

A report written by Col. Scott, defence attaché at the British High Commission in Lagos, commented on the fighting capabilities of the Nigerian army:

Tactics employed by the Nigerian Army are basically conventional but are poorly executed, ponderous, slow, but nevertheless in the long run they prove effective. This is an infantry war fought at

platoon or at best company level, with progress dependent upon the
going and the visibility in the various sectors. Units regard a vast
expenditure of small arms ammunition (the basic weapon being
fully automatic) as substitute for their acute shortage of leaders at
the lower level. Effective fire control and conservancy of ammunition are almost unknown throughout the Army apart from in a few
units in the 1ˢᵗ Division which are wealthier in junior N.C.O.s and
officers. Normally it is the cacophony of automatic weapons with
most bullets flying harmlessly high into trees, which carries the
Nigerian soldier forward. It has been said that the Nigerian Army,
in the advance is the best defoliation agent known.

The report also passed comment on the fighting qualities of Biafran
troops:

> The Igbo soldier has displayed latent military qualities which
> caused some surprise. This motivation stems from fear for sur-
> vival which follows the daily tirade of propaganda pumped out
> by Ojukwu's information service. In sheer guile he has proved
> himself adept at infiltration and by doing so, has forced the
> Federals to use caution in their movements and to expend a dis-
> proportionate number of men on purely security and defensive
> tasks. With the Federal formations acting in isolation and lack-
> ing in co-ordination, the rebels tend to turn the traditional dis-
> advantage any force has when operating along interior lines of
> communication to their advantage. Apparently this fundamental
> fact has never been fully appreciated by Federal planners, who
> consistently fail to move their three divisions in concert.[265]

This fact was borne out by the Federal forces' inability to join up along
the main road connecting Onitsha with Enugu throughout the war.
As Achuzia said: 'Because my troops found it easy to infiltrate with
theirs, and the Federal's inability to co-ordinate divisional attacks, it was
relatively easy to keep the divisions along the Enugu to Onitsha road
apart.'[266] Owerri proved a typical instance. Federal troops had advanced,
following main roads, to Owerri and had successfully secured the town.
However, because they made inadequate provision for protecting their
flanks over their lines of communication, Biafran troops found it easy to
break the Federal supply lines. Biafran troops were able to disrupt the

supply lines to Owerri and indeed, much of the time, were able to capture armaments. Thus over a period of weeks they literally laid siege to Owerri leading to a final surrender of Federal troops. The Biafrans, however, were not keen on capturing the Federal troops defending Owerri, so they arranged for a safe passage of these troops, having first relieved them of arms and supplies. Pragmatic as ever, Biafra was in no mood, nor was she able, to feed and look after additional captured Federal troops, hence the decision to allow them to escape. The retaking of Owerri was a great victory for Biafra and a serious setback for the Federal side.[267]

When the war began the Biafran air force consisted of two B26 bombers and a number of French Alouette helicopters. In 1968, following recognition by Zambia, she received two DC-3s from that country.[268] In May 1969 Biafra received a boost in its defence forces with the arrival of five Swedish Minicom light aircraft. According to the terms of their sale, they were delivered on 29 April to an airport in Paris and then dismantled and loaded on to a charter plane which delivered them to Libreville and then on to Uli in Biafra. The planes had been financed by Tanzania, who had officially recognised the state of Biafra on 13 April 1968. Count Carl Gustaf von Rosen, together with a group of Swedish volunteers, with the help of the Biafran air force, put these planes to considerable effect. They were classified as trainers, and although the Swedish Ministry of Trade stated that they were equipped with cameras for prospecting, what the ministry did not state was that they were equipped with 76-mm rockets. During May 1969 the Minicoms raided the airports at Port Harcourt, Enugu and Benin, destroying a number of Nigerian planes. Von Rosen and his team were also successful in attacking the oil refinery complex at Port Harcourt and the Shell-BP terminal in the Mid-West at Forcados. These attacks proved so successful that they had a serious effect on Nigeria's oil production. They also effectively attacked shipping near Sapele and Warri.[269] It is also interesting to note that according to Sqd-Leader Alfred Anowai, no Minicoms were lost throughout the campaign and they continued to be effective until the end of hostilities. The Biafrans in their usual imaginative way ensured that all these aircraft were safely stored when not on mission. The Biafrans built specially secure hangers for these aircraft into the side of a hill, ensuring their invisibility to Nigerian aircraft surveillance.[270] Von Rosen and his Minicoms represented a good example of how even a limited supply of armaments could have a disproportionate effect in one side gaining a stragegic advantage. Throughout the campaign both sides were constrained by the supply of arms, but because the war was effectively fought as a series of skirmishes and limited engagements, many of short duration, additional armament support could result in either side gaining substantial results. The effect of Von Rosen's aircraft was to paralyse the supply of oil from Port Harcourt and the Mid-West to Lagos.

Arms procurement was an ongoing problem for both sides. From the Federal position arms procurement should have been fairly straightforward. It had no constraints on access to the country either by sea, land or air or on her finances, due to ongoing Yoruba support for the war. It had competent administrative support from Awolowo and his ministry of finance, together with Adebayo, the Western military governor's ongoing commitment to defeating the Biafrans, and initially it had the support of Britain. However, as the war progressed and international pressure reviewed the human cost of the war, constraints were put on the Federal Government.[271] Added to this was the huge appetite the Federal forces had for the wasteful use of arms.[272] Biafra had different constraints, which meant that arms procurement was an ongoing issue throughout the war. Sources of supply in the early stages proved extremely difficult, but as the war progressed became less problamatic.

Gowon: control and logistics

Gowon had been elected as a compromise candidate following the second coup, and it took time for him to secure his power base. Although by the start of the war his position had improved significantly, he had massive manpower, logistical and topographical constraints to overcome if he was to successfully challenge the secessionists' determination to achieve sovereignty. Although initially he declared that the Federal Government's response to Biafra's declaration was only to be a police action, following the secessionists' unsuccessful incursion into the Mid-West he was obliged to expand the size of his army rapidly. Because the majority of the officer elite were of Igbo origin, Gowon was left with a very small group of experienced officers, the majority of whom were his peers in the army's hierarchy. Because of this, he said, 'They had had similar military experiences as I had had, mainly during their time as a United Nations support force in the Congo, and I tended to allow them a high degree of responsibility and autonomy for recruitment and expansion of the army.'[273]

This approach saw the beginning of his style of leaving his commanders with much independence, which was to prove in some cases successful, but in others less so.

At the start of the war the Federal Government appeared to be militarily superior to Biafra. On the one hand it had most of the original Nigerian army, both in equipment, arms and men. However it suffered from one weakness at the start of hostilities. It had an insufficient number of trained and skilled officers to conduct a war which eventually demanded the expansion of the army from 10,000 men to 200,000 men. Obviously during the course of the campaign it attempted to redress this imbalance, but this proved an extremely difficult task. As Scott pointed out, the 1st Division was fairly well supported by officers and non-commissioned officers (NCOs) of sufficient calibre, being the remnants of the original Nigerian army, but the other two divisions relied on newly trained and often inexperienced officers and NCOs. As Adekunle pointed out when he was given the task of creating his commando division, he was obliged to recruit from the student population, prison officers and ex-prisoners.[274]

Not only did the Federal Government have the daunting task of massive expansion of its army, but it also had to overcome logistic and topographical barriers. The logistics of supporting an army some four hundred miles from its base proved extremely testing, especially at the start of the campaign. As the war progressed, and especially after Federal forces captured Port Harcourt and seaborne support became available, this problem became less acute. However an intractable constraint was the territory over which the war was fought. Together with the weather these were to prove ongoing challenges for all Federal forces. This was especially true during the rainy season from April each year, when troops found that advances were extremely difficult to achieve, in spite of the army preferring to move only along the major roads. Added to this was the troops' deep superstition and fear of the dark, which meant that nocturnal activities were very limited.

As an example of Gowon giving his commanders a high degree of autonomy to create and control their own divisions, Adekunle was given the task of recruiting and training his men, and as he said he sought recruits from a variety of sources including released prisoners. He often exercised his responsibility for procuring arms and provisions.[275]

> The divisional commanders exercised supreme power over life and death both in military and civil matters within their commands ... The fact that their headquarters were a long way from Lagos and difficult to reach because of poor communications reinforced their autonomy. Adekunle was particularly fast off the mark when he

needed something urgently. On one occasion, he called the British Leyland representative (an Englishman) into his office in Port Harcourt and ordered forty Land Rovers on the spot. When the representative asked for the customary down payment, the 'Black Scorpion' promptly paid him £50,000 in cash over the top of his desk and promised the balance on delivery. On another occasion, Adekunle walked into a large store in Lagos and bought half a dozen typewriters for his divisional offices. He told the two expatriate salesmen to come with him to Ikeja where he would settle the account. They did so – it was in the morning – but when they got there Adekunle simply put them on his plane and flew them off to Port Harcourt, 400 miles away. There they were paid in cash and sent back to Lagos in his aircraft, arriving just before nightfall.[276]

However autonomy also led to great rivalry between divisional commanders, which proved detrimental to the Federal authorities in their attempts to secure their objective:

> The rivalry between the three Divisions ... covered every field ... from the capture of significant Biafran towns to competition for arms, supplies and reinforcements from Lagos ... the Shell oil depot in Apapa had permanent representatives, from each division, vying with each other over petrol supplies. Adekunle was especially prone to flying back to Lagos suddenly and personally supervising the routing and sometimes 're-routing' of ammunition and other supplies to his own Division .... . Yet more extraordinary was the fact that at least two Divisions had their own arms buyers operating in Europe independently of the Federal Government.[277]

However as the war progressed the divisional commander's style of independence proved to be ambivalent. Undoubtedly Adekunle enjoyed some spectacular successes at Calabar, Port Harcourt and Aba, but in an attempt to take Umuahia and Uli, in competition with his rival, Murtala Mohammed, the commander of the First Division, he lost Owerri. Murtala Mohammed also exercised autonomy from Lagos over his command, but he enjoyed much less success than Adekunle. On three occasions he failed to take Onitsha against the redoubtable Joe Achuzia's forces, succeeding in the end when he approached the problem by crossing the river Niger further north and attacking Onitsha from that direction.

By the middle of 1969 Gowon decided that these commanders should be replaced. It is possible that he felt that they were simply becoming too powerful and independent of his command and would potentially offer a threat to his power base. When questioned on this, his comments were ambiguous, but seemed to confirm that this sentiment was close to his thinking at the time.[278] Murtala Mohammed had been his closest rival during the traumatic days following the second coup, and of course he was to oust him from power in the future. Adekunle had become hugely popular with the Yoruba population, and although only half Yoruba, his mother was a Bachama, from the Middle Belt; his popularity with people in the Western Region was a potential challenge to Gowon's position. 'Regional pride being what it is, and Adekunle having acquired hero's status to many Yorubas, it was necessary that all three commanders be moved simultaneously.'[279] According to Adekunle, he still feels bitter about being replaced at a time when, as he said, he was in a position to bring the war to a successful conclusion.[280]

The end

Nigeria concluded the war, which had had many international ramifications and involvements, without a single foreign arbiter or force setting foot on its soil. This attested to the willingness of Nigerians to give peace a chance. The foreign press had prophesied a bloodbath. Even the Pope, as he saw the crisis drawing to a close, said that unfortunately in the Nigeria conflict weapons had leverage over humanity. He saw the Nigerian war reaching its end with the terror of possible reprisals and massacres of a defenceless population.[281]

By early January 1970, Biafra's situation had become virtually untenable. Its territory had been reduced to a small enclave barely 60 by 100 miles, a fraction of its original size. Many of its provinces were already under the jurisdiction of the Federal authorities. Those of its people who had remained were confined within smaller areas, and the territory was increasingly unable to support itself. In spite of these constrictions and privations why was it that Biafra collapsed so suddenly? Was the political will to survive simply draining away, or were there forces strong enough to continue the fight? There were reports that political support for Biafra was waning, but there were members of Biafra's administration who were keen and prepared to wage a guerrilla war in order to sustain Biafra's objective of independence. Until the closing stages of

the war, the sentiment still persisted that if more substantial international official recognition could be achieved then Biafra, even at this
late time, could achieve sovereign status. It was based on the assumption that the longer she conducted a guerrilla campaign the greater
opportunity she would have to secure a negotiated settlement and international recognition.[282]

Ojukwu called a conference of his war cabinet on 6 January 1970.
At the conference he blamed the army for Biafra's current predicament
and said that the people had lost confidence in its ability to defend its
sovereignty. At this meeting both the chief secretary to the Biafran
Government, N.U. Akpan, and the Chief Justice of Biafra, Sir Louis
Mbanefo, supported this argument. Ojukwu also made the point that
following the loss of Aba province and its main town, Aba, if Nigerian
troops crossed the river Imo, Biafra's position would indeed be precarious.
Various military representatives at the meeting voiced their opinion over
the army's loss of support, but it was left to the commander of the Biafran
Organisation of Freedom Fighters, Colonel Ebenezer Aghanya, to confirm
that Biafra should continue in its struggle to achieve its independence.
Ojukwu gave his whole-hearted support to this sentiment and then succeeded in producing a coup de grace. He explained that his government
had gained possession of top-secret Nigerian documents which confirmed
that Federal forces were under express orders to massacre all male Biafran
adults when, as anticipated, Biafra capitulated. He affirmed that these
documents were genuine by arranging for certified copies to be distributed. He also confirmed that there was to be a resumption of guerrilla
operations under Colonel Achuzia. Achuzia had been operating in Federal
territory in the Mid-West region for some months, during which time he
had encountered the Italian oilmen.[283]

On 10 January 1970 Biafra held its last cabinet meeting. According to
an eyewitness account, Ojukwu was insistent that everything should be
done to salvage what was left and end the suffering. He reluctantly agreed
to leave after he had ruled out the idea of 'a government in the bush'. He
left Uli airport on 11 January, with N.U. Akpan, the chief secretary to the
cabinet, Michael Okpara, advisor to Ojukwu and Major-Gen. Madiebo,
commander of the Biafran army. He said that he was leaving 'in search
of peace, leading a delegation, in order to give it maximum effect, and
to speed up matters, in order to save lives of the people and preserve the
concept of Biafra'. He continued, 'I did this knowing that whilst I live,
Biafra lives. If I am no more, it would be only a matter of time for the
noble concept to be sent into oblivion.'[284]

When questioned about his final departure from Biafra, Ojukwu confirmed that at the time, although it seemed on the one hand that he was abandoning a lost cause, he felt with his advisors and colleagues that this was the best course of action, which could have helped lead to a form of negotiated settlement which would have seen Biafra gaining some form of autonomy, although, as he commented ruefully, he had not expected Effiong to give up the fight so quickly and so readily.[285]

Achuzia's account of Ojukwu's departure is much more colourful: 'Ojukwu told me that a meeting had been arranged in Liberia by President Taubman, to negotiate a peaceful settlement between him and Gowon.'[286]

There are conflicting views as to why the war came to an abrupt end. As Hunt comments: 'Right up to the end he (Ojukwu) was winning the propaganda war, and he had realistic hopes that a combination of white European countries would come to his rescue and nullify his military losses.'[287]

Even the Scott Report states that its aim is 'to examine whether either side can reach a successful military conclusion before the end of the dry season'.[288] Scott defines this as the end of April 1970. His assessment concluded that the Federal forces were capable of achieving military success, but with a number of qualifications. Scott had based his report on a debate in the British House of Commons on the Nigerian Civil War on 9 December 1969. The motion read:

> That this House, in the name of humanity and realism, calls for a change in Government policy over the Nigerian Civil War, which after two and a half years cannot now be won by either side; and urges Her Majesty's Government to press through the Security Council of the United Nations for an immediate and total arms embargo on the supply of arms to either side.[289]

Gbulie is of the opinion that Ojukwu had lost support politically. As he says, by then Nnamdi Azikiwe had deserted him and was actively promoting the East's reconciliation with the Federal Government. Effiong, his military commander, was also wavering in his support for continuing the fight. Immediately after Ojukwu fled the country Effiong simply disappeared, and it was left to others, notably the chief justice Sir Louis Mbefano and Col. Achuzia, to broker a peace.[290] He is also of the opinion that many senior civil servants had reneged on support for

Biafra and indeed had been clandestinely communicating with members of the Federal opposition for some time. As Achuzia said: 'It was a fairly open secret that civil servants from both sides met throughout the war at Ukei, in the Mid-West. Trading went on at these meetings as well as intelligence swapping. I felt that this created doubts in our people's minds that we could ever win the war.'[291]

Ojukwu claimed that he had tacit and material support from a number of European countries, including Ireland and Holland, in the Middle East Israel, and in Africa, beside the countries which had already recognised Biafra, South Africa was ready to acknowledge her officially. He hinted that if France had not been so ambivalent in her relationship with Biafra and indeed had officially recognised her, all the other nations emotively backing Biafra would have fallen into line and the country would still be a sovereign unit today.[292] As the official Foreign and Commonwealth report pointed out, on 31 May 1968 France did in fact recognise Biafra, in a 'quasi' fashion, and from that time onwards she dramatically increased the supply of arms to Biafra. However, this was still not sufficient to encourage official recognition from other supportive nations. As Ojukwu pointed out, without that international support, Biafra's cause was lost.[293] Achuzia states that the Biafran army was far from defeated, and that he had received instructions from Ojukwu several months before the cease-fire that the army was to be divided into three sections, a defensive army commanded by Col. Kalu and an offensive army commanded by Col. Achuzia, with a third of these two forces to be rotated for training and support for the other two armies. In his opinion this force, consisting of 150,000 well-trained and well-armed men, would have been able to defend Biafra for many months to come. As he said, the army was far from defeated and the Federal forces never succeeded in overrunning Uli airstrip, allowing for an ongoing flow of arms and goods into Biafra. He is dismissive of the fighting strength of the Federal forces, confirming that his forces were more than a match for the opposition, and that he was prepared to continue the fight, as a guerrilla war if necessary, until inter-national pressure forced official recognition for Biafra. However, as he pointed out, he was induced by Biafra's chief justice, Sir Louis Mbanefo, to broker a peace with the Federal forces. According to Achuzia, who it seems by then had achieved popular folk hero status, the troops would only agree to a ceasefire if he ordered one. It was to take his English wife Ethel to ask him 'is this your war Joe?' for him to agree to a ceasefire.[294]

Because of its superiority in arms and because it was the 'status quo' authority throughout the war, and enjoyed the support of the former colonial power, it was perhaps inevitable that the Federal Government would achieve its objective and bring Biafra back into the Federation. However, Ojukwu's campaign to promote Biafra to the outside world proved very successful. Even late in 1969 when the British Conservative party sent Lord Carrington to visit both sides in Nigeria, he was impressed with the spirit of the Biafran army, commenting that he saw neither side altering their respective positions on Nigerian unity and Biafran sovereignty.[295] Frederick Forsyth commented that even Nigeria's third and final assault on Biafra had petered out.[296] In spite of losing much of its territory by the end of 1969, Biafra's ability to survive had proved conclusive. Her use of 'attack markets', boy soldiers and its ongoing superb intelligence network had all helped in this process. On the negative side, Ojukwu's style of running the Biafran state had arguably proved detrimental in sustaining its sovereignty, and it had certainly created problems of supply to its armed forces. The supply of arms had been problematic for both sides, but on balance the Federal forces had had much easier access to supplies from outside the country, and this had helped its achieve her objective. More arguable is Gowon's style of control, or rather lack of it, which had mixed results and eventually led him to replace his commanders with more compliant people who had less ambition and were therefore not a threat to his position. Logistics, land and climate also played their part in determining the outcome of the second part of the war. The Biafran army was perhaps better placed to benefit from these. It knew the territory, and although supplies were intermittent and often non-existent, they never had far to travel, and added to this the army knew the land well and had the support of the local people. Eventually, although the outside world felt that Biafra would not capitulate to the Federal Government, it seems that internally by the end of 1969 Biafra's sovereignty was highly questionable and that it was only a matter of time before she effected surrender.

CHAPTER 5

BIAFRA'S LONGEVITY

*Because they are convinced that 'no condition is permanent in this world'
{an Igbo motto} they are adaptable to a degree and prepared to learn new
ways . . . .*

*Ironically it is their hard work and their success that have contributed to
make the Biafrans so unpopular in Nigeria, and notably in the North. Other
characteristics are adduced to explain the antipathy they manage to generate;
they are pushful, uppity and aggressive say the detractors and energetic say the
defenders. They are money-loving and mercenary says one school; canny and
thrifty says the other. Clannish and unscrupulous in grabbing advantages, say
some; united and quick to realise the advantages of education, say others.*[297]

*Nigeria had vast petroleum resources . . . and was by no means irrelevant to the
course of events . . . and was subject to the influence of external factors directly
related to Africa's recent colonial past and to the present context of contest between
imperialist powers and the people of the newly independent countries.*[298]

How was Biafra able to survive from July 1967 to January 1970, a period
of 30 months, in the light of the Federal Government's claim that it
would defeat Biafra within weeks? During that time Biafra suffered
extreme privation, leading to mounting malnutrition, disease, illness and
death; diminishing land space, which caused severe reductions in food
and other resources, and homelessness and increasing numbers of refugees,
and mounting military opposition, putting further pressure on Biafra to
capitulate. Ongoing attempts at negotiated settlements and peace initiatives, Biafra's resourcefulness, ranging from extensive innovativeness

to brilliant sagacity, the support it received from foreign aid agencies and foreign countries, and the use of propaganda, which helped Biafra to promote and sustain accusations of genocide, all helped to prolong Biafra's survival, but it was perhaps its military resourcefulness and the innate weakness of the Federal forces, together with Biafra's terrain and the weather, which determined the length of the war. However, the most significant feature which linked all these factors was the effect that the international press and Biafra's overt and ongoing use of propaganda had on the longevity of the war. It is likely that without them the war would indeed have been a much shorter affair.

Attempts at negotiated peace settlements

Undoubtedly negotiated peace settlements played their part in sustaining the war, for four reasons. Firstly, at the start of the war neither side was strong enough to bring hostilities to a conclusive end, and therefore both sides demanded help from outside agencies. Secondly, these agencies were themselves not able to offer total support for one side or the other, due to internal and external pressures, and so sought compromise. Thirdly, the fact that outside agencies were ambivalent in supporting one side or the other meant that in their eyes compromise was the only way to secure a lasting peace. Fourthly, it is a reasonable proposition that at the start of the war the negotiating stance of both parties was strong, as neither side could claim physical superiority over the other. This in itself ensured the war's longevity, because the outside agencies sought compromise. As the war progressed, the balance of power edged more to the Federal side, thus weakening Biafra's bargaining position, and its demands were less well received by outside agencies intent on brokering a peaceful settlement.

In all there were nine attempts by the international community to broker peace, all of which ended in failure. The challenge for the negotiators, as in most wars, was that initially both sides treated peace negotiations as yet another way to achieve their respective objectives; many peace negotiators failed to appreciate this. Arguably it was this main fact that led to so many failed attempts to secure a peaceful settlement. As Ojukwu commented, 'The bargaining position of any of the peace negotiations was determined by our military position at the time.'[299]

The two sides' positions were also seemingly intractable. The Federal Government's demands were that Biafra should give up its right to self-determination and return to the Federation. It should accept the twelve-state structure, and the old Eastern region should be one of three regions, East Central forming mainly the heart of Igboland. Biafra took the view that its sovereignty was not negotiable and that its independence was permanent. Although from time to time there were minor variations to these opposing demands, both sides negotiated from these positions until the end of the war.

The first organisation which, under pressure from Biafra and support from Ghana, took an interest in brokering a peaceful settlement was the Organisation of African Unity (OAU). However, one of the OAU's founding principles was that it did not interfere in the internal affairs of a sovereign member nation. Nevertheless it did offer to appoint a consultative committee of six member states, which visited Lagos but not Enugu. Unsurprisingly, the committee reaffirmed its commitment to the sovereignty and territorial integrity of member states and therefore came firmly down on the side of supporting the Federal cause. This caused Biafra Radio to comment: 'By deciding to consult only one party to the dispute, the mission has demonstrated its lack of objectivity and doomed itself to failure.'[300]

At this early stage in the war neither side was in a mood to compromise, each feeling that their respective cause was justified, and each strong enough to win. However, the OAU was seen by Biafra as a biased agency which would not support their cause, and by other countries as an inadequate medium through which to negotiate a peaceful settlement.

A major breakthrough came early in 1968. The Federal Government asked Arnold Smith, the Secretary General of the Commonwealth, who had been contacted by Gowon, if he could negotiate a peaceful settlement which would keep Nigeria's sovereignty intact; an almost insurmountable task, in view of Biafra's demand to retain its right of self-determination. However, at this time Biafra was, arguably, on the defensive. Its army had retreated back to the river Niger not, it should be added, because of pressure from Federal troops, but because of its lack of leadership, following Banjo's decision to renege on his orders. Furthermore, Onitsha was being attacked by Federal troops and, importantly, Nigeria had changed its currency. The currency change, discussed later in the chapter, initially had a severe impact on Biafra's economy and its ability to conduct the war. Up until this time both sides had traded in a common currency. This new situation left Biafra in an increasingly vulnerable position. So arguably, at this stage, negotiations for peace, therefore, appeared an attractive proposition. Three of Ojukwu's most important and trusted advisors, Michael Okpara, former premier of the Eastern Region, Kenneth Dike, former vice chancellor of Ibadan University and C. C. Mojukwu, Ojukwu's uncle and home minister, were prepared to agree to a confederated Nigeria, providing there were guarantees for the Igbo people. Unfortunately, the Federal Government's attitude had hardened since the start of hostilities and it was in no mood for compromise. Furthermore it seems that Biafra was in reality simply trying to improve her international standing and to gain more outside support. To a point she seems to have been successful. Whilst negotiating a peaceful settlement, Mojukwu was also in France arranging for a supply of arms.[301] Not only was Biafra successful in negotiating a new supply of arms but in April 1968 through persuasive negotiations it received official recognition from a succession of African states. Tanzania, Gambia and the Ivory Coast formally acknowledged the existence of Biafra, to a large extent because of their frustration at the Federal Government's inability to secure a compromise peace internally. All of them were concerned with Igbo survival rather than the East securing victory over the Federal Government. Unsubstantiated evidence would seem to point to many other African countries having sympathy for Biafra's cause, and their inclination being to recognise her.[302] Even Niger and Sudan, although predominantly Muslim, showed sympathy for Biafra's plight, seemingly because of Ojukwu's personal friendship with both leaders.[303] A view from the time lucidly expressed recognition for Biafra:

It was not an approval of the political choice of Eastern Nigeria to secede. This was made clear by the fact that the first recognition did not come until months after secession. It was the magnitude of the war and the enormity of the suffering produced that made the leaders of these countries revolt against the method adopted by the Nigerian Government to solve the problem .... Like secession itself, [it] was more a reaction against than a decision for. Like most acts born of reaction it produced unexpected counter-reactions. Not only did it encourage the 'hawks' on the Biafran side to unnecessary intransigence as far as peace negotiations were concerned, it also provoked in the Nigerian government an increased determination to make nonsense of, by military means, whatever gains Biafra might have scored diplomatically.[304]

The Kampala peace talks, under the chairmanship of Arnold Smith, took place in May 1968. Each side had a contrary focus. The Federal Government was intent on its troops capturing Port Harcourt, an event which would arguably lead to Biafra's military collapse. On Biafra's part, having been recognised by four African states, with others showing considerable sympathy, it firmly believed that by this action the international community would acknowledge the status it was determined to achieve. The Federal Government offered the Igbos the opportunity to return to the confederation, with some safeguards but little else. This indicated its ascendancy on the battlefield at the time: it had overrun much of Eastern Nigeria, was in control of its major towns, including Enugu, and had control of much of its natural wealth, especially oil. Biafra insisted on a ceasefire, an end to the blockade and withdrawal of all troops to pre-war positions. The talks lasted for six days, but because of both sides' intransigent positions, they had little chance of success. Although the Kampala talks failed, both sides, especially the Nigerians, were under pressure from the international community to seek a negotiated settlement, and from the middle of 1968 the Organisation of African Unity took a focal role in these negotiations, under the chairmanship of the Ethiopian Emperor, Haile Selassie. On this occasion Ojukwu made a personal appearance at the peace talks in Addis Ababa. However, his speech did little to appeal to any OAU representatives and indeed may well have undermined support for Biafra's cause. Ojukwu was intent on trying to put Biafra on an equal sovereign footing with Nigeria. The problem at this stage in the war was that neither side was in a mood for compromise. The Federal Government still felt that it was militarily in the ascendancy and, because President De Gaulle had spoken of the necessity for Biafra to confirm its own identity, this implied that France would shortly recognise Biafra as an independent nation.

The annual OAU meeting in mid-September in Algiers saw a renewed effort at establishing a negotiated peace. At this time Gowon was intent on one of his final 'big pushes'; he said, 'I felt that our forces were strong enough to finish off Biafran resistance once and for all.'[305] With that objective in sight he felt he could persuade the OAU that the Biafran cause was lost, and gain majority support for his position. His problem appears to have been one of poor communication with his commanders. Adekunle had enjoyed a degree of success in South Eastern Nigeria, near Aba, but his counterparts in the North East, around Onitsha, and the North West, around Enugu, were still hopelessly pinned down by the Biafrans led by Colonel Achuzia. Biafra, fully aware of the Federal army's precarious positions, exploited this claim to the full at the OAU meeting, in the knowledge of France's ongoing support. However, the conference finally resolved to support the Federal Government's cause and demanded that Biafra give up its sovereign status. What followed was probably a defining moment in Biafra's fortunes, and, arguably, would eventually become one of the factors which ensured its collapse.

On 7 September 1968, in the Hotel Napoleon in the Avenue de Friedland, Paris, a crucial meeting took place between representatives of Jacques Foccart, General de Gaulle's special African envoy, and senior Biafran delegates, including Nnamdi Azikiwe, Nigeria's former president, Michael Okpara, former Eastern Nigerian premier, Kenneth Dilke, the vice-chancellor of Nsukka University and Francis Nwokedi, a senior Biafran diplomat. At the meeting the French representatives explained the level of French support for Biafra, for the present and the future. Although it offered substantial continuing aid no official recognition would be forthcoming until other African nations confirmed their recognition of Biafra. Arguably, this was a defining moment for France in the Biafran war, which effectively confirmed its ambivalence. Debatably, the motivation for France was that if the Federal Administration defeated Biafra then it would find its influence over the Federal Republic weakened. The result of this was that the delegates, apart from Nwokedi, felt that the time had come to open more accommodating negotiations with the Federal Government.

Unfortunately, Ojukwu was in no mood for compromise and his influence meant that the delegates' plans of moderation were moribund. Nnamdi Azikiwe felt, however, that the time was opportune for offering compromise and settlement with the Federal Government. Together with Ralph Uwechu, he abandoned his support for an independent Biafra and was to spend the rest of the war campaigning for a reunited Nigeria. His influence, following his change of mind, should not be underestimated and it can be argued that from this date the seeds of disenchantment with Ojukwu within the small ruling political elite were sown, and Ojukwu's political power base was irretrievably undermined.[306] On 16 February 1969 Azikiwe proposed a fourteen-point peace plan. In it he suggested 'international mediation and not regional conciliation', and that because America had followed a neutral policy throughout the campaign, it should move that the Security Council of the United Nations should constitute a committee to seek ways and means to bring the conflict to a conclusion. His sixth point suggested that he was in favour of a united Nigeria:

> That the Security Council should obtain acceptable assurance from Biafra of its unqualified acceptance of the principle of the creation of states, provided it accords with the wishes of 60% of the inhabitants of the area or areas concerned, without prejudice to the future modification of the present 12-state structure, as far as Port Harcourt is concerned.[307]

He also confirmed, however, that if political union between Nigeria and Biafra ensued, that it did so within the Aburi Agreement. This was a possible sop to Ojukwu and his Eastern colleagues, since Gowon's rejection of the Aburi Accord had been a major cause of the war. He also reaffirmed that should a plebiscite confirm support for an independent Biafra, then the United Nations should support this.[308]

In September 1969, the sixth conference of the OAU met in Ethiopia; this time there was a resolution:

> appealing solemnly and urgently to the two parties involved in the civil war to agree to preserve, in the overriding interests of Africa, the unity of Nigeria and accept immediately the suspension of hostilities and the opening without delay of negotiations intended to preserve the unity of Nigeria and restore reconciliation and peace that will ensure for the population every form of security and every guarantee of equal rights, prerogatives and obligations.[309]

However by then the international community were focused on providing consistent and organised relief for Biafra's increasingly beleaguered population; at the same time neither side was willing to compromise and make determined efforts at negotiating a peaceful settlement. There was one final effort at a peaceful settlement in December 1969, made by an extremely persistent Haile Selassie, who proposed to both sides two rather different versions of a basis for arranging a truce leading to a peaceful settlement. In retrospect it was a rather naïve approach at this late stage in the war. His hope was that once talks started, the gulf between the opposing sides could be bridged. Unfortunately, on the evening of the peace meeting Ojukwu broadcast on the radio a speech which obliterated all hope of a peaceful compromise. In it he said that Haile Selassie had assured him that the meeting would be under the auspices of neither the OAU, nor of previous resolutions passed by that organisation, and he confirmed that Biafra would not be forced to surrender its sovereignty in order to restore the integrity of one Nigeria. Biafra would regard such a move as unconditional surrender. This speech totally undermined the Emperor's compromise position, and it also confirmed the Federal Government's unwillingness to countenance any meeting with Biafra under these preconditions.

Arguably, peace negotiations were a useful tool in Ojokwu's armoury to help him to secure confirmation of Biafra's sovereignty; his unwillingness to compromise confirmed that such negotiations would not help him to achieve his objective, but undoubtedly they helped Biafra to keep its cause in the international arena and offered opportunities to help sustain the war, and thus were a cause of its longevity. Ojukwu played on international sensitivities to good effect. Not only did this factor increase his faith in Biafra securing her independence, but they helped to engender further attempts at negotiated peaceful settlements, hence the number which took place.

Not only was international concern and pressure brought to bear on Gowon to seek a peaceful settlement, but his own humanitarian and Christian spirit also played its part in his attempts to forge a peace. As one of his officers pointed out: 'We always knew when peace negotiations were in the offing because the supply of arms and ammunition would dry up.'[310] Throughout the war Gowon attempted to confirm his desire for a peaceful settlement, which is why at the end of hostilities he proclaimed the slogan of: 'No Victor No Vanquished'.[311]

Even as late as November 1969 he was still hoping for reconciliation with the Igbos:

> He prefers to wait for Biafra to run up the white flag. Throughout the front, empty beer bottles outnumber the spent cartridges in the trench litter. At the forward line of 16 Commando Brigade, the officers relate with increasing gusto how the roof of battalion headquarters was blown off in a Biafran air raid. The story is more than a month old but it suffices as nothing else has happened since to break the monotony . . . . Lagos has decreed that the army must do no more that hold its own, striking only when the Biafrans strike first.[312]

Unfortunately at each attempt at a peaceful settlement, both sides took it in turn to be intransigent, depending on which side had the military advantage at the time of negotiations. However, it was the international concern for a negotiated settlement which helped to foster ongoing attempts at agreement and which inadvertently ensured that, whilst they were pursued by all parties, the war would continue in its longevity.

Biafra's resourcefulness

Biafra was fortunate in having a well-organised regional civil service and part of an efficiently-run national police force, as well as an organised judiciary, and a well-established banking system. All functioned well and were part of the successful running of the regional government before the conflict. These agencies continued to run efficiently, but under wartime constraints, throughout the period and helped to ensure that Biafra functioned as an orderly state, and contributed to her longevity. Even two years into the war there was still evidence of the smooth and efficient running of the state:

> In the week I was in Biafra a new coinage was issued, the postal service was operating normally – taking four days from any part of the country to another .... The Africa Continental Bank reopened four branches in new locations (following the fall of Umuahia the seat of Government and the last sizable town in Biafra) bringing its total to 26, which includes a bureau de change at Ulli Airport. And the court of appeal established after six months of war in December 1967 was preparing for its next session .... The civilian nature of life, even in Biafra at war, is everywhere evident: arms are not carried even by the soldier, except at the front. Road blocks are, in the main, manned by uniformed police, often even by smart policewomen. There is no curfew and no restriction on movement. The army itself has the character of a citizen's rather than a militant force. Its officers seem to regard war as a subject for urgent study and practice, rather than a permanent way of life.[313]

There had been attempts under the Ironsi regime to centralise the civil service into a unitary arm of government, under Decree 34,[314] but due to the second coup and his overthrow, little had been achieved in this direction and the civil service remained an arm of regional government. When a military government had been formed following the first coup in January 1966, General Ironsi had appointed Lt-Col. Ojukwu military governor of the Eastern Region. When he arrived in the region he was fortunate in having a fully functioning state under his control, and although he took his orders from the ruling military government in Lagos, because of the way the country had been governed before and during its short-lived democratic period, the regions were semi-autonomous and remained so.[315] As Ojukwu commented: 'And for three-quarters of a century now, Biafra has been ruled as a single political unit; so that the vast majority of the population have grown accustomed to the fact of the uniqueness of the political entity which we now know as Biafra.'[316]

It was therefore easy for Ojukwu to take control of the reins of regional government and ensure that in the event of secession the functions of government remained intact and indeed gave weight and control to the new breakaway state, helping to ensure the efficient running and stability of a modern sovereign country. These apparatuses of state were to remain the backbone of Ojukwu's administration throughout the short life of Biafra, and arguably were important to Biafra's survival. It not only gave him control but, in the light of Ironsi giving him the military governorship of the region, it gave a legitimacy for his leadership, and although he ruled through a small group of advisors, and paid a degree of acknowledgement and respect to Biafra's Consultative Assembly of representatives and elders, his power in effect was absolute. His position, arguably, was therefore much more secure than that of Gowon, who throughout his administration had to rely on the support of many more factions within the Federal Government, which ultimately caused his downfall.

These factors are important when considering the war's longevity. Without Ojukwu's secure and legitimate power base it is possible that Biafra as a state would have collapsed far sooner, because in effect he was an unchallenged leader, a position he was to hold until the very end of Biafra's life. Even today, some forty years later, he is still held in awe and respect by the elders in the Igbo community.[317]

However, it was Biafra's ability to harness its creative inventiveness which was a major factor in determining her ability to survive so long. Biafra was indeed fortunate in having a well-educated minority whose skills, creativeness and inventiveness were brought to bear during the war. Colonel Ahhanya, a qualified engineer, was charged with the task of bringing together scientists, engineers and people with specialised skills who would support him in the challenging task of forming a group called Research and Production (RAP). Ojukwu realised early on in the campaign that Biafra's survival would depend on its resourcefulness to counter shortfalls which the young country would meet as the war developed.[318] RAP became involved in an extraordinary range of activities, ranging from the chemical group to the clothing and steel helmet group. Some were more effective than others, but all gave weight to Biafra's survival.

Under RAP a range of directorates was established in an attempt to provide for the well-being of the army as well as the civilian population. Some of these directorates were more successful than others, and some were accused of, and found to be, stockpiling and trading their goods in a black market, as mentioned in the previous chapter. However, others eventually, through a process of trial and error, helped create support for Biafra. Scientists under the leadership of Dr Okpala from Nsukka University were given the responsibility of developing arms and rockets for Biafra's army. They produced two types of rocket, ground-to-ground and ground-to-air, which were effective in defending Calabar and Onitsha.[319] However, their most successful development was an anti-personnel mine, 'Ogbunigwe' which means 'Kill 'em plenty', nicknamed 'Ojukwu's bucket'. It was nothing less than a metal container charged and filled with metal pieces. The Biafran Commissioner for Information, Dr Eke explained: 'The Ogbunigwe, which we are producing at the rate of up to 500 per day, is effective up to a range of half a mile, clearing an angle 60 degrees wide in front of it.'[320] It had a devastating effect on the Federal forces, achieving notoriety and building confidence amongst Biafran soldiers because it gave them an easily produced armament which they knew was an effective defence against their enemy. Its support was to make Biafran soldiers stand and fight rather than simply disappear into the jungle when attacked by a generally better armed and better supplied enemy, as in the battles at Awka and Abagana.[321]

Oil production and refining became increasingly important as the war progressed. Initially it was of little significance because Biafra had ready access to extensive oil supplies. However, following the loss of Bonny Island and Port Harcourt and the area's hinterland, oil supplies became scarce and production and refining became a priority. Under the Petroleum Management Board, the production and supply of crude oil and its refining continued and adequate supplies were maintained throughout the war. Indeed by its end almost every army contingent supported and refined its own fuel supplies.[322] A report in *The Times* dated 5 March 1969 explained:

> Far from supplying fuel to the Biafran Government or military, the churches and the Red Cross get a weekly allocation from the Biafran Government of 1000 gallons of diesel fuel. Since the taking of Bonny Island in July 1967, Biafra has been under naval and land blockade. ... Where does the fuel come from?
>
> At a Biafran Army divisional headquarters I saw one of their homemade refineries in action. The man in charge of it, an economics graduate of Durham University, Mr Nwofili Adibuah, aged 34 explained: 'The process we use is fractional distillation using these crude cooking pots. These are our mini-refineries'.... Mr Adibuah commented: 'The petrol comes off first, then the kerosene and final[ly] the diesel.'... This particular mini-refinery which consisted of three 'cooking pots', was producing 280 gallons of petrol and 100 gallons of kerosene and 250 gallons of diesel fuel per day ... this has since been followed by several others both at divisional and brigade level. There are even private citizens who are today refining their own fuel in their back yards so as to keep their cars on the road.
>
> Dr Ben Nwosu, a distinguished Biafran nuclear physicist, who trained in London and the United States and worked until recently at the International Atomic Energy Agency in Vienna, told me: 'Our main refinery, which is considerably more sophisticated than what you have seen produces 25,000 gallons of fuel per day and we are now investigating the possibility of making our own aviation fuel.' Dr Nwosu continued: 'But we do more than produce equipment for the army. We have decided [to produce] what we call survival gin, which has palm wine at its base. Until we lost Abakaliki we were able to produce our own salt. We make our own matches, dyes for military clothing, soap made from palm oil and caustic soda, shoe polish and farm implements.'[323]

In order for a modern state to function efficiently, circulation of money internally and externally is a priority. Biafra was no exception, especially when considering its needs for external commodities, in particular arms. When secession became a real probability the adequate supply of finance became an imperative. Indeed if the fledgling state was to survive, a secure financial base was essential. Initially this proved a problem, in spite of Biafran funds being based on Nigerian currency and Nigeria being a member of the Sterling Area. Eastern Nigeria was dependent on the central administration for its allocation of funds, and at the point of secession this allocation was quickly suspended. The challenge for Biafra was to create situations to ensure the ready circulation of internal and external funds. This at times was to border on the desperate, at others on the farcical, but throughout its independence evidence shows that given all its constraints it was able to retain a reasonable liquidity of funds. As Ojukwu commented: 'We were fortunate in having most of the machinery for running the state, because of the highly developed infrastructure, because of regional independence, long since developed by the colonial administration.'[324]

One of the first decrees made by the newly independent state of Biafra was No 3 of 1967, The Bank of Biafra Decree. The decree stated: 'The Bank shall carry out all the central banking functions in the Republic including the administration of foreign exchange and the management of the public debt of the Republic.' It also confirmed that the bank would maintain parity with the Nigerian pound.

Because Nigeria was not prepared to allow Biafra its sovereign status, establishing a defensive policy was priority, and the funds to secure adequate outside supplies of arms were paramount. Evidence suggests that initially some of this funding came from the population; indeed Ojukwu himself was rumoured to have put some of his family's fortune at the disposal of the state.[325] Other sources used were the issuing of ten-year bonds, although there is no evidence to show that this was successful. However, by far the most important strategy for Biafra in its quest for foreign exchange was its conversion of its holdings in Nigerian currency. On 30 December 1967 Nigeria's finance commissioner stated that '£37 million had been seized by the rebels in the East'.[326] Biafra, however, claimed that by January 1968 it had collected £53 million. Debatable though the amounts were, the evidence would point to a sizeable figure, and these funds, including a further £6 million raised at the start of secession, were all deposited in Europe.[327] This gave Biafra adequate funds to create good external arms supply lines to support its military defence force and to ensure her survival against external attack. There is documentary evidence to show that in July 1967 Biafra entered into an arrangement with Rothschild Bank in Paris to sell her oil and mineral rights for a period of ten years, for the sum of £6 million.[328] The British High Commission questioned the evidence but obviously felt at the time that it did have a degree of authenticity:

> A questionable piece of evidence is the mysterious document which the Federal authorities produced purporting to show that Ojukwu has assigned all mineral rights to the Rothschild Bank for a £6 million consideration.
>
> Paris suggested in their telegram No 428 that any such policy is likely to come elsewhere than from the Quai d'Orsay, presumably from the Special Department of African Affairs in the Elysee, reflecting therefore a policy more personal to General de Gaulle. Our impression here supports this suggestion.

Hunt, the British High Commissioner, then goes on to suggest:

> the Nigerian Authorities are convinced that the French are now firmly behind Ojukwu and that it is only the French subsidies, which by now have reached many millions of pounds, that keep Ojukwu going. I believe that neither the French Embassy in Lagos nor the Quai d'Orsay is involved; indeed my French colleague here continues to be vehement in his professions of support for the Federal cause. The Federal Government believe that SAFRAP, the state-owned French Petroleum Company, is the channel for the subsidies. The odds are against Ojukwu winning even the help of French mercenaries; but an oil company which is used to spending large sums on speculation in unproductive trial drillings is not likely to blench at risking £10 million or so when there is a chance, however slim, of acquiring properties which cost the present owners £200 million.[329]

When questioned on the authenticity of the Rothschild document and Hunt's comments to his Secretary of State, Ojukwu refused to be drawn into discussion on the matter. It is therefore apparent that whatever the truth, the fact was that there was considerable material support by France for Biafra and it seems reasonable to assume that either through Rothschild Bank or the French state-owned company SAFRAP, subsidies and or finance were forthcoming, and proved a valuable source of foreign currency to support Biafra.

A chance of further funding also came following Biafra's invasion of the Mid-West region. Some £2 million out of a total £12 million found its way to a bank in Asaba, from Benin. This money was collected by the retreating Biafran Army from bank vaults in Benin. It seems that the balance of £10 million was too difficult to transport at the time. However, it seems that little of this ended up with the central bank of Biafra. Some was probably spent funding the Mid-West invasion and retreat and some was simply stolen by Biafran soldiers. Achuzia recalls that his pay and records chief, Lt-Col. Morah absconded with a large quantity of money and caused him embarrassment over payment to his troops. According to Achuzia the money was part of the consignment of funds collected at Benin for transportation to Biafra's central bank. Morah was eventually arrested trying to affect his escape to Cameroon, and brought back to Achuzia for a summary court-martial but without the money. Achuzia threatened to shoot Morah for his 'despicable' behaviour. However, Achuzia was ordered by Ojukwu to return Morah to Biafra's army headquarters, where he was promptly promoted to a more responsible position.[330] It seems likely that very little of this money ever found its way to the vaults of Biafra's central bank; that indeed is what Symes records in his document *Bank Notes of Biafra*.[331]

By August 1967 the Federal authorities were becoming aware of the increased currency movements from Biafra to Europe and its conversion into foreign exchange. In an effort to control this, a decree was issued to the effect that Nigerian currency exported from Nigeria, including that from the East, would not be redeemed by the Nigerian Government. At the same time the Federal Government were taking further steps to make currency transactions even more difficult for the recalcitrant regime: it planned the introduction of a new currency. Once the new notes were in circulation it could stop the redemption of the old currency, eventually making currency held by Biafra worthless. The date from which the new currency would come into effect was 22 January 1968. Prior to this date there was an unseemly rush by currency speculators as well as the Biafran authorities to redeem old currency for new. Biafran currency holdings were sold at a heavy discount, and the proceeds were then repatriated back to Nigeria. In one case, on 12 January 1968 some twenty tons of Nigerian banknotes were flown into Switzerland, but only seven tons were allowed to be unloaded, since thirteen of the twenty tons had been shipped in a Rhodesia-registered aircraft; Switzerland did not have diplomatic relations with Rhodesia. The aircraft continued its flight to Lisbon. In another case, on 20 January, some £7 million of Nigerian currency was seized at Lome in Togo. This was repatriated to the Nigerian authorities. It was rumoured that Nigeria paid Togo a substantial sum of money for this service.[332] In the event the Nigerian authorities brought forward the date for introducing new currency to 3 January 1968. By late January Ojukwu announced the introduction of Biafra's own currency. Undoubtedly Nigeria's introduction of a new currency did much damage to Biafra's ability to gain foreign exchange. In a speech almost a year later he deplored the untoward action by the Federal Government:

> The government has long been aware of the terrible experiences of our people over the issue of currency. The present difficulties started when early last year Nigeria, on the advice of Whitehall, suddenly decided on its wicked and diabolical plan to dispossess our people of their wealth by means of the notorious currency switch. We had to do something quickly to save the near disastrous situation. New currency was introduced.[333]

An interesting development then occured, which helped Biafra's ability to trade abroad, but which hindered the Federal Government's attempts at controlling their currency's flow into the East. Although the Federal Government introduced her new currency towards the end of January 1968, the Federal authorities were concerned that it would fall into the hands of Biafra, especially in disputed areas which often changed sides. It was therefore decided that the old currency would be retained for those areas. This effectively allowed for three currencies to circulate in Nigeria. There is evidence to show that by retaining their old currency, the Federal authorities were powerless to stop Biafra trading in the new currency which was of particular benefit to Biafrans and their 'attack markets'.[334] Although the Federal Government's new currency caused currency shortages for Biafra and the old currency suffered severe devaluation, even as late as 1969 all currencies were still traded, and it seems likely that some of this new currency was used to secure ongoing arms supply from abroad. Because the first attempt by Biafra to introduce her own currency was carried out in haste to resolve an immediate need, the notes produced were of poor quality, but a second attempt was made in 1968, and efforts were made to ensure that the notes were of a higher standard (see Appendix). The evidence suggests that these notes were produced in Switzerland.[335] The Biafran authorities were quick to create a revenue-earning opportunity with the issue of their new notes which, along with their postage stamps, were sold at considerable profit to avid collectors throughout Europe.[336] Collectors paid £20.10s (in stirling) for the two notes of £1 and 5 shillings.[337] However, the conclusion drawn from attempts by the Federal authorities to curtail Biafra's use of its currency for foreign exchange is that, although it created shortages, it was unsuccessful. The other fact to be taken into account was that by mid-1969 Biafra had been compressed into 5,000 square miles and by that time there were a limited number of goods available, which meant that demand for currency was reduced.

Finally, the Biafrans, never slow to exploit a commercial opportunity, made landing charges for aid-agency aircraft flying life-saving goods into the beleaguered state. Consequently this levy charged on humanitarian aid meant that donors from the international community were not only funding the aid but were actually being charged for supplying support. It is doubtful whether any aid agencies considered this detrimental to their cause of saving lives, but the donor public might well have questioned Biafra's attitude to their benefactors, and such knowledge could well have affected the flow of funds destined to relieve Biafra's suffering. Even at the end of hostilities the Biafran Government had ordered the production, in Switzerland, of gold coins as collector's sets for resale. Biafra gained the royalties a few days before her collapse. It seems the only person to benefit from this exercise was William Bernhardt, the owner of Markpress, who commented that he offered some sets to Ojukwu but by then he had left Biafra and pleaded penury.[338]

Unquestionably Biafra's creative ingenuity helped it to survive. Eastern Nigerians have a great capacity to 'make do and mend',[339] and during the war every effort was made by the majority of the population to ensure that equipment was maintained or recycled. Of course, as Achuzia and Gbulie commented, there was some abuse by people in privileged positions and there was always a thriving 'black market' for all commodities, but as they added most of the population led a subsistence life before the war and therefore they were used to privations and hardship, so a war hardly changed their status, until perhaps towards the end when even basic food resources were in short supply. It was probably the middle and educated classes, at least those without official connections, who found the deprivation most difficult to bear. But Biafra's ingenuity and her people's ability to live life as normally as possible and to keep the institutions of state running undoubtedly helped to sustain its longevity.

Foreign support and aid agencies

The British, as the ex-colonial power, were concerned to retain as much influence as possible, before and throughout the civil war. Initially, prior to the war and on Gowon's accession to power, its policy was to try to prevent secession by the Igbos; when this failed its position, and that of the Americans, was one of neutrality. Its priority was to protect its substantial investments in the country, and one of its major commitments was to oil extraction. Shell had sizeable investments amounting to £200 million. At the outbreak of the war Shell had discovered that Nigerian oil production would exceed all planned expectations. In conjunction with the British Foreign and Commonwealth Office (FCO) it was decided that none of these new discoveries would be divulged to Nigeria or Biafra:

> Mr Stanley Grey, the Managing Director of Shell/BP in Nigeria had frank talks with the High Commissioner and the Dutch Ambassador on 28 October(1966) .... Mr Grey made the following points:
>
> 1. He confirmed what he had told us a month ago, that the scale of the Nigerian oilfield had been revealed in the last three months to be vastly greater than had previously been estimated. Shell/BP output was running far in excess of expectation. The revenue due to the Nigerian Government by 1970 was now practically double the figure estimated in the summer and previously.
> 2. In reply to the High Commissioner's enquiry, he said that he had not yet informed any Nigerian authority of this spectacular change. He felt that it was better at this juncture that both the Military Government and the Eastern Government should not realise that the oilfield was so much more valuable than had been reckoned. The High Commissioner said that he entirely agreed.
> 3. He confirmed that Shell/BP were investing an additional £40 million this year ....
> 4. He felt that the oil companies could adjust their relations to any set of political changes ....
> 5. He had had a friendly and satisfactory meeting with the Military Governor of the Mid-West (Ejoor), who had started by jocularly describing himself as a future employee of Shell/BP ....

6. He remained satisfied with his relationship with both the Military Government and the Eastern Government. Colonel Ojukwu was both capable and hard-headed, and showed a statesmanlike attitude towards the oil companies. Ojukwu said he would not wish to alter the arrangements for payment of oil revenue for 2–3 years … . No embarrassing pressures had been brought to bear by the Eastern Government on Shell/BP. Some time ago a secret approach had been made by Ibos to see if Shell/BP would finance a coup to overturn the Abubakar government. Mr Gray made it absolutely clear that in no circumstances was Shell prepared to play politics … .

7. Shell/BP were subscribing £1,000 to the Eastern Relief fund through the Red Cross. He realised they would not get away with as small a contribution as this.

8. He had a satisfactory first meeting with Colonel Gowon. He found that Colonel Gowon had only the most elementary knowledge of the subject of oil operations etc. He seemed to be very uncertain about the attitude that the oil companies were likely to take as the political situation developed. Mr Gray had said that Shell/BP would maintain their payments to the Military Government, and Colonel Gowon seemed to be agreeably surprised by this clear-cut assurance. He had also shown some signs of suspicion that Shell/BP might be supporting the Eastern Government financially, and Mr Gray had made clear that the company did not make political contributions.[340]

Initially, Britain's policy of neutrality ensured that, whichever side won, Shell's investment in oil exploration would not be compromised.[341] However, Britain was already Nigeria's main arms and armaments provider, and therefore it found itself in a very difficult position from the start. Its immediate decision was to continue supplying Nigeria arms as it had been, but restricting the supplies to small arms. Britain's official policy was at this stage: 'For the moment, therefore, the only policy for us is to wait, husbanding our limited influence with the Federal Government without antagonising the Igbos any more that is strictly unavoidable.'[342] The decision did not suit the Federal Authorities who, like the Biafrans, went exploring other potential suppliers. In an FCO document dated 20 November 1967: 'We know from secret sources that Ojukwu is still getting large supplies of arms from the continent, through Portugal and with the obvious connivance of the Portuguese authorities. His emissaries have also been in touch with French officials, and there are indications that he is trying to raise a force of mercenaries.'[343]

As the war progressed, Britain, under the premiership of Harold Wilson, did try to be more accommodating to the Federal Government's needs but never fulfilling their absolute demands. Wilson found himself following an increasingly uncomfortable path, supplying arms to the Federal Government whilst officially denying the amounts of these supplies.[344] At the start of the war supplying arms to the Federal Government was not a major political issue in Britain. The war did not feature highly in its public's mind and had not become politically controversial. However, once it became of major significance Wilson's Labour government found itself morally and politically compromised. It had decided to continue to allow arms to be sold to the Federal Government, because that was the traditional policy, but then found itself compromised as the war progressed when Labour Party members became antagonistic to the policy because of their, and their constituents', humanitarian consciences. Initially the policy was termed 'defensive armaments' and subsequently 'traditional armaments'. At the same time the British Government became increasingly concerned about and suspicious of other countries' attempts to gain influence over the Federal regime. This suspicion was at the time very real:

> We know also from secret sources that Ojukwu is still getting large supplies of arms from the continent, through Portugal and with the obvious connivance of the Portuguese authorities. His emissaries have also been in touch with the French officials, and there are indications that he is trying to raise a force of mercenaries . . . .'
>
> A major reason for the British Government's decision to supply the Nigerian Government with armaments has been the fear that the Soviet Union would move in lock, stock and barrel as she has already taken the opportunity of doing in several countries of the Middle East since the six-day war. . . . Although communism and the prospect of Soviet domination ill-accords with the western outlook and the free enterprise spirit of the Nigerians, the Soviet threat to the largest and richest country in all black-Africa must be viewed with the gravest apprehension.[345]

At the start of the war both sides looked to arms suppliers who could accommodate their needs, and they both achieved success and failures in their searches, but as the war progressed, humanitarian considerations came into play. Essentially, although Britain initially posed as neutral, its underlying sympathies lay with the Federal Government. Similarly Biafra had the support of Portugal and subsequently France took an interest in the fledgling state. Therefore, arguably even from the war's earliest days, both sides had the covert support of some of the great powers. Debatably, it was the outside arms support, balanced between both sides, coupled with the humanitarian concern over genocide and starvation, which was a major factor which ensured the war's longevity. It seems that throughout the campaign when one side was winning the physical war the other side was winning the moral war, and arguably it was this changeable state which ensured its longevity and even up to its final days gave Ojukwu confidence that Biafra would achieve ongoing sovereignty.

The aid agencies

When the war started it was seen by the west, if at all, as a localised tribal affair in a remote country in Africa. As the historian, Marjorie Perham, commented in the Oxfam *News*, April 1968, 'A terrible and bloody war is going on. Why do we hear little or nothing about it in the press or on the radio ... the need must be known. The strange silence in Britain about this war must be broken.'[346]

Her comments were about to be answered in a most dramatic way. The war came to the western public's attention initially in the *Sun* newspaper's picture reports in June 1968, and then through the Independent Television News (ITN) programme *News at Ten*, and its report about the starving and dying children of Biafra.[347] It is hard now to imagine how dramatically these images impacted on the western public, but the impression was so great that arguably it was a major reason for Biafra's survival. Because it struck such a strong cord of sentiment with people in the west, it enabled Biafra to mine a new source of ongoing material and financial support. Even today, when asking people in Britain about the war, a common response is: 'Oh! That was the war with the starving, pot-bellied black children?'[348]

Once the west became aware of Biafra's apparent plight there were determined efforts to come to the support of the underdog. Pressure was put on Harold Wilson's precarious government to stop the flow of British arms to Nigeria, which caused the administration to underplay the arms supply to the Federal Government:

> I have looked most carefully into the request for military supplies
> which you have made. There is nothing I fear we can do to help
> over jet aircraft and fast 30 knots patrol boats. These could not have
> been in any case made available in anything like the time to affect
> the current situation in Nigeria. We could however, if you wish,
> allow you to purchase twenty-four Bofors guns ... and we could
> arrange to train a sufficient number of Nigerian soldiers in their use
> by arranging courses in this country. ... We have also considered
> the general question of arms supplies, and I wish you to know that
> we do not intend to put any obstacle in the way of orders placed in
> this country for reasonable quantities.[349]

And:

> You may inform the Federal Authorities that Her Majesty's
> Government {HMG} are prepared to release 10,000 mortar
> bombs. ... It becomes progressively harder to go on releasing
> ammunition in the face of reports on bombing hospitals. A reli-
> able British witness who was in Umuahia until 1st March has told
> us that to his personal knowledge four hospitals have been bombed
> .... A motion has been put down in the House of Commons, over
> the signatures of forty-three members, welcoming the support
> HMG has given to the peace initiatives of the Commonwealth
> Secretariat but arguing that 'As a pre-condition HMG take all
> possible steps to prevent the supply of arms for use in the war in
> order to demonstrate genuine neutrality.'[350]

However, the main effect was to create funds for the aid agencies, in order to
help the suffering Biafrans. 'From June 1968 the allocation of funds under my
jurisdiction for Nigeria and Biafra expanded at a disproportionate rate.'[351]

Most importantly, it gave Ojukwu a new opportunity to put pressure on the international community to come to his country's aid, and to
stop Britain and other countries supplying arms to Nigeria. Through his
public relations company, Markpress, starvation and the genocide of his
people was promoted throughout the world to good effect. It was, therefore, this sudden revelation in the West's national press that brought great
support for Biafra's survival, but its incidental and unknowing effect was

to help Biafra survive for a further eighteen months and so prolong the agony of the war.

Foreign support came from a number of sources during the war and was extremely important to Biafra's survival.[352] Assistance came in most cases, France and Portugal being to a large extent the exceptions, because of the west's perception that it was a humanitarian imperative to protect and save lives from starvation, disease and the indiscriminate killing of innocent civilians. Information coming from Biafra was biased through the state-funded public relations company, Markpress, and from news reporters who were anxious to gain dramatic headlines, using exaggerated or unsubstantiated numbers, which arguably, created a biased picture in the minds of the populations of Western Europe and America. Ojukwu admitted that support for Biafra of this nature gained it international assistance at the expense of the Federal authorities. His primary aim was to stop the supply of arms from Britain to Federal Nigeria by gaining support from the British public to put pressure on the British and other governments.[353] Supporting him were three separate but closely entwined factors. First were the aid agencies, who provided large quantities of supplies throughout the war. The aim of all aid was to alleviate the suffering of the Biafran and the Nigerian people, and there is evidence that in the early days much of this aid found its way to its correct destination.[354] However, as the war gathered momentum and saw Biafra increasingly in need of supplies, much of this aid became misappropriated and redirected. Secondly, as the Biafran cause gained international support, arms and armaments were increasingly supplied by France. France never officially recognised Biafra but comments by De Gaulle, and recent confirmation from Ojukwu, showed where France's sympathies lay.[355] Thirdly, there were individuals who offered support to Biafra, either for their fighting prowess or because of their humanitarian conscience and belief in Biafra's cause.

In the early part of 1967, Oxfam had given help and aid to the Irish Holy Ghost Fathers, who were based in the Eastern region. However, Oxfam, keen not to be seen as partisan, gave support to both sides. Brierly, as Oxfam's Field Director for West and Equatorial Africa, emphasised the importance of giving help to both sides.[356] By February 1968 Oxfam had evenly donated the not inconsiderable sum of £59,300 in support of the war's victims, but, although Brierly was at pains to show no bias to either side, he had not taken into account the effects of the June press publicity about the Biafran people. Much against his wishes he found himself compromised over Oxfam's determination to break ranks with the other aid agencies, and establish its own airlift into Biafra. Having decided on a partisan approach to the problem, the net effect of this initiative was to put him in an extremely uncomfortable position with the Federal authorities, and it led to Brierly's resignation.[357] Gowon naturally was extremely sensitive to aid agencies deciding on independent courses of action, as was shown when the International Red Cross decided on unitary action.

Although the effect of the aid agencies was to help to prolong the war and Biafra's survival, their efforts were often frustrated by both sides' intransigence as to the best way of getting aid to the neediest causes. The reasons for this occurred from the middle of 1968 when Nigeria was in the ascendancy, militarily, and, having successfully overrun Port Harcourt, had effectively landlocked Biafra. How were the aid agencies going to supply the much needed aid to support Biafra's starving masses? The two schools of thought centred round air and land supplies, either direct supplies into Biafra, or supplies through notionally Federal-held territory. Gowon and the Federal Government supported a land corridor through territory which they felt they controlled. But their position was in fact being challenged by Biafran forces, which were still very much in evidence in the disputed territory.[358] Ojukwu and the Biafrans felt that this would make them far too vulnerable to attack from Federal forces. The fact was that the proposed land corridor ran straight through the middle of Biafra's existing, though challenged, territory, and however supportive the foreign powers might have been to make sure the corridor was only used for humanitarian purposes, the opportunity for Federal troops to infiltrate and overrun the area was simply too great.[359] Even the charity, Save the Children, came out against the idea:

> The Myth of Mercy Corridor. Lord Hunt's Mission to survey relief requirements in Nigeria and Biafra visited the area in July. In the House of Lords on August 28th 1968, Lord Hunt estimated the need for relief supplied to be 300 tons a day and he hoped this could be moved by five-ton trucks passing up and down the 'mercy corridor' – conceived as a 20 mile wide demilitarized zone down the middle of which would run the 57 mile long Enugu–Okigwi road. Sir John's solution would postulate 60 five-ton trucks doing the return journey each day and competing for space on the road

with army traffic. The Enugu–Okigwi road is flanked on either side by dense jungle, just 16 feet wide tarmac surface badly cut up by half tracks, armoured cars, and other heavy militant transport. There are countless blown bridges, some of which have been replaced by narrow Bailey bridges, and shell holes and mine holes pits the surface. The whole length is littered with destroyed cars, land rovers of all descriptions, mute witness to the tide of battle which has ebbed and flowed down the road in two years of war. The road now thrusts like a spear into the heart of Iboland and the advance of Colonel Shuwa's Nigerian First Division south is entirely in Ibo country. Biafran guerrilla activity continues in the area; to the West, the Enuga–Onitsha road is still unsafe and the 34 Niger River Bridge has not yet been repaired. To the East, the Biafrans move at will and forage deep into the North above Enugu for food. The road is cut and ambushed several times each week, and at the end of September a Nigerian truck was blown to smithereens with a home-made rocket, killing the driver and another soldier.[360]

Biafra favoured air support ideally from neighbouring countries[361] (St Tomé, Fernando PO and later Benin, were used by Biafra to supply arms). The Federal Government was against this because it left them with no control over the contents of the air supplies. The inference was that arms would be flown in with humanitarian aid, which to a greater or lesser extent was exactly what happened.[362] Ojukwu essentially won his argument, due to Gowon's Christian sensitivities.[363] There followed an uneasy truce, which continued until the end of the war, intermingled with the Federal Government's periodic attempts to control the airlift and carry out threats to attack aircraft not involved in humanitarian aid. These attacks were generally not very successful, not only due to the inexperience of some of the Federal pilots, but mainly due to the high rewards being paid to all foreign pilots willing to risk their lives on both sides. These pilots had a vested interest in making sure that their compatriots and their aircraft, many known to them on the other side, were not shot down and killed.

Fred Cuny, a foreign pilot, said:

All sorts of political agendas were being played out through this. Our discussions came down to one thing that is if you keep your aircraft going you save lives, if you don't the country's going to collapse ... but everybody was worried if the airlift stopped, the Nigerian forces who carried out a number of atrocities at the time would either seal the area off and let the country starve to death, or they would swiftly move in and there would be masses of massacres throughout the area and fear of retaliation. The Federal Government began hiring mercenaries to fly. They used Egyptians. They used some Brits, some South Africans and others were called to fly. And there were a few guys who were really willing to go out and shoot down people because they knew the pilots on the other side. It was actually a bizarre situation. There were times when our pilots would go over to Nigeria, to the Bristol Hotel, and meet their pilots in the lobby, have a few drinks and work out the rules of engagement. And the basic rule was, 'you shoot us down you'll be out of business and you're getting a nice lucrative contract so wouldn't it be better for you just to miss the interceptions and claim the radar sent you to the wrong place and whatever.' Often we'd be intercepted by MiGs on the daylight runs and they'd make passes and shoot like mad and then of course never shoot anything or whether these were the mercenaries who didn't want to hit anything ... firing off stuff and making claims on the radio, so that ground controllers would think that they were actually engaging the aircraft.[364]

In the middle of 1968 General de Gaulle confirmed his support for Biafra, stating that it had a right to self-determination, but, crucially, he did not give his official endorsement for the country. However, as discussed earlier in the chapter, French support and sanction for arms supplies to Biafra, although having no official endorsement, seems to have been condoned through the offices of the Secretaire-General aux Affaires Africanes et Malgashes aupres de Presidence, Jacques Foccart, whose brief by President De Gaulle was to look after the well-being of at least a dozen African presidents, and to keep them supportive of France and her colonial interests.[365] France had unofficially provided currency support with which to provide arms, and by mid-1968, was regularly supplying arms through Gabon into Biafra's Uli airport. By August 1968 two flights were made each night from Libreville. Each flight contained arms, ammunition and food supplies for the Biafran army. The aircraft were piloted by Frenchmen and their contents were funded by France.[366]

Personalities were also involved in supporting Biafra and although they might not have had much influence on the war's outcome, at the time they did have a limited effect on its longevity. The effect of support for Biafra from a new source in mid-1969 was to have a morale-lifting effect on Biafra as well as upsetting Federal oil supplies. This source was through the support of Count Von Rosen:

> Flying from a secret strip carved out of the jungle, a rejuvenated Biafran air force led by Sweden's most celebrated aviator now poses a significant military and economic threat to the war effort and the Nigerian Federal Government. Count Carl Gustav von Rosen and a small cadre of Swedish volunteers and Biafran airmen have carried out three raids on Nigerian airfields without any losses. Their aircraft are five small, 100 horse-power Swedish M.F.I. 'Minicoms' specially adapted for counter-insurgency operations. More are reported to be on the way .... Although no bigger that a Piper Cub, the Minicom has a formidable punch. Each can carry a dozen 76mm rockets or a combination of bombs and machine guns. 'The rocket sights we're using are fantastic,' said the Count after leading the first raid on Port Harcourt airport in which two Nigerian MiGs and an Ilyushin bomber were destroyed. Although 59 years old and near retirement as a commercial pilot, Count von Rosen flies the lead plane in each raid ... Neither the Swedes nor the Biafrans believe the new air force will tip the military balance in Biafra's favour. But the Biafrans ... are convinced that they can hurt Nigeria from the air far more than Nigeria air attacks have hurt Biafra.[367]

As Wing-Commander George Ezielo, the head of Biafra's Air Force, commented:

> There are really no easily identifiable targets left in Biafra that are worth bombing, except Uli airfield where the night-time relief flights land, and after a year of trying, the Nigerians have yet to knock Uli out. Our Government is now completely decentralized. Our industries and refineries are all well concealed in the bush.
>
> In contrast, the number of military and strategic targets in Nigeria is said to be almost endless, by striking at Federal airfields

the Biafrans have begun an effort to paralyse Nigeria's civil air traffic. Federal ports are thought to be vulnerable, as are the American
and European oil rigs and pipelines in the Mid-West region. Any
cutback in the flow of Nigerian oil exports could seriously imperil
the Federal Government's chief source of foreign exchange.[368]

Von Rosen had been an active humanitarian, flying first for the Red
Cross in Ethiopia and then in Biafra. His belief was that right lay with
Biafra and he was a keen supporter of Ojukwu. He went so far as to
claim that if his plans for more frequent and ambitious attacks on Lagos'
Apapa oil terminal and docks, and the Jebba road and rail bridge, the
South's sole link with the North, had been implemented, he would have
forced the Federal Government to make peace, presumably on Biafra's
terms. As he commented: 'Once you have seen something like Biafra you
cannot turn your back on it. It is really fantastic what they have done.
The Biafran struggle will go down in history like Thermopylae. I am
proud to have been associated with men who fought as they did.' This
was a sentiment shared with the Welsh South African Taffy Williams,
mentioned in chapter 4.[369]

It is interesting to note that none of Von Rosen's aircraft were destroyed,
and although he and his planes were of limited value and did not appear
until the later part of the war they did cause some oil-supply disruption
and damage to Federal aircraft.

The writer Frederick Forsyth was another person who unashamedly
supported Biafra's cause, mainly because he did not agree with Britain's
support for the Federal authorities and the biased attitude of the British
Broadcasting Corporation (BBC):

The BBC World Service was funded by the British Government, and I
was in Nigeria at the time, reporting on behalf of the BBC. As soon as
I tried to balance the picture by giving Biafra's position, problems and
issues, I was reprimanded by the Corporation and eventually recalled
to London. Once back in London I was effectively demoted and sent to
the House of Commons as an assistant reporter. Added to which I discovered that in my absence my London flat had been broken in to, and
although I found nothing missing, I did discover that some boarding
alongside a wall had been disturbed. I am convinced to this day that
the security services had entered my home looking for evidence to

incriminate me. Because of this break-in and my effective demotion I resigned from the BBC, and with my severance pay I booked a flight back to Nigeria and presented myself to Ojukwu, in Enugu. Ojukwu welcomed me and offered me the use of a caravan, as a home and a place to work, parked near to Ojukwu's home, state house, a car and driver and a commission in the Biafran army as a captain. I think the offer of a commission was to allow me the opportunity to freely move round the country in a protected way, so that I could report events as I saw them. I readily accepted this generous offer and for the following thirty months I stayed in Biafra, trying to give the outside world a picture of the country's condition and plight.[370]

Propaganda and genocide

Propaganda showing starvation and genocide was used by Biafra throughout the war to convince the international community that it should support Biafra. As a result, international journalism, describing life in Biafra and giving snapshot pictures of malnutrition, starvation, genocide and indiscriminate bombing of innocent civilians by Federal Government aircraft, led the Federal authorities to invite an international observer team to look into these descriptions and accusations.

All Biafrans live in real danger from being annihilated by the Nigerians, only yesterday my wife's half brother was killed.[371]

If the Nigerians come across anybody with any level of education they will be killed, this has happened before - anybody who can talk will be killed.[372]

An emergency debate in parliament shows growing, if belated, concern about the bloody tribal war in which Britain is simultaneously professing neutrality while supplying arms to the Federal Government.[373]

Not only was the press able to sensationalise the apparent atrocities carried out on the Biafran people, but the politicians from all political parties in Britain and other western countries sided with Biafra essentially for humanitarian reasons; Ojukwu was only too pleased to encourage and support this. At the time there was very little objective enquiry into the reality of the reported atrocities. Ojukwu was not prepared to disabuse the perception by many in Britain of the situation, and even politicians who visited Biafra often came away with a narrow, biased picture of the situation. However, the Federal authorities, backed by the British Government, continued to support positions which lacked foundations, or at best were assumptions, notwithstanding the fact that the Biafran authorities held contrary views. It became almost impossible to ascertain a relatively objective picture, and arguably these opposing views fostered divergent and opposing western opinion which unfortunately helped to sustain the war's longevity. A British newspaper reported:

It has become common practice for reports from Biafra – whether from journalists, relief organisations or the churches – to be dismissed as 'Biafran propaganda'. In many ways more disturbing have been some misconceptions that have been current in Lagos, which do not accord with what one sees on a visit to both sides.

1. 'Only three and half million people live in what remains of Biafra' ... The colonial office put the figure at seven million.
2. 'Deaths from starvation have been grossly exaggerated by the relief agencies' ... Few of those on the spot, including senior officials of the relief agencies, put the figure at less than one million. There are some who estimate it at one and a half million. It would be interesting to know what information sources of their own the British Government have.
3. 'Ojukwu seceded out of political ambition and greed for oil.' These were no doubt factors, but certainly the massacres in 1966, the failure to implement the Aburi Agreement, and the decision of the Federal Government to declare unilaterally the creation of twelve states ... played their part.
4. 'The Ojukwu clique' – From the Biafran side the war has all the aspects of a people's war.
5. 'Our side {sic} is winning, it will only be a matter of weeks now.' – I understand from journalists who preceded me to Lagos that this has long been a popular misconception shared by both the Federal Government and substantial sections of the diplomatic corps in Lagos.
6. Reports of the bombing of civilians by the Federal Nigerian air force are 'just not possible', pure Biafran propaganda.

7. 'There is no starvation in Biafra today. Dr Lindt, head of the international Red Cross relief operations, said so himself when he came through Lagos a week ago.' I was told this toward the end of January, but Dr Lindt has since assured me that he did not say this, and that anyway it would be incorrect.

8. 'Reports that the rebels have been eating seed yams cannot be true. There is no such thing as seed yam'... The normal practice is to eat about half of a small size yam, the other half is used to sustain the new shoot until its roots are developed.[374]

Many of these comments prevalent at the time, and depending on which side the report favoured, determined that view. Undoubtedly they created misconceptions and misapprehensions which led both sides to determine that their course of action was correct and honourable, however incorrect and biased were the facts at their disposal. For example, statements that bombing of civilians by the Federal Air Force were 'just not possible' were countered by Gowon:

I agree that there were incidents of indiscriminate bombing and accidental killings of civilians, but all pilots were under direct instructions from me that all civilian targets were to be avoided at all costs. I put these most unfortunate incidents down to the inexperience of many of our pilots and sometimes their desire to jettison their cargo of arms with little consideration for aiming their bombs on pre-determined military targets.[375]

Even a Commonwealth Office report to Lagos stated:

It becomes progressively harder to go on releasing ammunition in the face of reports of the bombing of hospitals. A reliable British witness who was in Umuahia until the 1st March has told us that to his personal knowledge four hospitals have been bombed (the Mary Slessor hospital and the hospitals at Itigide, Itukmban and Arochuku).[376]

Only four months earlier the British Government had been arguing:

Given our interest in a quick Federal victory, therefore, and the fact that Ojukwu is now implacably hostile to us, I think we should be justified in relaxing our policy on arms supply to allow FNG to buy from us items which seem to us to have importance in increasing their ability to achieve a quicker victory, particularly the quick capture of Port Harcourt.[377]

The argument of genocide was one which Biafra also used to help achieve an objective. Ojukwu's exaggerated claim that in excess of 50,000 Igbos had been mercilessly slaughtered in 1966 in the North was sustained by him and his government until the end of hostilities.[378] The numbers had grown from a notional 5,000 to this popular figure, purely to confirm in the Biafran population's minds that the Federal Government and her army was intent on genocide of the Igbo race, as well as fostering and maintaining this idea with the international community. A forceful article appeared in the British press articulating the notion of genocide:

'If the Ibos want to commit suicide', a Nigerian Federal commander is reported to have said, 'We will help them commit suicide.' This is just about what has happened. Western hopes that victorious Federalists will behave with 18th-century gallantry towards the fallen foe seem unlikely to be gratified. The Ibos put it to the touch and lost, and must pay the price of defeat.

This will not be genocide in the sense of mass extermination. What has been exterminated is the Ibo hope of self-determination and freedom. Gen. Gowon's plan to split Nigeria into 12 regions in the place of the former four will now be put into practice. Biafra will cease to be a rich and potentially powerful region, but three states, of which only one will be unequivocally Ibo. The plan will strip them of most of the oil fields, of Port Harcourt, and of their hegemony over four million non-Ibo now to be distributed between the new Rivers and South-Eastern States.

This is General Gowon's solution to the deep ancient enmity between the Hausa/Fulani mainly Moslem people of the North and the predominately Negro Southerners of bush and forest . . . . Along with material rewards they {Igbos} earned a heavy charge of envy and resentment which is now exploded in their faces, together with the British-made bombs.

Everything now depends how genuine are the good intentions expressed by Gen. Gowon not to seek revenge but reconciliation. And not merely how genuine, how possible to carry out ... and quite another to prevent Hausa soldiers from raping Ibo women in the bush and shooting down fugitives.[379]

Gowon was sensitive to detrimental reports of his regime and was conscious of world opinion and support by the international community for his determined objectives. Therefore, arguably, it was unfavourable reports by the international media which encouraged him to invite a group of international observers to report on the adverse charges made to the Federal Government about the conduct of its troops in the war:

> These included extensive looting, brutality to the population which would eventually lead to the destruction of the Igbo people. In essence, the terms of reference asked that the observers should examine the following accusations:
>
> 1. That of genocide: whether this strong word is in any way justified.
> 2. To examine the attitude of the Federal troops to the Igbo population and in particular to find out whether the assertion that the Federal army was intent on destruction of all Igbo property is, or is not, correct.[380]

Gowon's strong Christian sensibilities, as he said, made him react to detrimental comments in the international press that inferred that his regime was focused on genocide: 'I was deeply distressed that people thought that I even considered genocidal action towards the Igbo people. It never even entered my thought process.' Even forty years later, during the course of interviewing him, he became very agitated that his Christian spirit and sensibilities should be sullied with a hint in the conversation that it might even be thought that he had considered genocide against the Igbo people. As he said: 'It was not the Igbo people I was fighting but the small group of leaders who had led the East out of the Federation.'[381]

The international press's outpourings, often gained from Biafra's public relations company Markpress, were extremely vociferous, especially in Britain:

> In an ITN bulletin on Monday viewers saw the Biafran, who declared he was looking for his parents, bound hand and foot and shot by Nigerian Officer, Lt. Macaulay Lanurde.[382]

Col. Scorpion's *{Adekunle}* men attack refugee camp: Biafra women and children 'massacred'

Biafra last night accused Federal Nigerian troops of massacring more than 2,000 women and children at Owazza and Uguaku. The killings, Biafran Radio said, came as the Federal army crossed the Imo River during their advance on Biafran stronghold of Aba. Federal troops also killed 374 people at a refugee camp in the area.[383]

Nigerian Loyalties – Millions of people in this country saw on their television screens on Monday night the murder of an unarmed youth by an officer of the Federal Nigerian Army, who himself was shot in front of television cameras in Lagos on Tuesday. In this way, the bestialities of this squalid but destiny-laden African war are brought into people's living rooms ... . The country was British until only eight years ago. Generations of British missionaries have worked there, in particular in the areas of the present fighting. Their heartbreak at pictures of dying children is comparable to, and as honourable as, that of a parent forced to watch his own children suffer.

The Nigerian forces were raised and trained by the British. The many links to this country rule out any question of her present woes being a matter of indifference to us.[384]

Because of incessant propaganda about the Federal army's atrocities against the Biafran people, which led to increasing international support for Biafra, and concern in some quarters, and condemnatory attitudes in others, led the British Government to put pressure on the Federal Administration to counter these charges. The United Nations Organisation and the Organisation of African Unity were invited by the Federal Government to report independently on the many accusations. Gowon said that he wanted these independent observers to have a completely free and supportive hand and to give an objective and unbiased report on their findings.[385] It was agreed with Gowon that the teams should have complete freedom of movement, which meant they could change their plans according to the situation, as they saw fit. They felt that some' window-dressing' took place if a particular commander knew that the observers were about to visit, but that it was certainly not sufficient to conceal malpractices that had been recorded.

The major conclusions reached by the International Observer Team were:

> The word genocide is completely unjustified. There undoubtedly have been acts of brutality perpetrated by both sides in this Civil war. This is not surprising since on the Federal side their army expanded from approximately 5,000 to 85,000 in 18 months and on the Biafran side their soldiers only receive 3 weeks training. However it is absolutely clear that it is not the policy of either the Federal Government or its army to deliberately destroy the Ibo people. In fact, a great deal is being done to help those Ibos who are now behind the Federal lines.[386]

However, the observer team did investigate three areas where atrocities had been reported locally in the East and then been in the foreign press, emanating from Biafra's public relations company Markpress. The first area was around Mbaise, north of Aba, and the team confirmed after enquiry that no massacre or large-scale killings had occurred, although some civilians had been killed during the fighting. The second area was at Afikpo, where the team investigated 'irregular conduct' by Federal troops. The conclusion the team came to was that, although some civilians had been killed by Federal troops, the main reason for the atrocity was activity by the Biafran Organisation of Freedom Fighters (BOFF), which was responsible for killing 17 people and destroying 40 homes, due to an incident with the local head of the Muslim community. However, it did confirm the unlawful killing of some 70 people by Federal troops on 25 December 1969 at a village called Ndukwu. The third area the team visited was at Afikpo, together with five other villages in the area. Here the team did find that Federal soldiers had rounded up some of the villagers and forced them into a blockhouse in one of the villages, planted charges and blew up the building, and afterwards shot any who had survived the ordeal. With this incident the team concluded:

> The team is of the opinion that the behaviour of the Federal troops in the Amaseri area may not have been in accordance with the Operational Code of Conduct for Nigerian Armed Forces. ... The conduct of the Federal Military Government {F.M.G.} forces was as good as that of any forces during and after the war.[387]

The more this aspect of the war was researched it seemed to point to the conclusion that word genocide had been a useful promotional tool, firstly to instil in the Biafran population the ongoing fear that Federal troops were intent on destroying the Igbo race, and secondly to persuade the outside world that genocide, being contrary to international law, should be condemned by the international community, and that countries should offer their support to Biafra against the Federal Government's inhumane activity. The reality, as investigated by the observer team, was that the charge of genocide levelled at the Federal Government and her forces was completely unjustified. The idea of genocide had become a popular promotional thought which, alongside starvation, death and killings, helped foster the idea that Biafra should be helped for humanitarian reasons. Undoubtedly many people in the international community were convinced by the propaganda, and it helped perpetuate a myth and therefore prolonged the war, because, as with attempts at peaceful settlements, it encouraged the international community to pressurise both sides to agree on a compromise settlement, and this neither side was prepared to entertain. It is interesting to note that Markpress's public relations promotional propaganda was linked to five major news agencies, as well as all members of the British House of Commons and the United States Congress. Markpress became synonymous with Biafra, and because of its reputation it was able to promote Biafra and its cause convincingly to the international community, especially after the middle of 1968 when starvation and then genocide was promoted to the outside world.[388] The perception of genocide had grown from the uncontrolled riots which occurred in the North in the later part of 1966 against the Easterners who lived there, and which Ojukwu accused Gowon's administration of being unable to condemn or stop. As Ojukwu said, it was a useful weapon in Biafra's propaganda armoury and one which she used to good effect until the end of the war.[389]

As one article in the international press commented:

> Besides righteousness, however, the Biafran leader possesses a considerable talent for propaganda, and he has skilfully used that talent to promote abroad the notion that Nigeria is waging a genocidal war against the Igbos. In this effect he has received considerable assistance from the Nigerians themselves. Nearly every day Russian-made Ilyushin bombers piloted by Egyptians swoop out over Biafran territory. Almost always their targets are purely

civilian. One such, late last month, was the village of Ozu-Abam. 'The plane passed over very low,' recalls the parish priest, Father Raymond Mahar. 'I heard six explosions as it circled two or three times. When I got to the market every square yard was covered by a body or a part of a body. In all, there were more than two hundred bodies, not more than four or five of them were men.'[390]

One of the members of the International Observer Team commented:

I have been distressed by numerous letters from well meaning people telling me things which I know to be false: that the Federals shot every Igbo man, woman and children between Agbor and Asaba; that the minority peoples in the original breakaway state of Biafra were heart and soul behind the secessionists; that all the excesses in the war have been committed by the federals and none by the Igbos. I am sure there have been excesses on both sides.[391]

Conclusively, therefore, it seems that genocide was not a Federal Government objective, but it proved a useful tool in Biafra's armoury for encouraging the international community to support its cause, and thus was a contributory factor in the war's longevity.

Although the results of the International Observer Team's extensive investigations into indiscriminate killings by Federal troops confirmed that accusations of genocide and unlawful killings were unjustified, the international press continued to promote the notion that the Federal army was intent on killing innocent Biafrans. In March 1969 a report stated:

Deaths and damage caused, in Biafra, by 'indiscriminate bombing' by Federal Nigerian air force planes were described by Mr Frank Alluan, Labour MP for Salford, when he returned to London yesterday from an eight day visit to Nigeria. Mr Allaun said he had seen homes, hospital and welfare clinics had been shelled in many Biafran towns. In Biafra's capital, Umuahia, he visited air raid victims in the Queen Elizabeth Hospital. 'The matron, Miss Anne Bent of Lancashire, told me that on the weekend prior to my visit 60 civilian victims of a bombing raid were taken to the hospital for operations.' One air raid victim was a six year old boy. Doctors removed a piece of shrapnel the size of a matchbox from one eye.[392]

The problem for the Federal Administration was that although they had been exonerated by the International Observer Team from promoting genocide and indiscriminate civilian killings generally, incidents like this were continually reported in the international press, leading many people to believe that civilian deaths were still being condoned by the Federal army. These reports continued to favour Biafra and encourage people to subscribe funds to aid agencies. As Biafran territory became more restricted, through a process of attrition because of the ascendancy of Federal forces, mainly through increased arms supply, the well-intentioned aid increasingly went to support Biafran arms and troops, which prolonged the war.

It could be argued that balanced armies, one side with better-trained forces and the other with more firepower, could have created the conditions for a never-ending war. However, it was the effect of Britain supporting the Federal Authorities with her continual supply of arms, and then France's arms support for Biafra, which ensured the war's longevity. It is interesting to note that from the beginning of hostilities Wilson's government refused to countenance the supply of fighter aircraft, but that did not deter Gowon and his administration searching for a more compliant supplier. Unfortunately for Gowon, having achieved this objective, the perceived bombing of innocent civilians did little to endear him to the international press who, enthusing over a good story, were able to expose the horrors of this war to a sensitive and largely gullible public. This led the public to give funds willingly to the aid agencies which in turn created conditions of longevity. In spite of Gowon's well-intentioned attempts to have a disinterested assessment of unlawful killings and genocide, once the international press focused on their story of killings by Federal aircraft and undisciplined troops, it was never going to promote the cause of the International Observer Team to any great extent, primarily because good news does not sell newspapers.

It was therefore a combination of events which ensured that the war would last for thirty months, where, in retrospect, it seemed as though many of these events may well, on their own, have shortened the war, when sequentially put together they only added to its length.

CHAPTER 6

GOWON AND OJUKWU

An Appraisal of the Two Leaders

Both leaders were interviewed extensively, not only on the war, but also on their past, including their upbringing, and their opinion of the country in its present form and its present status. For Ojukwu corroborative interviews were made with several members of the Costain family, who knew Ojukwu as a schoolboy and as a young man growing up in Britain in the early 1950s, as well as Iro Hunt, the wife of the British High Commissioner, who was close to him during his early career in Nigeria. With Gowon the author used his own knowledge of him, when he was a young officer in the nascent Nigerian Army and was an intimate friend of the author's family. The appraisal has been divided, into their respective backgrounds, which have a bearing on the way they exercised their authority whilst in power, and their approach up to and during the conflict, how they dealt with the war as leaders on opposing sides, and finally their personal attitude to the war in retrospect.

Both Gowon and Ojukwu were two of the most important and significant people who held centre stage and controlled Nigeria's destiny during the period following the second coup in 1966 until the war finally came to an end early in 1970. Without their rise to power Nigeria's history might have followed a different path and conceivably a war might not have taken place. Although they held their respective positions throughout the conflict, both were challenged, but only once. Ojukwu finally lost his leadership when he sought peace or escape (the evidence is ambivalent), just prior

to Biafra's collapse, whilst Gowon retained his position until finally undermined by his ongoing rival, Lt-Col. Mohammed, in 1976. Unlike Ojukwu,
Gowon's position as Nigeria's head of state was always consensual.

> Murtala Mohammed and his Northern political supporters had
> been attempting to oust me from power from the early days in
> 1966. I feel it was these Northerner's political frustration that we
> the military were still in power after nine years, in spite of my
> attempts to return the country to civilian rule, and that the coun-
> try was no nearer to a political solution. Although I was concerned
> about Murtala's rather unstable personality I felt it was time for me
> to go, and let someone else try to resolve the seemingly intractable
> problem. So I resigned whilst I was attending an Organisation of
> African Unity (O.A.U) conference.[393]

The reality was that Gowon was removed in a relatively bloodless coup
by Murtala Mohammed, timed to coincide with the former's visit to the
OAU in Addis Ababa.

An FCO report on 11 November 1966 stated:

> I am now reliably informed that the old NPC led by Inuwa Wada
> did in fact attempt last week to get Gowon to stand down as
> Supreme Commander in favour of Lt. Col. Mohammed who, it was
> thought, would more actively further NPC interests. Gowon was
> apparently offered command of the army, but he refused to accept
> the deal and carried the day by emphasising his control over the
> Middle Belt elements in the army. Gowon is also supported by
> young Northern intellectuals. Mohammed has since been relieved
> of his post as Chief of Staff and was sent to Northern Nigeria by
> special plane on 9 November.[394]

Ojukwu's leadership was threatened when he recalled Banjo, after the latter's ill-fated invasion of the Mid West:

> Once Banjo had dislodged Gowon in Lagos, he planned to remove
> Ojukwu and appoint Lt.-Col. Emma Ifeajuna, the Olympic high-
> jump celebrity, to the office of Military Governor of the East. Biafra
> would have ceased to exist and the idea of secession would have been
> dropped. In the event Banjo, Ifeajuna, Alale and Agbam were made to
> stand trial for treason and were executed on 25 September 1967.[395]

Both men have admitted independently that if they had been given the time again they would have handled the situation differently and would have sought a negotiated settlement.[396]

How was it that two men from seemingly similar backgrounds (both men are Christian and had been exposed to British army culture) came face to face with each other over the seemingly intractable problems of the Biafran War? Ojukwu came from a privileged background, mixing freely with the Nigerian elite from all regions within the country. His father, who started out in life working for the United Africa Company, enjoyed a degree of success to the point where he felt secure enough to branch out on his own. His transportation company became the most successful in Nigeria, making him a rich and commercially powerful man. He thus associated with all the important people of the day, Nigerians and expatriates, giving him an entrée into the upper echelons of Nigerian society. He had a particularly close relationship with the Leventis family, who through several generations had established themselves as very powerful traders on the west coast of Africa, as well as all the leading Nigerian politicians and members of the British colonial establishment, including the governor-general. The young Ojukwu would automatically have enjoyed the benefits of this world from a very early age.

As a young man growing up in the North, Gowon enjoyed none of Ojukwu's privilages. He was also a member of a small ethnic group, the Angas people. His father was a Christian lay preacher and a farmer, who was intent on his children enjoying the benefits of western learning but who lacked the resources to secure them a good further education, leaving it to his children's own talents to secure that for themselves. Undoubtedly both men were ambitious, Gowon focusing on a successful military career, and Ojukwu aspiring towards politics. What motivated them to become embroiled in Nigeria's politics and how did both find themselves in commanding positions, but on opposing sides? To answer these questions and to enquire into the background and motivation of these two men it is necessary to look at their early development, the opportunities open to them, the political and social development of the late fifties and early sixties in Nigeria. It is also interesting and enlightening to investigate the status of these two men today. Both are in their mid-seventies, and essentially retired people, but living out their lives in totally different circumstances. Both reached the pinnacle of their careers in their early thirties, a time when most people are only just beginning to make their mark in their chosen activity.

Gowon's character

He is generally believed to be a modest man who reluctantly accepted the responsibility of Head of State as [a] military duty and to possess generally the opposite qualities to those required for success in the Nigerian political jungle. His experience of life was largely confined to the artificial environs of the officers' mess where he was more noted for quiet efficiency than for charismatic qualities. The fact that he had made his mark at Sandhurst was attributable to his absorption of the appropriate ethos and of itself not by any means necessarily an asset amongst his African colleagues and contemporaries. Moreover when he took office he was the youngest head of state in the world; his inexperienced innocence was glaringly exposed at the Aburi talks in Ghana ... . Few political leaders could in normal circumstances have survived being publicly outclassed to such a degree, but in this instance subsequent events proved their own commentary. Ojukwu disappeared into exile in the Ivory Coast, while Gowon's achievement of reconciliation in Nigeria was followed up by an increase in his external stature culminating in one year, in 1973, in unanimous election to chairmanship of the Organisation of African Unity, the state visit to London and an effective presence at the Commonwealth Conference at Ottawa ... . It was, however, the reunification of Nigeria ... which established his reputation in Western eyes. Portentous prognostications of massacre and genocide of Ibos were nullified in the first instance by his example ... . Not only were former opponents treated with magnanimity but he did not preclude the development of trust and loyalty on a personal level: his employment of Ibo pilots for his own plane might well have seemed foolhardy by some.[397]

When the author met him after a gap of many years, his opening question was 'How is your father?'[398] He was smartly dressed in a suit, formal but very friendly. He set no time limit to the meeting and at 4 o' clock tea was served complete with digestive biscuits. The feeling was that he was still in the officer's mess. Indeed his home could have been furnished by the British War Department during the fifties and sixties, comfortable but without ostentation. He is unassuming, diligent, persevering, compromising, religious, a 'doer' rather than a 'creator', a great family man, not endowed with a great intellect, but intelligent and caring. In his home he creates an image of a middle-class retired professional, with few adornments declaring any of his achievements or the positions he held in the past. When questioned about his assumption of power in Nigeria in 1966, he showed considerable embarrassment. When his wife Victoria explained that, because some of his subordinates in his new military government held more senior military positions than him, especially Colonel Adebayo, the newly appointed Military Governor of the Western Region, and Commodore Wey, the head of Nigeria's fledgling navy, the military council awarded him rapid promotion from Lieutenant-Colonel to Major-General. Whilst his wife was explaining this he showed modest diffidence, indeed a degree of embarrassment. Another example of his diffidence is the story confirmed by him, and reaffirmed by a student colleague of his when he was at Warwick University, after he was deposed as Military Head of State. The authorities at Warwick offered him the opportunity of following a PhD course with no preconditions; this he declined, because, as he said, he had no primary degree. He therefore joined the university as an undergraduate, and spent a total of nine years achieving his objective. Despite lobbying on his behalf, Oxford University declined his application.[399] Modestly he said: 'Achieving a PhD, from a British university, was so very much harder for me than running a country like Nigeria for nine years.'[400] He mixed freely with students considerably younger than him and with far less experience.[401]

His lifestyle today is comparable to that of middle-class people who have achieved satisfactory lifestyles but without the trappings of great wealth. He is now well rewarded by the Nigerian state because of his late position, and has for many years been fully reintegrated into Nigeria. On his return from enforced exile he made attempts at introducing himself as a potential political candidate for power, but his political expectations were short lived. Indeed comment has been made at his inadequacy for such political ambition.[402] When questioned about this he said that he had been proposed by former colleagues to make a political stand in Nigeria on his return, but although he accepted the challenge he lacked the political will to continue after his defeat. However, today he is still regarded with great popularity in Nigeria. Because of his former position and the ongoing state of politics in his country, where little has changed since independence in 1960, in spite of a civil war, and attempts at democracy, and because of some fairly objectionable military dictatorships, in the north of the country, which still holds immense political and de facto control, he is regarded as an elder statesman.

Following the civil war, Gowon was magnanimous towards the Biafran population, declaring that there would be 'No victor and no vanquished'. His status on the world stage was high, culminating in his being unanimously elected to the chair of the Organisation of African Unity in 1973, a state visit to Britain and a notable presence at the Commonwealth Conference in Ottawa.

Ojukwu's character

Political ambition complicates Ojukwu's character; it is interesting to note that during the first coup, as an Igbo he did not support the rebel leaders, who were later accused of executing an Igbo-inspired insurrection, and indeed as commanding officer of the 5th Battalion based in Kano he made every effort to contain the rebellion and remained loyal to the government and to General Ironsi when the latter assumed the role of head of state. There is also evidence to show that for a considerable period of time before secession he exercised caution on separating the East from the rest of Nigeria. He continued to negotiate for a confederal state, until finally the Federal Government issued the fateful decree dividing the country into 12 states, on 27 May 1967.[403] It is probable that even before this decree Ojukwu was simply trying to gain concessions from Lagos to create security for people in the East, rather than simply seceding.

When interviewed he gave the impression that he had been trying to resolve an almost intractable position.

> I was under immense pressure from hardliners *(in the East)*, returning refugees, and many Eastern Region civil servants who felt that separation was the only option. However, I was still hopeful, really until the declaration on 27 May, that a confederal compromise would be possible. I felt at the time that decree 8 went a long way by the Federal Government to implement the Aburi Agreement, and also felt that it satisfied the East's need for security and also gave each region a high degree of autonomy. Unfortunately, though, ultimately it was unacceptable to the East because a declaration of a state of emergency in any region of the Federation required the consent of only three out of the four military governors; the East felt vulnerable to the subjective sentiments of the other three regions. *(Of course, arguably, this was also true for the other regions, but*

in view of the fact that the other regions were tending to act with one voice,
the East felt increasingly isolated, especially over the real fear of the poten-
tial aggressiveness of the North towards the East.} So my conclusion was
that guarantees to protect the survival of the Igbo people were simply not forthcoming from the Federal Government. Not only were
these insecurities felt by the hardliners, but an increasing number
of people from all walks of life in the East felt the same way, even
those from the minority tribes in the region.[404]

Ojukwu's opening comment at his interview was 'Any true friend of
Nigeria is a friend of mine.'[405]

His new home is very imposing, with large reception rooms, richly furnished and well appointed, indeed the dining room could accommodate
some fifty people and the main reception room could comfortably hold a
social occasion for 100. He has a substantial number of servants tending
visitors' needs and his home gives the impression of ostentatious wealth,
but tempered by his delightful, beautiful, and gracious young wife and his
young precocious children. His wife is the younger daughter of the late C.C.
Ono, a well-respected lawyer and ex-politician. Indeed one is struck by the
incongruity of the situation: on the one hand his extremely hospitable wife
and on the other Ojukwu's somewhat austere and haughty demeanour.

The interviewer waited for about an hour, witnessing other people
going to meet Ojukwu, before being ushered in to meet 'His Excellency'
as he prefers to be called. Ojukwu demanded to know the purpose of the
meeting, although his chief of staff, Colonel Nwobosi, had briefed him
beforehand. Ojukwu also insisted that a time limit be set, although once
he had settled into recounting his knowledge of events at the time he
seemd to disregard this constraint. The differences between the meetings
with Gowon and Ojukwu was stark. However, Ojukwu is a politician and
a man of the people and, amongst his Igbo countryman, still a leader held
in high regard, but, and this is most important, from the past, as though
he is 'an emperor with no clothes', holding court and meeting supplicants
as though he still omnipotently ruled his people. There is, however, a
vulnerability about Ojukwu, which suggests he is a man of compassion
and sensibility.

I feel he was very distressed to hear of Iro's marriage to David
Hunt, and I think much of his antipathy towards Britain during
the war emanated from the fact that he and Iro had had an intense

relationship, and that his sentiment for Britain was coloured by this union. The fact was that David Hunt was hopelessly insolvent. Marrying Iro, who was heiress to part of the Leventis family fortune, gave him financial security for life.[406]

There is definite acrimony between Iro Hunt and Ojukwu, because he always sends her Christmas cards, signed with his love, and she gets very agitated on receiving them because, as she said, of the way he behaved towards Hunt during the war. Ojukwu seems to have come to terms with the past, but Lady Hunt is in an unforgiving mood, even intimating that Ojukwu's vitriol towards Hunt led to his health being undermined. Obviously too much can be read into these personal comments made by those involved at the time, but some elements do seem plausible, because there was hostility between Ojukwu and Hunt at the time, and maybe its origin was personal. Certainly Hunt's deputy as High Commissioner, in Enugu, took a much more sympathetic line than Hunt towards the plight of Easterners.[407]

> Because he was an extremely able politician and knew this fact too well, he tended to trust only his own judgement. This fact, coupled with an exaggerated personal ambition, blinded him to the sickening realities of Biafra's last days. In Biafra two wars were fought, simultaneously. The first was for the survival of the Igbo race. The second was for the survival of Ojukwu's leadership. Ojukwu's error, which proved fatal for millions of Igbos, was that he put the later first, A good deal of the war effort was diverted into promoting Ojukwu and his leadership. Be it the question of starvation and relief or other vital matters affecting the population at large, propaganda considerations took precedence over cold realities. Calculation as a method was replaced by hopeful interpretations of ambitious wishes.[408]

As Lt.-Col. Effiong, General Officer Commanding Biafra's army, said, 'He was no devil. Everybody admired his personal courage, his infinite ability for hard work .... He was quite courageous – although he escaped. But he had one weakness – he did not know when to apply the brakes. But it's because he was ambitious. He was a very able chap.'[409]

After the war Ojukwu went into exile and spent thirteen years in the Ivory Coast. It was not until May 1982 that he and Gowon were offered an amnesty, at the time of the Shagari administration, and he returned to Nigeria. Although he remained involved in politics and was still well regarded in the East, he was to enjoy little success in that area, although in 2007 he was a presidential candidate.

Gowon's background

Gowon's formative years were spent at Wusasa, just outside Zaria, a Christian island in a sea of Muslim Hausaland:

> Honestly they really went out to give us a good all round education. At least I would say this for our mission in Wusasa – they tried to make us into human beings; to make men of us. Honestly they did not try to make us inferior black people, etc. They tried to get the best of character, upbringing and ideals in us. That I would say for the C.M.S. mission at Wusasa. Yes I am grateful to each and every one of them; and I am sure all of us are grateful to them.[410]

Instructed in Hausa, his own tongue, Angas, became difficult for him in later years. He describes growing up in an atmosphere of Christian love in Wusasa, 'Where the Muslim boys were part of us. There was mutual respect for each other's religion and we played together as friends.'[411]

He had an extremely strong Christian upbringing, his father being a lay preacher working with the Church Missionary Society.

> My father was a farmer and after he converted to Christianity he returned to farming, not because he wanted to but because of financial need. I come from a large family and throughout my upbringing family funds were always in short supply. It was this situation which made me want to get out into the world in order to earn an income and help the family. I suppose this condition has remained with me to this day, in spite of the fact that I now have a lot more financial security today than I had in those early years. We chose to educate our children in England and that has proved expensive, so you might say that wealth is always relative.

To this day he lives in a modest but comfortable house.[412]

This was set to continue throughout his education and was to fit well with his induction into army life, his time spent at Sandhurst and with

British army officers up to 1960 when Nigeria gained its independence. His firm Christian belief forms an integral part of his character and was apparent during his leadership at the time of the Civil War, arguably causing him to refuse a totally aggressive offensive towards Biafra which, as remarked in the previous chapter, helped to extend the duration of the war. Meeting him today, one is aware of his Christian belief; it is not overt, rather it is subtly exposed in casual conversation. 'This is a very potent force in his life. Sometimes his faith seems to verge on fatalism, but his approach is profoundly religious. He believes that God overrules in the affairs of men and that His commands are absolute and must be obeyed.'[413]

The community of Wusasa, where Gowon spent his formative years, was created during the 1920s by Hausa Christians who were determined to build a church of their own in Zaria. This was not without its difficulties: 'For reasons which concern the administrator's own responsibility, it was found necessary, both for Lord Kitchener in the Sudan and myself in Nigeria to prohibit for the time being the establishment of Christian missions in Muslim districts.'[414] In the 1920s this was still the prevalent view in Northern Nigeria, and therefore extensive negotiations took place between government administrators and the Emir's court before some land just outside Zaria was sanctioned for development of a centre for Christians and their religion.

At 15 he went to the Government College at Zaria, having passed the entrance examination. He was to spend four years there, from 1950 to 1954. In December 1953 he sat an entrance examination for the army. His report stated that he was an excellent boy who should turn out to be a good army officer.[415] Having passed his army examination he was told to report to Captain Bassey, the Brigade Commander at Kaduna. He was then sent to the Regular Officers Special Training School at Tessie, Ghana. Amongst his colleagues there were Alexander Madiebo, Arthur Unegbe and Michael Okwechime, all of whom were to be his agonists in the Civil War. It is perhaps worth commenting that his education was modelled on Britain's educational system at that time, and especially at Government College the style of education was similar to that of Britain's public schools. His colleague and then future opponent was receiving a very similar style of education in his secondary school, Epsom College, in England, the only difference being that the English public, as well as grammar, schools of the day were elitist and the opportunity for those pupils to gain entry to universities and the military institutions as junior officers were good, while the opportunities for young people receiving a similar style of education in Britain's colonial empire were limited. However, because of Britain's requirements for defensive forces in her colonies, in whose ranks a slow indigenisation was taking place, the opportunities for entry to the local armed forces at officer level was greater. This was particularly true in Nigeria, where at the time, however, a career in the armed forces was seen as inferior to a career in government service. This is not to denigrate Gowon's achievements; in order for him to be selected for training at Sandhurst, not only did he pass an examination in Ghana for officer training in England, he also had to pass the War Office Selection Board (W.O.S.B.), followed by the Regular Commissions Board examination. He says that he very much enjoyed his time at Sandhurst, and he comments that it was there that his first name of Yakabu was shortened to 'Jack', as it remains to this day.[416] Once he had graduated from Sandhurst, after further training in England he was posted to the 4th Battalion, at Ibadan, of the Nigerian Regiment in the Royal West African Frontier Force; the Nigerian Regiment was shortly to become the Royal Nigerian Army, following Ghana's independence. He had hoped for a posting closer to his home near Zaria, but to no avail. By 1961 he had become a staff officer in Lagos and shortly after service in Zaire in 1963 he became the Nigerian Army's first indigenous Adjutant-General.

By early morning on 15 January 1966, Nigeria awoke to new political order. In spite of the first coup's failure its resonance conclusively changed Nigeria's political landscape. Ironsi, as General Officer commanding the Nigerian army was asked by the remaining Federal Administration to take charge of running the country in order to quell the rebellion and to restore the country to political normality. There are conflicting reports as to whether or not Gowon was implicated in this first coup, but the evidence points to his non-involvement. Indeed, but for a change to his temporary accommodation in Lagos at the time (he was due to take up a new posting as commanding officer of the second battalion from Lt-Col. Njoku), he may well have suffered the same fate as his colleague Lt-Col. Pam. Gowon's comments about the first coup are that he had had no involvement with the coup conspirators and indeed had been driven, as he said was his duty, to ensure that the attempted overthrow of the elected government failed. He had been in England attending the Joint Services Staff College from May until the end of 1965 and he did not return to Nigeria until 13 January 1966, only a few days before the first coup. Apparently as a reward for his support for General Ironsi, after the military had been invited by the civilian government to take power, he was appointed to the senior position of Chief of Staff of the army. As Gowon pointed out. because the troops, coming mainly from the Tiv region and further north, had been most affected by the coup, and because many Northern officers, as well as their political leaders, had been killed, he was also a Northerner and he had been the army's Adjutant-General and was well known to the majority of the army's rank and file, maybe Ironsi was simply being pragmatic in appointing Gowon to this position.[417] The consequences of this appointment would seem to bear out Ironsi's pragmatism, because during this first short period of military rule Gowon spent an inordinate amount of time touring the country visiting all the army establishments in order to appease the rising anger and disquiet over Ironsi's inaction in bringing the coup's perpetrators to justice. The fact was that the soldiers had become difficult to manage and cases of insubordination were becoming commonplace.

The grounds for a second coup were essentially laid as a result of Ironsi's prevarication over prosecuting the leaders of the first coup, his attempt to unify the country's civil service through decree 34, and an increasing perception that the first coup had been an Igbo-inspired insurrection. By May 1966 communal riots against the Igbo population in the North had broken out and unrest in the army's Northern troops was still prevalent. Indeed Ironsi had to order the police to quell the May riots rather than allow the involvement of the army. The army unrest culminated in the coded call sign of 'Araba', which simply means 'divide' and had been used in the Northern May riots.[418] It seems that the second coup had been planned within the army to remove Ironsi and was scheduled to coincide with his visit to Ibadan. At the same time fighting broke out in the garrison at Abeokuta, where Igbo officers and soldiers were killed. Major Danjuma and Lt Walbe were detailed to arrest Ironsi which they did and, according to Danjuma, he ordered that Ironsi be taken to the nearby Bida Prison and held there pending an official enquiry over the issues. Unfortunately other troops in Danjuma's detail, being highly suspicious of Ironsi's 'ju-ju' powers, had him stripped and, disobeying orders, took him and Fajuyi, the Western Military Governor, and Ironsi's host, into the bush where they were shot. Danjuma was extremely distressed at this turn of events as he showed during his recent interview; he confirmed to the interviewer that during this traumatic exchange he received a telephone call from Gowon demanding that there should be no more bloodshed.[419] When questioned about his telephone call to Danjuma, Gowon said that he simply could not remember,[420] in spite of the fact that Ojukwu makes comment about it in his book.[421] However, he did state that in his position as the army's Chief of Staff it was his duty to attempt to quell unrest and stop further bloodshed.[422] According to him, he was then asked by Brigadier Ogundipe and Colonel Adebayo to take a troop of loyal soldiers to the Ikeja barracks and attempt to quell the rebellion there. Again there are conflicting reports as what transpired at Ikeja, but suffice to say that after protracted negotiations lasting three days, during which time the baton of leadership passed to various people, Gowon said that he was finally persuaded to take charge, being the only candidate who could restore order and whose leadership the majority would accept.[423]

Ojukwu's background

Ojukwu's upbringing and background are in contrast to those of Gowon; his was one of privilege and advantage, albeit in the confines of the small elitist group of Nigerians and expatriates in Lagos at the time. Although both men are of similar age, whose formative years were experienced during the closing years of colonial authority, so that aspects of colonial rule touched them both, Gowon's relationship with the colonial power centred round his religion and education, whilst Ojukwu's centred round initially his awareness and then his knowledge of those in colonial control, from the Governor-General downwards. These included important Nigerian politicians of the day, from Azikiwe, a future president, to Awolowo, the leader of the Action Group, as well as the Northern rulers, including the Sardauna of Sokoto, arguably the most important and senior politician in the immediate post-colonial period. This meant that even from an early age politics and political involvement were important features in his life. His father, Sir Louis Ojukwu, who was one of the first Nigerians to be honoured by the crown, was an extremely successful businessman. He came from Nnewi in Eastern Nigeria and had built up his business empire from small beginnings, having been an employee of the United Africa Company, and then branching out on his own. By the time Emeka Ojukwu was born, Ojukwu senior was a very well-established businessman, having sold his transport business at a very auspicious time and at great profit. He had put his wealth into property and development projects, and had become involved with and closely connected to many of the substantial expatriate companies investing in Nigeria after the Second World War. One particular company with which he had a close relationship was Costain, a British civil engineering business which had 'bribed its way, as was the custom at the time', into ensuring that it was awarded substantial development projects within the country. 'In order for my father to obtain contracts he had to travel to Nigeria not with a suitcase of clothes but of money.'[424]

Ojukwu senior's relationship with Costain, especially with John Whiter, the managing director, grew, and he was eventually invited to join its board of directors. Whiter and he became close friends and with his friend Azikiwe they were invited to visit his home in England.

> When Louis Ojukwu and Nnamdi Azikiwe used to come to London my father would always accommodate them in Dolphin Square, at the time it was the largest apartment block in Europe and was owned by Costain. This was the early days of television and Azikewe and Ojukwu were always provided with the latest television receiver in their apartment. They would happily while away many hours watching television or indeed a blank screen due to limited broadcasting in those days. Another memory I had was of the two men playing tennis at my family home, but dressed in their traditional long robes.[425]

The intimacy between the men and their families grew, and when it was time to consider Ojukwu's education, because he was considered a bright boy he, together with his sister, was sent to England under the guardianship of the Whiter family. He commented that his first impression of England was that he felt 'completely lost in a sea of white faces'; this as he said created in him a desire for self-reliance and self-sufficiency.[426] Prior to this in 1940, he was sent to the Catholic Mission School and then to King's College in Lagos, an institution with an excellent reputation, modelled on the British private educational system. Once in England he was sent to Epsom College, where he proved himself an adequate pupil and good sportsman. From there he gained a place at Lincoln College, Oxford, initially to read law, which much against his father's wishes he changed to modern history – Sir Louis had wanted a lawyer in the family. He received a very privileged education, similar to Gowon's in content, but much more elitist. During this time he was very much dependent on the Whiters for a home, so not only did he receive an extremely good English education, but he also enjoyed the privilege of a very English middle-class upbringing.

Again unlike Gowon, whose family funds were very limited, the young Ojukwu could indulge himself because of his father's great wealth. With the background of a good English education, access to the family money and an interest in politics, he chose to join the Nigerian civil service and although he had hoped to be posted to the North, because of regional bias for employing indigenes the North was for Northerners, and he was sent to the East, to his homeland. Unlike Gowon who had had to assert himself from an early age to achieve his position, Ojukwu was almost able to claim by right of birth his position in the elite of Nigerian society, although with due credit to him he did not elect to join one of his father's companies, where position, status and success would almost have been guaranteed. Indeed on one occasion in the Whiter household, he proclaimed that there would be uprisings and a war in Nigeria and that he would eventually become king, such was his confidence and arguably his arrogance.[427]

He was to spend two years immersing himself in Igbo life and learning to understand the people, their aims, ambitions and fears. It was this, as he said, which stood him in good stead when he was asked by General Ironsi to become the East's regional military governor, and when he was the leader of the breakaway state.[428] There is perhaps an anomaly, considering that he led the East in its attempt to seek sovereignty, when in fact he confirms through conversation that he is a great Nigerian nationalist, and this was shown in his next career move.[429] He confirmed that the East was too narrow and restrictive for his ambition by joining the army, giving him more opportunity to be involved at the centre of the Federal state as the country came closer to independence.[430] Unlike Gowon, he did not go to Sandhurst, but was sent to Eaton Hall from where he emerged as a Second Lieutenant. By 1961 he was posted to Teshie in Ghana, to lecture in military tactics and military law. By 1963, after further training in England at the Joint Services Staff College, he returned to Nigeria and was appointed Quartermaster General, the first indigenous person to hold this post in the Nigerian Army.

At the time of the first coup he was serving as the commanding officer of the 5th Battalion, stationed in Kano, where it is an interesting fact that, with support from the Emir of Kano, he ensured that there was no rioting in the Kano district and that the area remained unsullied by the coup. As he commented, he had no involvement in the coup, indeed he was early in declaring his loyalty to Ironsi's new administration. 'Because I was considered far too much of an establishment figure the coup leaders did not confide their plans to me.'[431]

His loyalty to Ironsi was rewarded with his appointment as Military Governor of the Eastern Region, alongside Ejoor, Katsina, Fajuyi and Gowon, who were each appointed to vital positions to help stabilise Nigeria's fractured state. They formed a group of young men who had very limited experience of positions carrying such power and responsibility to help to run and administer a country destabilised by the first coup and its abandonment of democratic government. Ojukwu, however, unlike his colleagues, had the distinct advantage of having spent time and gained experience in the East in the civil service there, and he was now able to put this experience to good effect. However, one aspect in the early days of his appointment was his efforts at persuading Igbo refugees from the North, who had fled to the East because of persecution following the first coup, to return to the North. He bitterly regretted this in view of the subsequent outbreak of killings of Igbos in the North as reprisals by Northerners against the actions of the first coup, and Gowon's inability to control this after his election as the country's leader after the second coup.[432] Ojukwu commented that in his new position, although he had the responsibility of running and controlling the Eastern Region, he was still treated by Ironsi very much as his subordinate, inferring that although Ironsi had awarded him this position Ironsi was very much in command and regarded him as simply one of his junior officers. Gowon made similar comments about Ironsi.[433]

Both men had therefore achieved meteoric rise in their chosen professions. In the same year, 1963, Ojukwu became Quartermaster General and Gowon had been appointed Adjutant General. Both positions were the first to be held by Nigerians. They both held battalion commander appointments and both saw service in the Congo. Circumstances then opened up new opportunities for them which, under normal conditions, they would have been denied. Thus Gowon's appointment as Chief of Staff of the army gave him, as he said, a most rewarding opportunity where he had the effective control of the army, but this was to be the pinnacle of his army career. From the time he assumed control and responsibility as head of state, his military career was over, as he said, and from then on politics played an increasingly important role in his life, although this was to return partially during the war when he assumed the role of commander in chief of the Federal forces. He admitted that a political role was not of his choosing and he would have relished the opportunity to remain a soldier in his beloved army.[434]

Unlike Gowon, Ojukwu's ambitions were being fulfilled: at 34 he was in effective control of the Eastern Region and after his humble role as a junior civil servant in the East, he was now able to put right the wrongs as he saw them when last in the region, and set about minimising the endemic corruption. Circumstantial evidence points to success in this area.[435] Furthermore, having grown up in a political atmosphere his new role was beginning to fulfil his ambitions in that direction.

An interesting appraisal is given of Ojukwu at this time by the British High Commissioner, David Hunt:

Power he has now got in full measure and he is clearly enjoying it; he also enjoys very much contemplating the superiority of his own intelligence and the lack of brains of the Head of the Federal Military Government and the other Regional Military Governors. If I had any confidence in my ability to tell character from appearances I should say that there was some mental instability in him; apart from his appearance there seems to me a touch of paranoia in the ease with which he believes unbelievable stories about the secret manoeuvres of his enemies .... In spite of the defects of character to which I have alluded above, I think that Ojukwu is basically sensible and probably moderate by current Nigerian standards. He even has a certain amount of regard for his old comrades in arms. He certainly plays on their old associations when he appeals to Ejoor and Adebayo, who are the two he believes most likely to assist him in reducing the intransigence of the North .... I remember meeting him six years ago as a young Lieutenant when I thought him polished and intelligent far beyond the average of the Nigerian officer. There seems therefore good reason to hope that he is the sort of man who will agree to compromise when he sees that he cannot have everything his own way. The Federal Military Government and the other Military Governors have come a long way to meet him; if he now rejects their latest proposals it will be evident either that his extremist advisers have intimidated him or that unrestrained power at an early age has turned a head already prone to conceit.[436]

His assessment is arguably somewhat unfair; his comment on Ojukwu's intelligence is perhaps acceptable but his questionable mental state is a poor assessment from an experienced diplomat who knew Nigeria well.

Arguably it points to Hunt's misunderstanding of the true depth of feeling and despair experienced by the East at that time, and fits in well with his disparaging view that the East would be quickly defeated in the event of a war. His bias in favour of the Federal Government is evident; perhaps it was sheer frustration at the East's seeming inability to compromise which led him to this assessment. It is evident that from another source, and indeed from Ojukwu's own comments, that he did not want a war but that the frustration of the East through their consultative assembly was leading them inexorably in that direction.[437]

Towards war

Further turmoil in the Nigerian body politic then ensured that both men were thrust into the national and then international limelight. The second coup or counter-coup can best be described as a reaction by Northern politicians to re-establish their authority, initially over the North, with the intent of re-establishing it over the whole country. The disappearance of Ironsi and Fajuyi and the subsequent actions appalled Ojukwu.

> I got in touch with Brigadier Ogundipe on the telephone and tried to persuade him and arrest the situation. His state of mind was one of helplessness, incoherent and inept. He abandoned his responsibility and fled his post. Later I got in touch with Gowon, the architect of the mutiny. I impressed on him the need to stop the bloodshed. On his insistence that he assume supreme command, I made it clear to him that I would not recognize him as Head of the Federal Military Government and Supreme Commander. I urged a meeting of the Supreme Military Council to regularize the question of leadership in accordance of military practice . . . . In spite of this warning Gowon went on the air and announced himself as the Supreme Commander and Head of the Military Government.
>
> Gowon personally told me over the phone {and the conversation was duly recorded} that the North wanted to secede . . . . I told him that if that would lead to peace, they could go ahead. Gowon left Lagos Island to go to Ikeja barracks, where the Northern flag of the new republic of the North was flown. A speech had been prepared for him announcing the secession of the North . . . It was the

British and the American diplomats who intervened and stopped
the North from seceding ... . There is evidence that the British
High Commissioner *(confirmed by Cumming-Bruce)*, after expound-
ing to Gowon the opportunities now offered to him and the
Northern people for the domination of Nigeria, also assured the
British government's pledge to give him every support to maintain
that domination.[438]

When Gowon came to power on 1st August 1966 and made his first
broadcast to the nation, there was ambiguity in his speech, leading to
ongoing speculation as to his precise meaning when he stated:

> I have now come to the most difficult part, or most important part
> of this statement ... ..
>
> As a result of the recent events and other previous similar ones, I
> have come to strongly believe that we cannot honestly and sincerely
> continue in this wise, as the basis of trust and confidence in our
> unitary system of government has not been able to stand the test of
> time ... suffice to say ... the base for unity is not there or is so
> badly rocked, not only once but several times. I therefore feel that
> should review the issue of our national standing and see if we can
> stop the country from drifting away into utter destruction.[439]

When questioned on this he recalled the pressures of the time, and said
that his own position was especially precarious and that there were various groups who wanted to get their point of view across with regard to
the recent turmoil and to give their opinion as to the direction of the
country. His comment about 'the basis of unity' was simply to placate
the North and to reassure them that Ironsi's unpopular decree 34 would
be rescinded (which he did not actually state in his speech, but was to
rescind on 31 August 1966 when he restored the federal system of government), but also, that because of the upheavals, a new assessment should
be made as to how the country should be ruled in the future if Nigeria
was to remain a sovereign state. He then went on to comment that this
was why he went to Aburi with such an open and conciliatory mind and
was the reason for the agreement at Aburi, where in essence he went along
with Ojukwu's assessment and plans for the future.[440] It is important to
remember that by this stage Cumming-Bruce, the High Commissioner,

had through his personal contacts with the Northern emirs convinced the North that separation from the rest of Nigeria would have been an unwise option for them.[441]

It is interesting to comment on Ojukwu's assessment of the situation at that time, because as he said he had had no involvement in the second coup, and had observed it as an innocent bystander, although he did make efforts to ensure that Northern troops stationed in the East were not involved in any disturbances. In his broadcast on Enugu radio on the evening of Gowon's speech to the nation he commented on the realities of the new situation, as he saw it. He said that the country was now divided into two, the North, the West and the Mid-West, where the second coup seemed to have been successful, and the East where it had failed. As he rightly said the East was still in the hands of the legitimate government. He was adamant that he could not accept Gowon's elevation to Supreme Commander, firstly because Ironsi's fate had yet to be determined and secondly that there were other more senior people in the army hierarchy who should assume the supreme commander's position.[442] His comments reaffirm his British conservative ideal and a sense of fair play, undoubtedly imbued through his education and upbringing and in confirmation of an article he wrote whilst at Oxford:

> Colonial state generates a colonial posture. This posture automates a series of complexes which remain with the African long after the colonial stimulus has ceased to have direct contact. The continuation of these complexes is seen in a state of mind which permits colonialism as a reflex. During this period the remoteness of the stimulus is often misinterpreted as nonexistent, thus generating a false sense of security in the minds of Africans recently out of bondage. The stimulus exists, its virulence undiminished. In fact what happens is that the imperial power at this time, finding itself undisturbed, conserves energy, spreads its contagion, prepares the ground, and concentrates all its efforts toward the achievement of its main objective – that of economic exploitation.[443]

He was, he said, of the opinion that Gowon's assumption of power was 'de facto and not de jure' and therefore his position was untenable, especially since the whereabouts of the former Supreme Commander was unknown, and he urged Gowon to arrange a meeting to establish who in fact should take on the ultimate responsibility.[444] Questioned on whether or not he should have been that person, he refused to be drawn on the subject. Even today Ojukwu gives the impression that if he had taken on the responsibility, the series of events which then ensued would have been very different. However he was hardly well positioned to challenge Gowon's assumption of power, in the light of the serious unrest occurring throughout the army at the time. Ojukwu remained firmly in the East, where he ensured that there was no military disorder, in spite of the fact that most of the battalion of troops stationed in the East at the time were from the North. However, the effects of the subsequent attacks on Igbos in the North made him realise that 'Firstly it was imperative that Gowon exercise control and quell the desire by Northern politicians to stop them inciting mob rule to attack and kill Northern Igbos, and secondly that there had to be a period when the regions should adjust to the new reality of regional discord.'[445]

Looking in retrospect at the situation, Ojukwu was disingenuous over Gowon's position. Although Gowon talks lightly of his assumption of power, the reality was that that his position was extremely precarious, in Lagos at Ikeja barracks. It was at Ikeja that the drama of what action should be taken to control the country was played out. Gowon admits that although he had been ordered by Brigadier Ogundipe to take some loyal troops to Ikeja to restore order, the fact was that although the troops there were prepared to listen to him, they were in no mood to compromise and were intent on encouraging the North to secede from the Federation. As Gowon pointed out:

> For three days events at Ikeja really did determine which direc-
> tion the country would take and that the power of the country was
> firmly in the hands of this small group of soldiers at Ikeja. The sol-
> diers there were simply not prepared to obey orders from the army's
> remaining hierarchy but were prepared to listen to and eventually
> agree the argument that in order to bring the country under control
> a compromise was imperative.[446]

Gowon said that this line of thought eventually gained majority support and he reluctantly took control.

Having gained agreement that Gowon should assume the role of head of the armed forces and de facto head of state, with considerable support from the American Ambassador and the British High Commissioner, and getting agreement from the Northern politicians and Northern rulers that secession was a disastrous course of action for the North, the army rank and file was brought under control.

> Gowon contacted me for support. He told me that he was just a simple soldier and had no political ambition, but he wanted guidance on how to proceed. It was at that point that I decided on the policy of discouraging the North to secede, and I thought I would be successful because of my personal relatioships with the Northern Emirs.[447]

However the violence against the Igbo population continued in the North, and Gowon found bringing this violence under control almost beyond his power. In his impromptu address to the Ad Hoc Constitutional Conference on 3 October 1966, he reacted to the Northern tragedy:

> Certainly there has been damage. I think that is what we never seem to admit when there is something like that. There is damage and I am very, very sorry about it. I regret it and I am doing every-thing I can ... As I said, for God's sake, don't lose hope. If we are alive and if we are determined, we can get this country back to its proper shape. I am determined to do that even if it means my life. I give you my word for it .... To our Eastern friends, for God's sake please don't lose hope. Let us try and see what we can do to mend up what has happened. Give me a chance and I am quite convinced I will be able to do something very shortly.[448]

Although this impromptu speech confirms the sincerity of the man, which is arguably one of his great strengths, and was to feature con-stantly throughout the war, it hardly instilled confidence in those being attacked, killed and maimed, as Ojukwu confirmed. At this stage during this eventful time Gowon and Ojukwu held regular telephone conversa-tions, and from the interviews I held with them they both confirmed their sincerity in wanting to ensure that Nigeria remained one entity. This approach, with the support of Malcolm MacDonald, the British intermediary, laid the foundations for informal talks between Gowon and the regional military leaders, which were held at Aburi.

Both Gowon and Ojukwu confirm that these talks were successful and produced a compromise. Ojukwu is adamant that the agreement allowed for the regions to disengage from each other and exercise greater autonomy. As he said, he essentially gained agreement that Nigeria would become a confederation. The transcripts show that Ojukwu had put in much effort and produced a logical plan of action to allow for regional divergence within a national state. They also show that the other members of the meeting agreed to Ojukwu's proposals. The real failure of the Aburi Agreement was the fact that Gowon, whose power at this stage was not secure, was persuaded by his senior civil servants that the arrangement concentrated too much power in the four regions and left little authority at the centre of the Federation, and it was this fact which made the agreement unworkable. Ojukwu comments that if all the parties had stood by the agreement, secession would have been unnecessary, and a war would have been avoided.[449] From conversations with both Ojukwu and Gowon comes confirmation that they deeply regret that they did not take more care and consideration in leading both of them down a path where the inevitable result was a clash of arms.

How they dealt with the war as leaders

Ojukwu's style of leadership was to refer to his Consultative Assembly. It is interesting to note that when he was appointed by General Ironsi as Military Governor of the Eastern Region, the political regional assembly was disbanded, and Ojukwu, after the second coup, was able to develop a consultative group through which the people in the region could express their views. There were twenty-nine divisions within the region and each was asked to nominate four representatives as well as six elected delegates and added to this were forty-five representatives elected from teachers', lawyers', farmers' and most importantly market traders' associations. This group was known as the Consultative Assembly and together with the advisory Council of Chiefs and Elders was regarded as Biafra's parliament. Ojukwu consulted with this group over every major issue during the war and on most occasions followed their wishes. However, he also formed an Executive Council which met weekly, and it was this body which wielded the country's executive power.[450]

As Ojukwu commented, his aim was to create a democratically elected system within Biafra.[451] This would point to Ojukwu's desire not to run a military dictatorship, but to institute a meaningful democracy. Arguably, this is borne out by the fact that the Consultative Assembly was consulted at each stage as the East considered secession as its only option, and that nearly half of its members were from the non-Igbo minority. This also demonstrates that when it came to deciding on secession, Ojukwu's government had the overwhelming support of the minority groups.[452]

When the war started, both sides were ill-prepared for a long confrontation. Gowon's approach was that it was simply a police action to bring the recalcitrant East back into the fold. Ojukwu's and Biafra's agenda was to secure the country as a sovereign nation, recognised by the international community. Within Biafra it was felt that this would be easily achieved. However, as Ojukwu commented, it became very obvious shortly after hostilities broke out that the country's aspirations would not be achieved simply by seceding. As he said, in the light of the disastrous reverses during the opening stages of the conflict at Nsukka, dramatic action was called for, either to subjugate the Federal Authorities, or at least put Biafra in such a strong position that all parties would agree to Biafra's sovereignty.[453] This was the background to the Mid-West invasion. Although Victor Banjo was not Ojukwu's first choice he was considered a good candidate to lead the invasion, firstly because he was a close friend of Ojukwu, and secondly by being Yoruba, providing he remained loyal to Biafra, he would be able to negotiate on her behalf in the West through mutual colleagues, to achieve a satisfactory result. Unbeknown to Ojukwu Banjo's plans were totally at odds with his orders, and as described in Chapter 3 the invasion although a resounding success, and as Achuzia commented, 'Lagos and Ibadan were ours for the taking',[454] resulted in a disorganised retreat by the Biafran Army. Ojukwu was distressed by Banjo's duplicity, having put great trust and faith in his ability to achieve the objective. However, it transpired that there was a further agenda which appeared in sequence with the failed invasion, and that was a planned coup to oust Ojukwu and achieve a peaceful settlement with the Federal Authorities. How extensive the plans were is a matter of conjecture, but it proved to be the one and only time that there was a planned rebellion against Ojukwu:

> At 0600 hours on 19th September 1967, Majors Ifeajuna and Alele paid me a visit at my tactical headquarters .... Having gone to bed only two hours before I was pretty angry to be awakened at that

time of the morning .... Major Alele first asked me if I would like to see the war end immediately. I said yes without hesitation. He revealed that he and his group had been in touch with the British and American government officials who had a peace formula for ending the war.

According to Alele, the only condition demanded by these two countries was the replacement of Ojukwu .... he ended by saying that Ojukwu had to be told to step down ...

I thought the whole story exciting ... I pointed out that the whole affair ... would amount to a coup d'état ... I was about to go to my headquarters at Nkalagu when I was summoned to state house by Dr Ibiam and Mr Mojekwu ... I told them about the visit of Majors Ifeajuna and Alele. It appeared as if I had hit the main point, for I could see quite easily the bright glow of joy and relief in their eyes and faces ...

I did not know for certain that Ifeajuna's peace plan was in effect to topple Ojukwu until I heard the news that those involved had been executed for attempted coup.[455]

The effect of this attempted coup was to undermine the confidence the Biafran public had in their army and particularly their trust in the officer corps, especially those officers who had served in the original Nigerian Army before the war. As a result, throughout the remainder of the war there was a general paranoid fear of saboteurs, all emanating from the public's distrust of the officer corps. Ojukwu was seen to be above criticism and his status and position rose in the public's confidence, after his attempted overthrow. However, the affair did lead to the replacement of the head of the army, not because of his involvement in the coup but because he was seen as an unsuccessful army commander. There is also no doubt that following the coup Ojukwu's attitude to the army changed, and often throughout the remainder of the war he was seen to sideline the army and its hierarchy in favour of specially selected groups who came under his direct authority. When asked, he confirmed that the coup had undermined his confidence in the army's loyalty to him and Biafra, hence his use of Steiner and other mercenaries and the indomitable Joe Achuzia, and other trusted colleagues from whom he felt he could demand absolute loyalty.

Gowon's style of leadership during the war was different from Ojukwu's. Although both leaders faced similar problems and challenges, their scales of operation were different, and whilst Ojukwu's had greater immediacy, Gowon had the luxury of being able to take a more objective view of the war. However, Gowon had the constraint of continuing to convince the people that victory was achievable within the near future. He conducted all his military command and control from Dodan Barracks at Ikeja, and his style was to keep in touch with his military commanders on a regular basis by telephone:

> He is a man who believes in Government by telephone. If you are able to go upstairs from the drawing room in Dodan Barracks you will see the telephone room from which he controls Nigeria. In this little bare room, not more than 20 feet by 10 he sits alone for much of the time with ten telephones and three wireless sets. By this he keeps in touch with each field commander and with other vital levers of governmental power. He believes that it was by the use of the telephone that he has succeeded in dealing with the crisis in Nigeria's history. In January 1966 he rallied the loyal commanders and warned Ojukwu in Kano to be loyal, by the use of the telephone.[456]

As he commented, it was not his job to interfere with their own commands and he therefore gave them a considerable amount of leeway in executing their own objectives. This approach to leadership leads to the view that Gowon showed weak leadership and was unable to control his divisional commanders:

> Day by day he revealed himself a very weak man and a man of indecision. A few instances will suffice to demonstrate the weakness in the character of Gowon. During the war years it was common knowledge in military circles that Gowon was completely unable to control the three divisional commanders responsible for the actual fighting in the field. There was no co-ordination between the three divisional commanders and each one acted entirely independently of each other. As a matter of fact, elements of jealously crept in among the three commanders and each one resorted to decisions and actions that would impair or jeopardise the progress and prospect of success of the others. Such reprehensible conduct was known and reported regularly to Gowon. But throughout he did nothing

to coordinate the activities of the three commanders or call them to order ... . Otherwise how could anyone ever explain the fact that the man who could be said to rank next to Gowon ... during the war years never once visited the front throughout the the two and a half years of civil war? Not only this, this same man was known to have occupied himself at the time with reading for a law degree on part-time basis in the University of Lagos. Gowon knew of this but was too weak to call Major-General E.O. Ekpo to order.[457]

However his leadership style is interpreted, he was intent on conducting the war as humanely as possible, and he introduced a 'Code of Conduct' for his army.[458] The code commented that the troops were not fighting a war against a foreign enemy, nor were they fighting a religious war or jihad, and that they must remember that they would come up against soldiers who were formerly their comrades in arms and that in the future they might resume that position. The document comments that the aim of the offensive is simply to subdue Ojukwu and his 'clique'. It detailed how to treat civilians, prisoners of war and foreigners and also property, especially churches and mosques, and finally went on to state how a high standard of loyalty, discipline and patriotism was demanded and that troops would behave humanely. Finally it reminded the army that Africa and the rest of world was witness to the war and they would watch to see how well the task was achieved. When questioned about this document, Gowon said that he had had first-hand knowledge of how chaotic conditions could become, because of his experience during his time in the Congo, and that he was determined that his army would not behave in the way that troops had done during that disastrous clash of arms.[459]

The pressure on Gowon, firstly to convince many of the people to retain an interest in the war and secondly to secure a sustainable victory, was immense throughout the campaign. His problem was that for most ordinary people on the Federal side the war was simply too remote to particularly effect their day-to-day lives, and he was obliged, as he said, to keep people's interest by confirming that victory was in sight. His problem was, as he readily admitted, that his quarrel was not with the Igbo people but with Ojukwu and his close advisors. Initially, before the start of the war, when he had assumed power his relationship with Ojukwu was friendly, indeed they spoke regularly on the telephone and referred to each other as Jack and Emeka, they joked about the old days and the girlfriends they had known, but later as Ojukwu and the East secured more arms he became more arrogant and less friendly towards Gowon, who naturally took exception to this. By 1968 Gowon's attitude to Ojukwu had changed dramatically. He 'felt him wicked and that he was up to many tricks'. Fundamentally, Gowon, who has a firm belief in loyalty and straightforwardness, felt that Ojukwu did not behave like an officer and a gentleman. As he confirmed, loyalty and honour were instilled in him from an early age; he commented 'You are British and I learnt my dealings and experience with the British … you must understand what loyalty is.'[460] Because he had no grievance against the Igbo people he continually felt that he should constrain his army over too much aggression towards its foe. This dichotomy, as he said, effected and constrained him throughout the war. It restrained him from defeating Biafra by force of arms, his preference, as he said, 'was to achieve a negotiated peaceful settlement'.[461]

Indeed, by the autumn of 1969 Gowon found it necessary to explain to the world why he had not brought the campaign to a successful conclusion. He was coming under increasing pressure from the international community, mainly because of the humanitarian aspects of the war. On 6 September 1969 he told the OAU Assembly of Heads of State at Addis Ababa that there were four reasons for the delay in bringing the military operation against Biafra to a successful conclusion. Firstly, he accused the racialists of a conspiracy and said that they were committed to the disintegration of Nigeria following their failure to achieve that in the Congo. Secondly, he focused on the activities of some of the humanitarian organisations, who he said were helping to sustain the secessionist regime through moral and material support, the supply of foreign exchange, arms and military equipment. Thirdly, he said that a delay to the conclusion of the war was being caused by 'vicious propaganda and unparalleled falsehood being dished out by the secessionist regime'. This, he said 'was making the common man in the area feel that he was fighting for survival – against genocide.'[462] Fourthly, Gowon pointed out that the war was being fought to quell a rebellion, not to destroy the people. When asked about his Addis Ababa statement, he said that at that stage in the war he and his colleagues had become extremely frustrated by the seeming failure of the Federal army to bring the war to a successful conclusion and, as he pointed out, it was at that stage that he had replaced his divisional commanders, hoping that fresh input would swiftly conclude matters. However, he went on to comment that it was against the background of his frustration that he made the remarks. In retrospect he said that his comment about an international conspiracy of racially motivated groups to destroy a unified Nigeria was spurious, and it was to his regret that he had not put more faith in and more support for using his public relations company Galitzine, Chant and Russell, to promote the Federal cause to the outside world. He admitted that Biafra's use of William Bernhardt's firm Markpress had proved in retrospect to have been remarkably successful in convincing the international community that Biafra had the right to a sovereign existence.[463]

During the war the Federal authorities, like Biafra, used a public relations company to promote their cause to the outside world. However the efforts of Galizine, Chant and Russell were far less intrusive and therefore less successful than Biafra's Markpress. As Gowon pointed out: 'I trained in the British tradition, and I believe that in the end the truth will prevail. I do not want any public relations firm to help me to do this.'[464]

Arguably this was an extraordinarily naïve comment made by a head of state, who needed to make use of all available facilities in order to achieve his objective of defeating Ojukwu and his breakaway state, and later admitted that his comments about 'truth prevailing' were rather naïve. However it is such a telling statement, proving the sentiment and the status of this incredibly unassuming man. A final quotation about Gowon should be included, which perhaps confirms why he was able to survive in the leadership of the Federation in spite of accusations of poor and weak military control:

> It was during this period that Gowon paid his first visit to Port Harcourt ... when Gowon finally arrived, the citizenry erupted with joy. Gowon's high spirits were infectious. He spoke off the cuff cheerfully and eloquently to the leading citizens, and I noted in my diary later that day 'The idea of One Nigeria is right in his marrow. One could not but be impressed.'[465]

One of Ojukwu's great strengths throughout the campaign was his overt use of propaganda, whether for external or internal consumption; it undoubtedly had a major bearing on support for Biafra's cause and her potential success until an armistice was declared at the beginning of 1970. Externally, from February 1967 some six weeks after the Aburi meeting, Ruder and Finn in New York, and their London affiliate, Brook Hart, Ruder and Finn, were hired by the Eastern Region, at a monthly fee of $5,000 to promote their cause to a wider world. At the same time the East intended to establish missions in nine countries.[466] As Ojukwu commented, the East's objective at that stage was to bring to the world's attention that the killings in the North had been a form of genocide and that the East had never shared a common culture with the North, but he admitted that this public relations approach was ineffective and did little to create awareness of the East's condition at the time to a wider world. Towards the end of 1967, he had the good fortune, although he admitted he did not know this at the time, of being informed by his Paris mission of a company based in Geneva who could potentially offer public relations support for Biafra. From February 1968, the Biafran Overseas Press Service, under the name of Marketing Press (Markpress), came into existence, and was to prove substantially beneficial in support of Biafra. As Ojukwu admitted, one of Markpress's great strengths was encouraging him to allow journalists, members of Parliament, and other opinion-makers to visit Biafra and write reports which were then channelled through Markpress for international distribution. This was particularly effective when the issue of starvation was brought to the world's attention through the efforts of Michael Leapman and the *Sun* newspaper.[467]

Their personal attitude to the war in retrospect

Gowon and Ojukwu share the same sentiment that in retrospect they would have been more accommodating to each other and would have sought a solution to the seemingly intractable issues of the day. In their defence, one is drawn to the conditions of the time and the constraints which both men found themselves under during those increasingly tense months which led to the outbreak of war. They both consider that having gained a series of consensual agreements at Aburi they should have been more compromising and worked out a way forward which would have placated the majority of the interested parties and achieved a satisfactory settlement. However, as Ojukwu commented, the main issue the East had at the time was the uncontrolled and inhumane acts being perpetrated on the Igbo people who lived in the North, where they had settled for generations. These people were confronted with daily terror attacks which the Federal Authorities seemed powerless to control and indeed, as Ojukwu pointed out, many in the Eastern region were questioning the culpability of the Federal Authorities and began to believe that they were supporters of these inhumane crimes. Therefore in Ojukwu's eyes the only option the

East had at that time was to draw apart from the rest of the country, not with the idea of secession, but with the idea that the only solution to stop the killings was for the East to insulate itself from the North.

Gowon's perspective at the time was equally convincing. Whilst agreeing to the Aburi conditions, his opinion of them changed when it was pointed out that under the agreement all power in the country was vested in the regions, and not only would minority voices be overwhelmed by the power of the four major regions, but the authority of the Federal Government was totally undermined. It was this feature which Gowon was persuaded to find unacceptable. Whether or not the proposed system would have proved unworkable is open to debate, but as time went on this became an intractable situation which neither side was willing to accommodate or compromise over, in spite of the efforts of people like Awolowo, Ogundipe and Ejoor to find a way forward through the impasse.

Both leaders enjoyed a degree of success throughout the war and they both ended the war with their reputations intact. It can be argued that Ojukwu simply 'ran away' at the end, but as he said when he left the country, 'While I live Biafra lives'. There is an argument that Ojukwu was advised and agreed that with a final onslaught by Federal troops expected imminently and with Biafra's territorial area diminishing on a daily basis, the country would simply cease to exist. The fact was that although he left under very chaotic conditions, he left without the traditional fortune that many rulers in Africa accumulate when in power, and it is apparent that even today he is referred to only with respect and affection. Although Ojukwu through his publicity machine sought to expose the apparent barbarity of the Federal Army, forcing Gowon to investigate the falseness of these accusations through the International Observer Team, there was in fact very little proven inhumane conduct by either side. This can therefore be considered a tribute to both men's leadership and to their concern to ensure that acts of inhumanity were condemned. As Gowon commented, he had no quarrel with the Igbo people, only with Ojukwu and his colleagues, and it was this factor which disinclined Gowon to allow an overwhelmingly aggressive policy towards Biafra, and seemingly often led to lulls in the fighting.

Ojukwu says that his main disappointment during the war was the lack of recognition by more states within the international community, although as he pointed out there were many countries who were on the verge of giving Biafra official recognition. He feels that if this had been more forthcoming Biafra would still be an entity in the world today. His other disappointment was the lack of material support which he gained from the international community, and with Britain who sided with the Federation from the beginning, selling them an ongoing supply of arms which eventually, together with Russian support, led to a military inbalance between the two sides. This, in his view, meant that Biafra could never win the war militarily but as he pointed out, once the East had decided to secede, excepting her invasion of the Mid-West, international recognition rather than a force of arms would have determined Biafra's sovereignty.

Acknowledging the accepted premise of Ojukwu's de jure control over the East and Gowon's de facto control over the Federal Government, Nigeria was fortunate indeed to have two competent, honest and well-meaning leaders, albeit on opposing sides, to see the country through its civil war. Ojukwu long argued that Gowon had no legitimatcy to his claim as supreme commander of Nigeria, but equally Gowon could have challenged Ojukwu's right to take the East out of the Federation. The fact, however, was that neither men, finding themselves in positions of power, allowed themselves to be carried away by any sort of omnipotence. Power for its own sake never seemed to have had a corrupting influence on either of them. The fact remains that both of them, after a suitable period of estrangement from their country, were allowed to return with no preconditions, and indeed both were free to involve themselves in the politics of the day. Gowon attempted this with disastrous results, causing him to seek opportunities within the current political regime that did not involve controversy. In Ojukwu's case he is involved in politics to this day. Indeed at one of the interviews with him he explained that he was extremely busy because of the forthcoming presidential elections, in which he was a candidate.[468] One can only admire the tenacity of the man, but it is arguably a sad reflection of his wish to regain his powerful position from the past. One was reminded of a sportsman who having achieved ultimate success in his chosen field, retires, and then returns to that sport in an attempt to emulate his past glory. Because his discipline has changed and moved on beyond his past ability and understanding, he fails.

Arguably, Ojukwu came closer to exercising dictatorial power, firstly because he had been appointed under the Ironsi regime as the East's military governor, and that in itself gave him powers that in a democracy would only have been available to the most demagogic of politicians, and even then without the power of arms, and secondly because the people in the East looked to him as their protector from the evils of perceived and promoted genocide from the North. As a result, throughout the war his position was practically unassailable. Even the plot to overthrow him in order to make a peaceful overture to the Federal Government failed for lack of substantial support. What followed was a military embarrass-ment, with Biafra's withdrawal from the Mid-West Region, leading to a replacement of the commander-in-chief of the army and the permanent popular notion of saboteurs, undermining the state's power and its fragile sovereignty. Even then Ojukwu's popularity did not diminish and indeed arguably was on the ascendant.

A further strength of Ojukwu was his ability to choose his advisors, although he was not above nepotism – his father was chosen to advise him on various Eastern regional boards and his uncle C.C. Mojekwu remained a very close advisor throughout the war. Astutely, many came from the minority peoples in the region. His Chief of the General Staff and his acting Head of State in his absence was Major-General Philip Effiong, an Efik. The Chief Secretary and Head of Biafra's Civil Service was Mr N.U. Akpan, an Ibibio, and Mr S.J. Cookey, who was Commissioner for Special Duties, was from the Rivers Region. Even Colonel Achuzia, Ojukwu's highly successful army commander, although an Igbo, is an Asaba Igbo and a man whose natural leanings are to the Mid-West State, not to Enugu.

On assumption of power Gowon, like Ojukwu, was in effect sim-ply taking over an already established regime, but, unlike Ojukwu, one which had suffered extreme turmoil. Although the machinery of gov-ernment through the civil service was still in place, the military force which had effectively brought him to power was in disarray, and unlike Ojukwu he had to placate and accommodate many divergent factions, not the least the three regions, including a belligerent and politicised North led by the unpredictable Lt-Colonel Murtala Mohammed. Gowon's move to release Awolowo was certainly a wise decision which effectively, albeit slowly, gained the support of the Western Region for his regime. He also commented several times when being interviewed that, having no polit-ical ambition for ultimate power, he was not motivated by power for its own sake but rather to protect the stability of the country and his beloved army. It is easy to underestimate the strength of emotion and sentiment this man has for his ideals and his sense of tradition and heritage. As he said, his wish was to stabilise the country and protect the army; Murtala Mohammed could have taken charge, if there had been support, as indeed he was to do in 1976 under benign circumstances. At one of the interviews he was asked if he ever felt fear for his safety or for his life. He looked at the interviewer as though he had raised an inconceivably stupid notion and replied, 'No.'[469] An interesting observation is made of Gowon, which concurs with the writer's impression and understanding of the man:

> When you meet someone it is very important to know what their value system is. The value system of Gowon is a rather simple one. It springs from the imposition of ethics of Sandhurst and on the ethics of a very religious C.M.S. upbringing. He is not as complex a character as yourself! The values that he has are like yours, genuine ... the value system for Gowon is loyalty, straightforwardness, and the qualities of an officer and a gentleman. On the four occasions I have met him he continually used the words loyalty and honour. He spoke of the debt of Nigeria to Britain, not for the material things but for certain standards of loyalty.[470]

A final consideration must be made of both men's upbringing and background. Although from a class perspective, Ojukwu can claim to have the advantage, the fact was that his father enjoyed success and all the trappings of wealth through his own efforts. His son was therefore the first generation to inherit and enjoy those benefits. This arguably put him at an advantage over Gowon, whose father and family were poor, but their attitude was that success could be achieved through a good western education. It was in the field of education that both men's backgrounds were similar, not only through their respective schools but also through their religious upbringing. Gowon obtained his through his father's conversion to Christianity and his own subsequent initiation into the Christian faith through the Church Missionary Society, and through his schooling, all of which gave him a deep and long-standing commitment to Christian ideals, which he promoted throughout his time as leader of the Federal Government. Likewise, Ojukwu also had a Christian upbringing through his formative years in Lagos, where his family were members of the Roman Catholic community and during his time in England, when he was taken under the guardianship of the Whiter family. Although religion did not play as significant part in Ojukwu's upbringing as it did for Gowon, nevertheless it was important to him during the war, and still is today, indeed in a more overt way than Gowon.[471] It is a forceful argument that religious considerations were important to both men as they wrestled with their consciences over the rights and wrongs of the confrontation. Both have confirmed that although perhaps not uppermost in their minds, Christian beliefs played a part in the manner in which they approached and conducted the war.[472] It is also an anomaly that here were two men from similar religious backgrounds, confronting each other over a war which arguably was ethnically and religiously orientated, yet neither had an ethnic or religious orientation towards the Muslim North against whom the war was focused. However, that idea challenges the argument that this was an ethnic war, when the facts seem to point incontrovertibly to the war being commercially orientated, and to the international powers whose commercial considerations were under threat. Arguably Gowon was the protector of those commercial interests and Ojukwu, the protagonist who sought to protect those natural resources for Nigeria, or perhaps Biafra if she had survived, not for the international powers.

CHAPTER 7

CONCLUSION

In the final analysis the Nigerian tragedy has been bedevilled by a set of oppositions – generalised, stereotyped, not necessarily of the same order and maybe imaginary, yet each widening the wound and reducing the hope of healing it; North vs South, Islam vs Christianity, alleged feudalism vs assumed socialism, federal vs unitary preferences, traditional authority vs achieved elitism, have vs have nots, each with sinister undertones of tension, irreconcilability and threatened withdrawal. None was quite entirely accurate. Nevertheless each opposing set had sufficient seeds of truth within in it to permit, and even fertilize, the growth of feared fact from the semi-fiction of its existence.[473]

This book has investigated and attempted to answer five major questions. Firstly, why should a country endowed with so much optimism, economic potential and a rich and diverse energetic population have allowed itself to be dragged into a conflict which outwardly could only be to the detriment of the country's development and its people? Secondly, how realistic was Biafra's determination to achieve sovereignty? Thirdly, what caused the war's longevity and why did it take so long for the Federal Government to subdue the recalcitrant region? Fourthly, was genocide a reality or a myth? Fifthly, how important were the two leaders to the conflict?

However two important features occupied the thoughts and comments by the international press of the day. First was copy documents confirming that Biafra had offered to sell oil and other mineral resources to Rothschild Bank in Paris, in return for a substantial consideration.[474] No documentary proof could confirm this transaction, and in interview Ojukwu refused to be drawn into a conversation about the copy documents, but he did confirm that France had been the mainstay in supporting the supply of arms throughout the war.[475] It seems, however, that whatever the truth about the Rothschild documents, intensive negotiations had been going on with potential supporters and arms suppliers even prior to the war. Colonel Achuzia confirmed that he and colleagues had been to Europe in search of necessary arms and ammunition to conduct a war as early as October 1966.[476]

> I think it would be worthwhile recording that the first large-scale arms delivery to the East arrived in October 1966. It was Czech small arms and light machine guns, shipped from Szeczyn, in Poland.[477]

The second feature was the proposed land corridor. During the later stages of the war this became an important consideration for some aid agencies and the Federal Administration, but was totally rejected by Biafra. The reality, which appears not to have been grasped by the international media, was that the proposed land corridor went straight through the centre of land which formed a strategic part of the remainder of Biafra. At the time it was a disputed piece of territory which Biafra was intent on holding, therefore any move which weakened her attempts at retaining this territory were bound to be disputed. It seems that there was a fundamental misunderstanding of the position of this proposed so-called 'mercy corridor' which however well policed by the international community would have increased Biafra's vulnerability and her insecurity, and therefore was never going to gain approval from Biafra.

> The scheme proposed by the Nigerians was intrinsically an absurdity, being based on a shipment of supplies to Lagos, thence by 1000 mile journey to Enugu then 'corridor' into Biafran-held territory. They did not mention of course that they could not use the direct road route of roughly 300 miles only from Lagos to Enugu because they did not control it throughout the Mid-West or between Onitsha to Enugu. The Biafrans objected to the 'land corridor' south of Enugu because they relied on broken bridges and other obstacles for defence and feared that the Nigerians in the field would take advantage of the passage of relief convoys to penetrate Biafran defences. The idea of a 'neutral zone' on either side of

the corridor road was an absurdity to anyone with even a moderate knowledge of the country unless controlled by a large neutral force well-equiped with air reconnaissance, the provision of which was not suggested.[478]

The problem of relief and how to get it to those most at risk exercised all parties throughout the war, but became a cause cèlébre after the fall of Port Harcourt, which created a land-locked Biafra. This meant that all outside support had to be airlifted into the country, and as the war progressed the Federal Authorities became increasingly obsessed with the idea that much military aid was being airlifted into Biafra with the humanitarian aid. Their obsession was justified, and evidence comes from pilots' reports confirming that often the only way humanitarian aid could reach Biafra was in aircraft chartered to carry arms.[479]

Why was there a conflict?

Undoubtedly the meeting held in Aburi by Gowon and his military colleagues was an opportunity for the new leaders, following the second coup, to settle their differences and compromise over what had become an extremely intractable problem. It is also true that the creation of Nigeria by the British was an arbitrary decision, taken at a time when Britain's concern was protection for her West African trade rather than the indigenous people. A further consideration was the divisive rule exercised by the British over Nigeria. The political development also led to the tragedy of identifying the political parties with ethnicity rather than with popular mass appeal. Finally and most importantly was the nepotistic and oligarchic style of government which not only engendered favouritism rather than promoting ability but, more importantly, corruption.

Although they met as colleagues and brother officers and with great familiarity at Aburi, many of them, especially the military regional governors, had positions other than their own interpersonal relationships to consider. For example, Adebayo and Katsina were constrained by their regional and underlying ethnic responsibilities. It is easy to forget that until the first coup the Western Region had been in political turmoil, and following that coup, the Northern Region had seriously considered breaking from the Federation. It had involved Cumming-Bruce in much persuasive diplomatic pressure, to convince his friends, the emirs and sultans, not to secede. Gowon, who on his own admission, had little idea as to how to control and govern Nigeria, was grateful at this early stage in his assumption of power, to accept Cumming-Bruce's advice to keep Nigeria united.[480] At the time, following the first coup and Ironsi's unifying decrees, which seemingly undermined the North's position of power, she felt isolated, for the first time in the country's history, from the rest of Nigeria. Furthermore, as Adebayo commented, in view of the North's ambivalence about remaining in the Federation, the West was also considering its position. As the economic centre of the country, the Western Region, together with Lagos, had every reason to suppose that it would achieve economic success and prosperity without the encumbrance of the other regions, especially the North. As Adebayo said, the North had always been an economic drain on the West, and in view of the traumatic conditions at the time there was gathering sentiment in the Western Region for greater autonomy and distancing from the rest of the country.[481] Ojukwu's position was even more pressing. Firstly, as he readily admits, he was the only member at the Aburi meeting who had political ambitions. However, his involvement, following the second coup, had been marginalised because of the events which unfolded at Ikeja. Not only was he not consulted, but also he disagreed with Gowon becoming the new military head of state, because, he argued, there were other more senior men within the army who should have assumed that responsibility. Indeed at Aburi he confirmed that he had spoken to Ogundipe by telephone, and confirmed that if Ogundipe had stated on air that he had taken over the government, Ojukwu would have affirmed his support for him.[482] He disingenuously forgot that during the days following the second coup, the government of Nigeria had virtually ceased to function and was in danger of totally breaking down, leading to a state of anarchy. Gowon at that point in time was simply a compromise candidate for the post of military head of state. Secondly, and most importantly, following the second coup the North had embarked on the systematic destruction of Igbo life and property in the North. This had led the people of Eastern Nigeria as a whole, and the Igbo people in particular, to fear collective genocide by the Hausa-Fulani people. This fear was very real, as confirmed by accounts and pictures of the atrocities carried out in the North.[483] It led to a natural feeling that Eastern Nigeria was better placed to separate from the rest of Nigeria. Indeed Ojukwu's main argument at Aburi was that each region should move away from the others, with greater regional autonomy. As he commented, his objective at Aburi was not the disintegration of the Nigerian state but an agreement on confederation with greater regional autonomy. Indeed to this day he remains a firmly committed Nigerian nationalist. As far as he is concerned the seeds of secession were sown only because of the intransigence of Gowon and his administration and the Northern rulers.[484]

Gowon and Ejoor looked at the whole problem from a different perspective. Both men shared a love and respect for the Nigerian Army, and as Gowon commented, one of his main concerns was to see the unity of that army restored and maintained,[485] although he admits that at the time of Aburi this was an extremely difficult objective to achieve. However, his other main concern was to pull Nigeria back from the brink of anarchy and total disintegration. In this he had the support of the ex-colonial power. For his part Ejoor, as military governor of the Mid-West Region, not only supported Gowon in his objective but also was also concerned for the survival of his region. At Aburi both men were extremely keen to see compromise achieved. Arguably this is exactly what happened in Ghana: a compromise was agreed but very much in favour of Ojukwu's objective. It was agreed, as the transcripts prove, that the regions should move apart, with a high degree of autonomy, forming a confederation rather than a federation. Ojukwu could argue legitimacy, and feel certain of his position because after the first coup, Ironsi appointed him to the military governorship of the Eastern region. He took on the responsibilities of a region which already had a high degree of autonomy, and was still run much in the style established by the British during the formation of Nigeria. The tragedy of Aburi was that Gowon simply reneged on the agreement. Arguably he had little choice. Pressure from his own senior civil servants, who pointed out that the agreement left him with little centralised power, as well as their own consideration for their own minority ethnic backgrounds, led him to compromise over Aburi. Many of his senior civil servants came from small indigenous groups, and they could see that greater autonomy by the four regions would lead to the denigration of the smaller ethnic groups in Nigeria. Isaac Boro's attempt to form individual states in the Delta region was an extension of this real fear; a fear which even today proves an intractable problem. Furthermore, the North, having agreed to stay in the Federation, could see their oligarchic power being threatened should Nigeria become a confederation with greater autonomy for the regions.

Nigeria's formation was an arbitrary decision taken by Britain at a time when Europe was vying for control of trade in Africa. There was limited consideration for the peoples contained within those boundaries. Britain's concern was for the protection of her trade, which at that time was centred round palm oil. Frederick Lugard had been appointed by Chamberlain to command Sir George Goldie's defence force, formed to counter rivalry from other European countries especially the French, and to quell insurgency from non-compliant local rulers. He was eventually appointed Governor of the Northern Protectorate of Nigeria. He had witnessed the workings of indirect rule from his time in India and found that such a system was equally applicable in his Northern Territory, where there was a well-established hierarchical order, and he was able to couple Britain's suzerainty over and together with this rule. Where local rulers refused to cooperate he simply replaced them with people who would support Britain through the process of indirect rule. When he became Nigeria's first Governor-General in 1901 his attempts at extending this type of rule to other regions ended in failure, especially in the East where people simply refused to accept the imposition of so-called Warrant Chiefs. Lugard and the British administration had failed to appreciate the great ethnic distinctions and divide between the many peoples of Nigeria.

The divisive rule exercised by the British over the diverse people of Nigeria can also be seen as a contributory factor in engendering distrust and hostility between the various ethnic groups, and can be considered an underlying cause of the war. Although they were able to rule in the North because of a compliant hierarchy, they inadvertently laid the seeds of dissension and discord because of their support for the Northern hierarchy's traditions, customs and way of life. This led to an extremely unbalanced educational infrastructure. British rule in the North actively discouraged the spread of evangelical Christianity, which had been the source of western education in the southern part of the country, especially in the South East. Consequently as the country developed under British rule and after independence many senior roles were filled throughout the country and especially in the North by people from the South. This infiltration of people from southern Nigeria, particularly Easterners, into many aspects of Northerners' lives led to a general resentment of these people who felt that they were being exploited. It can be seen as the root cause of civil rioting leading to the death of many Easterners in the North, together with the destruction of their property, culminating in the Northern riots from

July to September 1966. Two further actions confirmed that the North resented the intrusiveness of Southerners, especially Igbos. First was the fact that during the lead-up to and following independence, rather than encouraging Nigerians to assume roles formally taken by Europeans, the North actively sought to keep Europeans in many of the roles rather than see them being taken by Igbos and Southern people. The North realised at the time because of their ill-developed western education, there were simply no suitably qualified Northerners to assume many of these roles, and rather than see Southerners occupy positions they allowed Europeans to continue in these roles. Second, with regard to the army, a determined effort was made to recruit Northerners into the officer ranks. However, again this proved problematic, basically because Northerners suffered a lack of western educational opportunities, and many potential recruits to the army found the entry requirements simply beyond their academic abilities. In order to ease this problem the standards of entry were lowered to accommodate these candidates. This led to much resentment from better educated officers who had been subject to more stringent educational standards. The final area which should be considered with regard to regional divisiveness was the way people from the South who settled in the North found themselves segregated from Northern mainstream society and encouraged to live in their own areas, called Sabon Garis. It may well be that many of these people found it more conducive to live segregated from the host people, but the fact remains that when there was racial tension the perceived cause was easily identified in the Strangers' Quarters.

In the 1940s during the early period of emerging Nigerian national political awareness, together with the formation of the National Council of Nigeria and the Cameroons (NCNC), attempts were made to ensure that politics would be a national affair and would gain support from all people rather than become ethnically divisive. Indeed before the Richards Constitution of 1945, Nigerian politics was based on unification towards a centralized state and the realisation of a common nationality.[486] Unfortunately the constitution allowed for the creation of regional councils in the West, East and North, which in retrospect have been criticised for introducing ethnicity into Nigerian politics. Because the Igbo people were the first ethnic group of Nigerians to embrace western education they found themselves in great demand to fill clerical vacancies in government administration and within the railways as workers and storekeepers, and because of population and land pressure they migrated in large numbers throughout the country. For their mutual benefit these people formed themselves into societies to promote education within their ranks and extended families. By 1944 these associations had developed into a national body with the formation of the Pan-Igbo Federal Union, with Dr Nnamdi Azikiwe as president.

At the same time, Yoruba students in London formed the Egbe Omo Oduduwa and although initially a cultural organisation it soon became politically orientated and was to lead to the formation of the Action Group, which initially was only interested in securing Western Regional interests. Indeed in the first general election of 1951–2, although the NCNC won seats in the West, the results for the Action Group and the Northern Peoples' Congress were decisively supported in their own respective regions. Although the NCNC continued in its policy of achieving a unitary Nigeria, the other two parties were determined to promote their regions. This was especially true of the North who had had little integration with the South and who feared Southern domination.

The Macpherson Constitution of 1948 allowed for popular elections in all three regions, resulting in the ethnically dominated parties being elected in each region, and this gave weight to national politics being conducted on ethnic lines. By 1959, in the final national elections before independence, Nigerian politics had decidedly assumed the mantle of ethnicity and racial divisiveness. All three parties gained majority support from their regional origins. Even the NPNC, which had started out as a national unitary party, became dominated by support from the Igbo heartland. This politically ethnic divide helped foster notions of ethnic segregation and state separation within the Nigerian federation.

Arguably the British, under their rule, had encouraged loyalty to the establishment with rewards for lucrative government contracts for indigenous people who were compliant and supportive of the colonial regime. Indigenous political development was gradually taking place, but on ethnic lines, as previously noted. However, control was firmly held by Britain through the services, and the indigenisation of the civil, military and police services was only gradually and slowly promoted. There was of course much competition from Nigerians to gain acceptance into these services, especially in the upper echelons. Having achieved these positions of perceived power and success, the traditional responsibility of supporting an extended family of relatives, friends and supporters was considered mandatory. Thus the indigenisation of these positions encouraged favouritism, bribery and corruption. Furthermore, the British had always rewarded their expatriate workers with generous remunerations and perquisites, far in excess of those paid to Nigerians of equivalent rank. This led to much resentment among the indigenous. However, once independence came Nigerians could reward themselves with the same emoluments accorded to expatriate workers.[487] Generous housing, vehicle and travel allowances became the norm. This situation was obviously acceptable to the few who enjoyed these benefits, but to the masses it was simply an unfair distribution of wealth. Independence was supposed to have brought benefit to all Nigerians, not just a few. The elite were increasingly accused of corruption. Nigeria's media became increasingly vitriolic over this perceived abuse of power. The evidence would point to this being one of the main areas of grievences amongst the young and well educated, who could see their opportunities of advancement being held back by the few who were in positions of power and influence and who were seen to be enriching themselves at the expense of the ordinary Nigerian citizen.[488] It was this that confirmed the popularity of the first coup, which in retrospect can be seen as the first practical step towards the country's disintegration and the start of the civil war.

How realistic was Biafra's determination to achieve sovereignty?

There were a number of reasons for Biafra's confidence that it would achieve its objective. They can be divided into two. First was the fact that initially Eastern Nigeria had access to and control of the country's nascent oil industry, as well as having good port facilities and extremely fertile land, and most importantly the support of the people for the seceded state. Secondly were a series of reasons which consecutively gave Biafra confidence that it could achieve its objective. First was the state of the opposition's army, second was an audacious invasion, third was Biafra's overt use of propaganda and publicity, fourth was the strength and consistancy of the humanitarian support it received, fifth was the ongoing supply of foreign arms, supported with its own armament production, and sixth was Gowon's reluctance to destroy the Igbo people.

Initially, control of Nigeria's oil industry played its part in giving Biafra confidence that its sovereignty could be sustained. Although oil had not achieved the significance it was to find in the future, it played an important part in providing foreign exchange, and in the country's ability to sustain a healthy trading balance for exporting and importing goods and services. The evidence, though not conclusive, would point to Biafra's attempts to secure funds from the French, through Rothchild's Bank.[489] The land also played its part in giving support to Biafra's sustainable independence, providing the necessary arable and protein products to sustain a healthy and growing population. Support by its people was, of course, the paramount consideration, but more important was the large numbers of educated people within its economy who could offer their skills in almost any field for the sustainability of Biafra. However, the fact was that the oil quickly lost its signifance as a source of foreign currency once the Federal forces had invaded and taken control of Bonny Island and Port Harcourt. As the Federal forces made increasing inroads into Biafran territory, limited land access meant that the provision of food became much more problematic, and as they overran the minority ethnic areas within the region, so the support by these people for the nascent state diminished. These actions nullified major reasons for Biafra's confidence in gaining its sovereignty. However, the second set of reasons then took priority. From interviews held with many Eastern participants in the war, there is common agreement that they all gave them confidence that Biafra would achieve its objective, but to varying degrees.[490]

Ojukwu, Gbulie and Achuzia, all commented on the perceived weakness of the Federal forces, who, they felt, were in no position to wage a successful war against Biafra. In their opinion Biafra had more qualified officers, and was better able to recruit supportive Easterners than were the Federal authorities, in spite of reverses during the opening stages of the war.

The chronic shortage in the Federal forces (now totalling about 70,000 in the Army and 1,000 in the Navy according to a reliable source who should be fairly well informed) was shown by the fact that when 500 freshly trained reinforcements were moved down from Makurdi into Enugu they were commanded by a corporal.[491]

As they all admit, initially there was a shortage of arms, but this was gradually remedied by fresh imported supplies, their own ingenuity at producing arms, like the very successful 'Ogbunigwe' anti-personnel mine and the Federal forces' habit of retreating and leaving behind arms which were then used by the Biafrans.[492] Unquestionably, Biafra's invasion of the Mid-West and its successful penetration as far as Ore in the West gave the country supreme confidence that it was on the verge of total victory. Because of Banjo's perfidiousness, this resulted in Biafra's retreat back to the river Niger, and its confidence was severely shaken. However, although Federal forces made inroads into Biafran territory from the south, Biafra was able to maintain a strong defensive position, and indeed often successfully attacked its foe.

Biafra's position was strengthened by its ongoing and successful use of publicity, through its agency Markpress, which not only created awareness throughout the international community of the plight of Biafra's population, but gave it access to aid on an unprecedented scale, both in armaments and humanitarian support. From the middle of 1968 its position strengthened again. Following its recognition by a number of African nations, France offered it more determined support, and although this fell short of giving it official recognition, it continued to give substantial supplies of arms, until the end of hostilities.

In a conversation dated 17 September 1968 between Mr Tickell of the British Embassy in Paris and M. Joel le Theule, the French Secretary of State for information, over French support for Biafra, Tickell reported:

> I asked who had laid the framework of the General's thinking about Biafra. M. le Theule recalled our previous exchange on this subject and said he had been interested to trace the origins of General de Gaulle's very strong feelings. So far as I could tell, they followed from a discussion he had had with M. Houphouet Boigny, the President of the Ivory Coast, who had subsequently given the General a paper on the subject. M. Houphouet Boigny was obsessed with the southward movement of the Moslem and Arab population of West Africa and presented the Biafrans as a sort of Christian rearguard of high intelligence and ability who were threatened with racial extinction. M. le Theule said that the General had been able in extraordinary fashion to communicate his feelings about Biafra to the French as a whole. As public opinion polls well showed ... the French felt even more strongly about Biafra than Czechoslovakia .... I asked

whether M. Foccart or M. Debre was responsible for carrying out French policy over Biafra. M. le Theule said that he knew nothing about M. Foccart's role and was sure that M. Debre was responsible (Professor Wahl said afterwards that M. Debre had recently told him that French policy towards Biafra was entirely General de Gaulle's. Professor Wahl had no doubt from this conversation that M. Foccart was effectively in charge under direct instructions from the General).[493]

These facts gave Biafra confidence that it would achieve its goal. Indeed, arguably, it is reasonable to comment that pressure from the international community would eventually oblige Gowon and the Federal authorities to agree to Biafra's independence, albeit within a Nigerian confederation. Indeed Gowon's own Christian and ethical stand determined that he had no wish to see the annihilation of the Igbo people.[494]

Undoubtedly there were times when Biafra came close to achieving permanent sovereignty. The invasion of the Mid-West came close to being a total success, which would probably have resulted in a settlement confirming Biafra's right to exist. Even that failure did not diminish its determination to confirm its independence. Support from the international community gave it belief in its independent destiny, which would probably have been confirmed if France had given it the official recognition it so determinedly sought. Ultimately, however, the balance of support from the international community increasingly favoured the Federal authorities, and this determined that Biafra's objective would be denied.

Why we support the Federal Government. Our aim is to do everything possible to restore peace, stability and prosperity in Nigeria, but we must do this in a way which keeps us on good terms with the Nigerians and their rulers. This is a Nigerian and African problem first and foremost. Nevertheless we have a great deal at stake in Nigeria. Shell BP have sunk at least £250 million in Nigeria ... . Our other investments are worth about £150–£175 million, and we have an export trade worth £90 million a year .... The whole of our investments in Nigeria ... will be at risk if we change our policy of support for the Federal Government. The French would be glad to pick up our oil concessions if they could.[495]

This statement, arguably, confirms why Biafra would ultimately be denied its right to self-determination. The old colonial power simply had too much at stake to allow Biafra its independence, and the underlying force of this argument meant that in the final analysis the pragamatic power of trade would not allow a recalcitrant region the right to self-determination, if it risked the loss of assets.

What caused the war's longevity?

Possibly the single most important factor which determined the length of the conflict was Biafra's creative use of propaganda. This was carried out with a high degree of success through its agency Markpress. A telling comment on this agency was made: 'Every day produced numbers of good, hot, news stories. They were not often true; but they were always colourful and sensational.'[496]

Initially Gowon's approach was very different: 'The Federals began with the idea, very congenial to Gowon, that the truth would prevail. Whenever they announced any thing it was always long after the event and consequently of no interest to the press.'[497] Gowon admitted that it was Biafra's unashamed use of publicity that so often gave it the moral high ground in the conflict. As he commented, he was too naïve at the time to appreciate this, and it was only later in the war that the Federal Authorities made more effort to promote their cause to the international community, through the medium of propaganda. He spoke specifically of Biafra's attempts through the media to accuse the Federal Authorities falsely of a determination to commit genocide on the Igbo people (discussed later in this chapter), and how damaging this was to the Federal Authorities in the eyes of the international community.[498] Coupled with Biafra's use of propaganda was the international support, in the form of arms and humanitarian aid, given to both sides. In the final analysis both appreciated that without external support they would not succeed in their objectives.

Initially, at the start of the conflict, there was arrogance on the part of both participants that victory would be achieved quickly and with ease. Ojukwu regarded the Federal army as easily defeatable:

> Everyone knows it is not possible for what remains of the Nigerian army to make any successful attempt on the East .... Jack {Gowon}

would never dare attack him *{Ojukwu}* .... I think it is about time
I sent my troops to Lagos to clear up the mess there. I can do it easily; I only have to give the order.[499]

The Federal army thought that victory over the Biafrans would be immediate: 'Victory was forecast in days rather than weeks. In the North Colonel
Katsina sneered at the Biafran "army of pen pushers" and forecast a swift
victory as the largely northern Nigerian federal infantry marched in.'[500]

Both sides were quickly disabused of their opinions. In spite of this
Biafra was singularly determined to achieve its objective of sovereignty.
It made extensive use of propaganda to gain international support. This
support revolved around a series of attempts to broker a satisfactory
peace settlement, and foreign aid. Furthermore, Biafra's innate resourcefulness also played an important part in its survival, and helped create
the war's longevity.

Of the nine attempts at achieving a negotiated settlement all proved
to be failures, mainly because both sides had incompatible objectives and
neither side was willing to compromise, because Biafra's sovereignty was
non-negotiable and the Federal Authorities were committed to the East's
return to the Federation. However, all attempts at a peaceful settlement
helped to sustain the length of the war, because they gave each side the
opportunity to explain their cause to the international community and
this tended to increase or decrease international support, depending on
either side's status at the time. Foreign aid was of course paramount for
both parties,[501] but Biafra was able to convince an ever-cynical world
of the rightfulness of its cause, especially in the light of a starving and
increasingly disadvantaged population, so support from the international
community increased, either with arms or humanitarian support. Once
de Gaulle had stated that Biafra had the right to determine her own destiny, French support for the beleaguered territory, whilst with no official
sanction, became ever more overt:

On 31 July 1968 a French Government statement declared: 'The
Government believes ... that the present conflict should be resolved
on the basis of the right of peoples to self-determination.'[502]
      On the basis of the data which is now in the hands of certain
Western Governments, the lifting capacity of the arms airlift from
Libreville to Biafra is not less than 60 tons a day.[503]

The supplies of light automatic French weapons and the ammunition to go with them are technically being taken from the stocks
of the Gabonese Army. However, it is clear that the replenishment
of these stocks comes from France.[504]

It is also reported that each night French registered planes with
French pilots fly from Libreville in Gabon to 'Biafra' carrying a
mixture of arms, ammunition and food.[505]

Because Biafra had lost its sea access after the fall of Port Harcourt, this
support had to be airlifted into the landlocked country, and increasingly
the humanitarian aid was mixed with armament support. This factor
in itself supported Biafra's survival and encouraged the war's longevity.
Conclusively it was these factors acting in sequence and together which
ensured the longevity of the war.

Was genocide a myth or a reality?

Arguably, there was little substance to Biafra's accusation that the Federal
Authorities were intent on committing genocide on the East and specifically on the Igbo people. However after the second coup there was a period
when determined efforts were made by the North to attack Igbo people,
many of whom who had settled in the North. Ojukwu accused Gowon of
being unable to control these attacks which went on unabated for several
months. Indeed Gowon admitted his inability to bring these attacks under
control. The verbal evidence and pictorial accounts bear out that these
uncontrolled riots led to many Igbos being maimed, losing their lives and
losing their property. Ojukwu, however, took every opportunity to exag-
gerate the numbers of people killed, and he was to use this in an ongoing
attempt to discredit the Federal Government, using the word genocide as
a pretext to prove the Gowon government's intention to kill the Igbo race.
It would seem that propaganda was used to promote the idea of genocide,
firstly to instil it in the Biafran people, in order to strengthen their resolve
to defend their homeland against Federal forces, and secondly to convince
the international community that annihilation of the Igbo race was the
Federal Government's intent. So persuasive did this argument become that
Gowon felt obliged to counter the accusations by appointing an independent international committee to determine the truth. The outcome of this
investigation confirmed: 'The word genocide is completely unjustified.'[506]

There was, however, a further report commissioned by Biafra and carried out by an international commission of jurists in 1968, which did confirm acts of genocide by Federal troops against people from the East.[507] Unsurprisingly, both findings did come across a number of isolated incidents where a degree of uncontrolled killing of innocent Easterners had taken place. One report considered these incidents genocide and the other did not. Looking at both these reports the conclusion was that the word genocide was unjustifiably used and that unlawful killing might be a more apt description, especially in the heat of battle or where troops lacking discipline behaved barbarically. The only other piece of documentary evidence regarding genocide was produced by Biafra's Directorate for Propaganda, in November 1968. It lists reports of genocide, from members of Britain's parliament, monitored reports from world radio stations, publications from foreign journalists and statements on genocide by independent foreign observers. On examination almost all the comments are based on unsubstantiated reports, without any witnesses being present at the time. Many are subjective and very biased and arguably should be treated with a high degree of suspicion.[508]

What impact did the two leaders have on the conflict?

Both men had spent their formative years during the closing days of colonial rule and were imbued with a sense of Britishness from their upbringing, their schooling and their careers in the army. Ojukwu had, by his own admission, political ambition based on the rule of law and democratic government, but he found himself charged by the Ironsi regime with ruling and administering a developing territory which had a well-run administrative and legal sytem and a large degree of autonomy within the federation.[509] Arguably his brief was to run an established country, within whose boundaries were a mix of ethnic tribes dominated by the Igbo people. Gowon's brief from the Ironsi regime was to run the army, a challenging opportunity, given the unrest within its ranks following the first coup. However for a young man it was an opportunity to make his mark in his chosen field, which under normal circumstances would probably have paved the way for him to achieve the ultimate position of responsibility within the military. Arguably that was the extent of Gowon's ambition, indeed as he commented, the opportunity for him to take charge of the country was totally unexpected and he would have been happy not to have had that responsibility if a more suitable candidate had been proposed and accepted by the army's rank and file. As he said, at the time he was the only acceptable person to take charge.[510]

Both men were ambitious in totally different ways, but arguably both had at heart the protection and well-being of the Nigerian state, albeit from totally different perspectives. This meant that although initially both were determined to forge a way forward that would have ensured the security of the state and of all the people, as ensuing events unfolded, their differences gradually became apparent, until they no longer felt able to compromise. Discussing this at length with both of them has led the author to feel that, although they were both clear in their respective objectives, each had respect for the other's position. Neither Gowon nor Ojukwu show any animosity towards other today, indeed they both still refer to each other by their first names. Arguably, therefore in spite of the tumultuous war which ensued, Nigeria was fortunate to have two leaders who conducted their campaign with a high degree of Christian ethics. It seems that the two men, chosen by default not by design, exercised restraint on their forces and compassion for their foes, in spite of their mutual determination to achieve their respective objectives.

EPILOGUE

By spending a year travelling and visiting all the major centres through-out the country, it is striking that there is little to remind the visitor of Nigeria's civil war. True there is the national war museum at Umuahia, which is indeed a remarkable assembly of armaments that were used by both sides during Biafra's struggle for independence. They are well looked after, as is the surrounding area, but it is disturbing that according to the curator the museum receives very few visitors and is severely short of funds for maintenance, and there are no thoughts of expansion. To the visitor it seems a forlorn assembly of metal, sited as a memorial to a long-forgotten piece of history, although that is maybe how the authori-ties thought the war should be remembered. However, throughout the rest of the country there is a dearth of war memorabilia; indeed even the national museum in Lagos makes scant reference to the war. It focuses on Nigeria's history and heritage, as it should. Much significance is given to all the heads of state since the country's formation, and pride of place seems to go the bullet-ridden motorcar ridden in by the murdered mili-tary ruler Murtala Mohammed.

The country makes no further reference to the war. There are no memorials to the event. Little seems to be taught in schools about the war, as is evident from interviews with teachers and past pupils. It seems as though a certain air-brushing of the event has occurred in the minds of the population and throughout the topography of the country. Of course it is arguable that memorials and preservation of the past is not an activ-ity much indulged in in Nigeria, and the consensus among interviewees would confirm that. However it also true to say that many of the inter-viewees when probed, are very emotional about their experiences during the war. Essentially, it seems that Gowon's slogan of 'No victor no van-quished', has been a popular sentiment with the majority of Nigerians since the end of hostilities, and has continued in this vein to the present.

In Eastern Nigeria, however, in discussion with many Igbo people, it is apparent that the people are disillusioned with their government and treat it with due disdain. As Professor Sydney Emezue commented little has changed since the British left and the military came to power.[511] The North is still in charge and her influence forms the centrepoint of the all-powerful NPC political party. The country seems to be a one-party state. The main concern for Easterners, however, appears to be that the country still lacks a national consciousness. As Chief Jerome Udoji commented in 1996, thirty years after the war: 'A country without national conscious-ness ... torn apart by cleavages of tribe and ethnicity; ... with frequent religious riots ... {and} widespread corruption ... is a country where the governed have lost hope and confidence in the government.'[512]

The Biafran War created conditions for Nigeria to come of age as a nation. It enabled it to assert her independence from the colonial power. For the duration of the war it had for the first time to become controller of its own destiny. It lost its dependence on the colonial power, initially because of Britain's refusal to supply the arms, particularly fighter planes and bombers, to subdue the rebels. It therefore had to look to other nations for support. Russia in particular filled a gap. This did not mean that Nigeria was in danger of becoming a client state of Russia; it was simply being pragmatic, in spite of Britain's misgivings. It demanded arms to finish the job of subduing the rebels and it found support from Russia, and indeed from whatever source would support its needs to bring the conflict to a successful conclusion.[513]

This war had a number of distorted images and facts. Firstly there were very few major military engagements, but there were a series of hard-fought but minor battles, which the media from both sides inten-tionally sensationalised and exaggerated, to the point that myths and impressions developed which have misrepresented the war over the years. This does not denigrate the seriousness of the conflict, as indeed there were many heroic actions carried out by both sides. But there is evidence that the essential character of Nigerians as a collective of peoples kept on surfacing throughout the campaign. Their natural sociability was a regu-lar occurance: 'September 1967, two sides in Biafran war declare truce to watch Brazilian team Santos, starring Pele, play two matches.'[514] Secondly the numbers involved would appear to have been seriously distorted. The number of those killed in the July-September 1966 Northern riots, as portrayed and promoted by the East, seem to have been incorrect. The figure of 50,000, as suggested by Ojukwu, was a serious exaggeration.

Even he admits this today, but justifies it because he was trying to bring attention to the Igbo Northern atrocities.[515] The fact that they did indeed occur is borne out by newspaper reports and pictorial evidence at the time. The same is true of the numbers of people escaping from the North to the East. The number of 1.5 to 2 million refugees does seem to have been an exaggeration. The most informed opinion would confirm a figure of 150,000:

> The Eastern Regional Government called on all refugees to register at special offices set up throughout the region; these offices were under the control of a British Civil Servant, a Mr Savile, who told Mr Parker *{British Assistant High Commissioner, in Enugu}* that the total registered was 150,000. This is the only solid and official figure in existence. According to Mr Parker the authorities manipulated it in the following way. First they doubled it 'because only about half the people who could have registered did so' (though it could be argued also that some people who were not refugees registered in the hope of benefit); then finding 300,000 an insufficiently impressive figure, they assumed falsely that all those on the register were men, made the assumption that all these men were married and had an average of three children, multiplied by six and produced a figure of 1.8 million. This of course was always rounded upwards: I remember with amusement Ojukwu saying to me at our interview in March 'and then we have two million refugees – no, I must not exaggerate, 1.8 million.' Two million became the classical figure, then 'over two million'.[516]

Finally the numbers killed or dying during the war again seem to have been exaggerated, especially by aid agencies and the international press. Numbers are very hard to substantiate, but both Achuzia and Adekunle have put a figure of 50,000 as war casualties for both sides, and suggested that 30,000 were the number of fatal casualties.[517] The other figure, which is very hard to substantiate, is the number of civilian deaths through the war and through disease and malnutrition. Both Oxfam and Save the Children[518] feel 2 million is untrue, and Professor Murray Last makes the compelling comment that after the war the numbers of children in the East of educational age were very much at pre-war levels.[519] Arguably, therefore, a comment that 'the total casualties were about 100,000' is more plausible.[520]

The final feature which became increasingly apparent was Gowon's desire throughout the campaign to seek a compromise solution and his unwillingness to obliterate the Igbo people. This is borne out by his own comments and also by some of his subordinate officers and the western press.[521]

In 1974 most of the Biafran detainees who had been involved in the war were released: Colonel Nwawo, Lt-Colonel Nwajei, Majors Okonkwo, Asoya and Ademoyega, Captains Gbulie, Udeaja, Okonkwo and Isichei, Lieutenants Okocha, Amuchienwa, Oyewole, Nwokocha, Ikejiofor, Onyefuru, Egbikor and Azubuogu, and Second Lieutenant Ngwuluka; all were dismissed from the army. Interestingly, Colonel Achuzia was not on the list and he remained in prison until 1980. Captain Gbulie has recently been notified that he will receive his army pension.[522] In 2009 it was confirmed that Lt-Col. Ojukwu was to receive and had accepted his army pension from the Nigerian Army. Colonel Achuzia confirmed his disapproval over this action.[523]

As a footnote to the story, in Lagos the newspaper the *Daily Sun* published the following announcement: 'It has been announced that army pensions are to be paid to Nigerian soldiers who fought on the Biafran side. A gesture by the new president Umar Musa Yar'Adua thirty seven years after the end of the war.'[524]

Arguably this war was a conflict between northern Nigerians who have a strong Middle-Eastern culture and religion stretching back several hundred years, and eastern Nigerians: a pragmatic people who had readily grasped European ideas, education and religion. However, crossing these two main cultures was western Nigeria who were ambivalent in their support for either of the two main groups. Overlaying this was a thin veneer of British upper-class attitudes to ruling subjective people. When the British left, they left this thin veneer of rule to the only group who could offer a heritage of class and subservience similar to their own. Therefore this brittle thin veneer of ruling power was always going to find it difficult to control a people as divergent and different as the Nigerians; and so it proved. The result of the war ensured that this thin veneer of power retained control, but with the backing of military force, leading, even to the present, an oligarchic power structure consisting of a one-party state, where the focus of power is still with the original ruling elite as left by the British, but always supported by the military. The divergence of the two main groups which created conditions for the conflict have not been put to rest, and the losers are the Igbos. Despite Gowon's proclamation of 'No victor no vanquished' the ongoing reality has been very different, and the undercurrent of dissent and disquiet with the ruling oligarchy is never far from current day-to-day life.

Travelling from Lagos to Enugu in 2007, the author reached the river Niger early one morning and found the bridge closed and guarded by the military. On enquiring for the reason, he was told that a state curfew had been imposed on Onitsha, the great Igbo trading town on the Niger's other side. Several days later, in the company of Igbo friends, the discussion came round to the reasons for the curfew and the comment was that a group of Igbo politicians had flexed their muscles against the ruling party and were being brought into line with the status quo. Their view is that the Igbo people, ever since the January coup of 1966, have always been subjugated by the ruling party, which is still controlled by the North.

POSTSCRIPT

'No victor no vanquished' was the slogan promoted by Gowon's administration at the war's conclusion and arguably the Igbo people should have had their position secured as a major contributor to the Nigerian Republic. However certain factors ensured that this was not to be a reality. The North had defeated her recalcitrant neighbour and since the war there has been a political determination that no other part of Nigeria would be allowed to challenge the authoritative power of the North. Therefore, considering the period from the end of hostilities to the present, constraints have been imposed on the East to secure the North's ascendant position. Looking at three main areas relevant to a county's successful development and sustainability, politics, education and economics it would seem that restrictions have been imposed on the Igbo people, in all these areas.

The creation of twelve states by the Gowon administration set in train a process by which the north could exercise political control over the rest of the country. Together with the unashamed use of oil revenues by the North's ruling party, the People's Democratic Party (PDP), it secured sufficient wealth to ensure an ascendant position outside its home territory. It became dominant in the East and even in the West, until the West threatened secession. This saw the establishment of the Action Congress of Nigeria (ACN), the successor party of the Action Group (AG) in the West. However, in an attempt to gain political control over the PDP, due to lack of finance and the fragmentation of Eastern Nigeria into more states, the All Progressive Grand Alliance (APGA), the successor party to the Nigerian People's Party, stood little chance of gaining a majority of the popular vote, within the East let alone the rest of the country. Furthermore, since the war the military has remained the guardian of the North's dominance. Whenever this has been threatened the army has assumed control, giving rise to a series of military dictatorships.

During the war much infrastructural damage had been done to the East's educational establishments, lack of finance and the North's focus on funding to bring its educational levels up to those in the Southern Nigeria, ensured that re-establishing the East's pre-war academic excellence was very slow in being restored. Indeed many teaching posts were awarded to Yorubas and expatriate Indians in preference to Igbos. Underfunding and restricting Igbos into the teaching profession was detrimental to education, which had a negative impact on development in the East. This state of affairs has continued to the present. Furthermore, teachers' remuneration in the East is often three months and more in arrears.[525]

Economic prosperity has also played its part in constraining the rise of the East again, although arguably in a most subjective manor. Although Igbos were and often are better qualified for the job, the North and to a lesser extent the West generally seem to secure the top jobs, especially the country's public utilities, and large corporations. These appointments gave people the opportunity to accrue considerable wealth. Most of this wealth was retained for the benefit of the individual and his extended family. It was also used to extend political influence. As few appointees came from the East, and even fewer were of Igbo origin, little benefit went in supporting political parties in the East.

Furthermore, most major infrastructural development has been focused outside the East, which has meant that the East has been unable to take advantage of community wealth which accrues from such development.

It has been Nigeria's determination to fragment into thirty-six states which has been the main reason for marginalising the Igbo people. Twelve states have now become thirty-six and it is no surprise that of the six geopolitical zones formed, the Igbo people only have influence in one of these, the South East, and there only over four states, while the North holds sway over nineteen states. The imbalance is obvious in view of the fact that the country's wealth, mainly generated from its oil production, is distributed fairly evenly to each state. This has meant that attempts by the APGA, the East's main political party, to gain ascendancy in Igboland, let alone in other parts of Nigeria has been frustrated, through lack of funding. This position has been exacerbated, as stated, by the lack of Igbos controlling the country's major corporations and industries, allowing them to accrue wealth, which could be used for political benefit, as has been the case in the North. Even the position of the country's presidency has been denied to an Igbo, in spite of some Igbo politicians attaining the governorship of some Eastern States. Arguably this will be the case for at least the next sixteen years, in view of the fact that Goodluck Jonathan, who is not an Igbo, and comes from the Southern state of Bayelsa, has been elected as president, and should he secure a second term, and a Northern candidate serves as president for a further two terms, which is the convention, then an Igbo will not have the opportunity to stand for president for the foreseeable future.

Following the West's attempt at secession, the ACN, a successor party to the Yoruba-dominated Action Group, with support from the country's president, Obasanjo, and the writer Wole Soyinka, saw the rise of the ACN, over the PDP. This gave rise, in the East, to the formation of the Movement for the Actualization of the Sovereign State of Biafra (Massob), which has attempted to secure political ascendency over the PDP in the East. Also, one of its objectives has been, and is, to secure independence for Biafra. To date this has proved a forlorn hope. It is hard to imagine the East's lack of control over its own destiny changing much in the foreseeable future. There is a limited amount of discussion on the internet about Biafra and its claim for independence, and Massod seems fairly active in this area, but the will and resource seems to be lacking to have much positive appeal to most people who live within the old boundaries of Biafra.

The recent presidential election, which internationally has been seen as the fairest in the country's post-independence history, bodes well for the country's future. The incumbent president, who comes from the south, was re-elected with an overwhelming majority, in spite of the fact that arguably it was the turn of the North to have a Northern President. It has also just been announced that the new army chief of staff is an Igbo. This is the first Igbo to be appointed to this sensitive post since 1960. In January 2006, the then president, Obasanjo, visited Armichi, in Anambra State, Eastern Nigeria. Out of the four reasons for his visit, significantly one was 'to thank the people for the role the people of the town played in the unfortunate civil war, and their contributions in the peace and reconciliation of the country after the war.'[526] Arguably, therefore, the country does seem to be moving, albeit very slowly to reconciliation with the Igbo people. This will be particularly true if the newly elected president Goodluck Jonathan is able to contain corruption.

The Igbo peoples are irrepressibly optimistic and talented, they will always find ways round their disadvantaged position, and although they have had to suffer restrictions and control by the North since the end of the war, they have continued to excel in many walks of life. The only tragedy has been that the bulk of Ojukwu's people have been unable to enjoy even some of the riches and benefits accruing from Nigeria's only real source of income, oil. As Senator Uche Chukwumerije said during an interactive Senate press corps session, 'Although the civil war ended almost 34 years ago, Igbos are still treated as a conquered people. They are still being marginalised.'[527] Perhaps this will change as Nigeria, wanting affirmation and support from the rest of the world, realises fair distribution of the country's wealth for the wellbeing for all her people, not just a select few, is paramount to a sustainable and fair society.

CHRONOLOGY OF EVENTS

JANUARY 1966 TO JANUARY 1970

1966

15 January: Military coup overthrows First Republic. Prime Minister, finance minister, two regional premiers and senior army officers assassinated.

16 January: Acting President hands over power to Major-General Ironsi. Supreme Military Council established.

18 January: Military Governors appointed: Maj. Hassan Katsina, North, Lt-Col. Fajuyi, West, Lt-Col. Ojukwu, East, Lt-Col. Ejoor, Mid-West. Lt-Col. Gowon appointed army chief of staff.

24 May: Ironsi abolishes the regions and establishes a unified civil service under a unitary government, set up by decree 34.

28–31 May: Riots in Northern Region.

29 July: Northern troops mutiny; Ironsi and Fajuyi murdered.

1 August: Gowon emerges as national leader.

12 September: Ad hoc constitutional conference meets in Lagos.

1 October: Several days of intense rioting in the North, leading to a breakdown of law and order, and the deaths of Igbos living in the North, and some killing in the East.

16 November: Constitutional conference adjourned indefinitely.

1967

4–5 January: Military Governors and Gowon meet at Aburi, Ghana.

25 February: Ojukwu threatens unilateral action before 31 March.

30 March: Eastern Region directs that all revenue collected in the region on behalf of the Federal Government should be paid to Eastern Region.

29 April: The Federal Military Government announces suspension of all postal and money order transactions between the Eastern Region and the rest of the Federation.

6 May: Chief Awolowo and others visit Enugu to find a solution to the crisis.

27 May: Gowon declares a state of emergency. He abolishes the regions and creates 12 states.

28 May: Twelve governors appointed for the new states.

30 May: Ojukwu declares the former Eastern Region a sovereign state to be known as the Republic of Biafra.

6 July: Fighting breaks out between Federal and Biafran forces on the borders of Benue Plateau State and East Central State.

15 July: Nsukka captured by Federal forces.

25 July: Federal forces capture Bonny.

9 August: Biafran forces invade Mid-West Region.

11 August: Russian Mig-17s arrive in Kano. Biafran aircraft bomb Lagos.

17 August: Biafran leader, Lt-Col. Ojukwu, names Major Okonkwo Military Administrator of Mid-West region.

23 August: Biafran troops reach Ore, 100 miles from Lagos.

2 September: Gowon announces 'total war'.

21 September: Benin recaptured by Federal forces.

23 September: Lt-Col. Banjo and colleagues found guilty of treason and executed by Biafran government.

4 October: Enugu falls to Federal forces.

19 October: Calabar captured by Federal troops.

22 November: The Organisation for African Unity (OAU) mission, headed by Emperor Haile Selassie arrives in Lagos to open peace negotiations.

1968

3 January: Federal government introduces a new currency.

29 January: Biafra issues its own currency.

11 February: Commonwealth Secretary General Arnold Smith visits Lagos, to explore ways of ending the conflict.

30 February: Azikiwe's press conference in Paris.

25 March: Destruction of Federal force at Abagana.

13 April: Tanzania recognises Biafra.

15 April: Federal Government chooses International Committee of the Red Cross to co-ordinate all relief aid from outside Nigeria.

8 May: Gabon recognises Biafra.

15 May: Ivory Coast recognises Biafra.

20 May: Zambia recognises Biafra.

23–31 May: Kampala peace talks.

27 May: Czechoslovakia announces arms embargo on Federal government.

5 June: Gowon announces that there will be no advance on Igbo heartland until all peace talks fail.

12 June: France announces arms supply embargo to Federal government. Michael Leapman's report, on Biafra's starving children, appears in the *Sun* newspaper.

5 July: Belgium announces arms supply embargo on Federal Government.

6 July: Lord Hunt flies to Nigeria to assess relief needs.

31 July: French cabinet supports Biafran claim to self-determination.

5–9 August: Addis Ababa peace talks, attended by Ojukwu.

28 August: Federal Government nominates an International Observer Team to investigate charges of genocide.

31 August: Biafran troops reinforced by French army supplies.

10 September: Federal forces capture Aba.

15 September: Biafra retakes Oguta.

16 September: Owerri falls to Federal troops.

2 October: International Observer Team reports no evidence of genocide.

30 October: Count Von Rosen appointed to oversee arms airlift into Biafra.

11 December: British government gives £700,000 to ICRC for relief in Nigeria.

13 December: British members of Parliament, Lord Brockway and James Griffiths, make private visit to Biafra and Lagos.

15 December: Rioting in Ibadan, Abeokuta and Ishara.

17 December: Ojukwu rejects daylight flights.

1969

10 February: Azikiwe publicizes 14-point peace plan.

27–31 March: British Prime Minister, Harold Wilson, visits Nigeria.

9 May: Foreign oil men captured by Biafran troops at Kwale.

12 May: Federal army replaces all three divisional commanders.

22 May: Biafran air attacks by Swedish MF1–9B minitrainer aircraft led by Count Von Rosen, on Port Harcourt, Benin and oil fields in the Rivers and Mid-West states.

1 June: Ojukwu issues the Ahiara Declaration.

23 June: Federal forces mount another major offensive.

28 August: Azikiwe declares support for a united Nigeria at a London press conference.

6–10 September: Sixth OAU summit held in Kampala.

14 September: Ojukwu rejects ICRC's Lagos daylight relief agreement.

22 September: More riots in Western state.

1 November: Ojukwu issues peace proposals.

9 December: Lord Carrington visits Biafra and Nigeria.

15–18 December: Efforts to launch peace talks in Addis Ababa.

27 December: Federal forces link up at Umuahia, cutting off more than 500 square miles of Biafran enclave.

1970

9 January: Owerri falls to Federal troops.

10 January: Ojukwu holds final cabinet meeting and leaves Biafra.

12 January: Effiong announces Biafra's surrender.

13 January: Gowon accepts Biafran surrender. British government makes £5 million available for relief to Nigeria.

14 January: Biafran mission arrives in Lagos.

15 January: 'The dawn of national reconciliation', Gowon's victory message to the nation.

PEOPLE FEATURED
IN THE BOOK

Achuzia, Joseph. Igbo. Unorthodox but successful military commander in the Biafran Army. He was not a regular soldier, but had undergone national service in the British Army.

Adekunle, Benjamin, Major. Yoruba/Bachama. Came to prominence during the civil war as a divisional commander for the Federation. Enjoyed military success and was a popular hero with the Federal people. Was, arguably, removed from his command because of his popularity; seen as a threat to the Federal Authority's position.

Aguiyi-Ironsi, Johnson, Maj. Gen. Igbo. First indigenous general officer commanding of the Nigerian Army, and military ruler of Nigeria following the first coup.

Akintola, Samuel. Yoruba. Awolowo's deputy in the Action Group and Prime Minister of the Western Region.

Akpan, Ntieyong. Ibibio. Secretary to the Biafran government.

Azikiwe, Nnamdi. Igbo. Formed the National Council of Nigeria and Cameroons (NCNC), with Herbert Macaulay; first indigenous governor-general and first president.

Anowai, Alfred Sqd-Ldr. Igbo. Nigerian-trained airforce officer, fought for Biafra.

Awolowo, Obafemi, Chief. Yoruba. Leader of the Yoruba-based Action Group political party.

Balewa, Sir Abubkar Tafawa. Hausa-Fulani. Federal Prime Minister.

Banjo, Victor, Lt-Col. Yoruba. Sandhurst-trained Nigerian army officer. Led the Mid-West invasion by Biafra. Executed by Ojukwu.

Boro, Isaac. Ijaw. Student political activist, aimed to form a separate Delta Region state. Fought for Federal Government during the war.

Brierly, Tim. Oxfam director for Nigeria at the start of the civil war.

Burrows, Julia. Daughter of managing director of Costain, 1955–1964.

Crowther, Samuel. Yoruba. First indigenous Christian bishop.

Cumming-Bruce, Sir Francis. High Commissioner to Nigeria before Hunt; later 8th Baron Thurlow.

Danjuma, Theophilius, Captain. Hausa-Fulani. Thought to be responsible for killing Ironsi during the second coup, but denied culpability.

Effiong, Philip, Lt-Col. Ibibio. Chief of staff of the Biafran army.

Eneje, Dr James. Igbo. Member of Biafran Organisation of Freedom Fighters (BOFF).

Ejoor, David Lt-Col. Urhoho. Sandhurst-trained regular officer in the Nigerian Army, appointed Military Governor of the Mid-West Region by Major General Ironsi, when he came to power following the first coup in January 1966.

Fajuyi, Adekunle, Lt-Col. Yoruba. Appointed Western Military Governor by Major-General Ironsi, and killed in the second coup.

Foccart, Jacques. Gen. de Gaulle's special advisor on African affairs.

Forsyth, Frederick. Writer and Biafran supporter during the civil war.

Gbulie, Benjamin, Captain. Igbo. Sandhurst-trained officer of the Nigerian Army and one of the officers involved in the first coup. An Igbo who fought for Biafra.

Goldie, Sir George. Created the United Africa Company during Nigeria's early colonial development.

Gowon, Yakubu, Lt-Col. Angas. Military leader of Nigeria after the second coup.

Haruna, Ibrahim, Major. Hausa-Fulani. Commanding officer of the Federal forces 2nd Division.

Hunt, Sir David. British High Commissioner during the war.

Katsina, Hassan, Major. Hausa-Fulani. Sandhurst-trained Nigerian army officer and appointed by Major-General Ironsi as Military Governor of the Northern Region after the first coup.

Kalu, Ogbugo, Major. Igbo. Attended Staff College, Camberley, in Nigerian Army, then fought for Biafra; trained militia in Port Harcourt before the start of the civil war.

Leapman, Michael. Reporter for the *Sun* newspaper.

Lugard, Lord Frederick. First governor-general of Nigeria.

Macaulay, Herbert. Early Nigerian nationalist, formed the Nigerian National Democratic Party (NNDP).

MacDonald, Malcolm. Son of British Prime Minister Ramsay MacDonald, and Cumming-Bruce's roving unofficial ambassador in Nigeria, following the second coup.

Madiebo, Alexander, Lt-Col. Igbo. Sandhurst-trained Nigerian army officer, commander of the Biafran army.

Mbanefo, Sir Louis. Igbo. Biafra's chief justice.

Mojekwu, Christopher. Igbo. Cousin and close advisor of Ojukwu.

Murtala Mohammed, Major. Hausa-Fulani. Muslim Northerner, who came to prominence after the second coup. Led a division for the Federal Authorities during the civil war. Was a contender for Gowon's position following the second coup, and ousted him from power in 1976.

Njoku, Hilary, Lt-Col. Igbo. Nigerian army officer and first commander of the Biafran army.

Nzeogwu, Chukwume, Major. Igbo. Sandhurst-trained Nigerian army officer and one of the leaders of the first coup.

Obasanjo, Olusegun, Major. Yoruba. Assumed command of 3rd division of the Federal Nigerian army from Adekunle.

Ogundipe, Babafemi, Brigadier. Yoruba. Most senior army officer still alive following the second coup. Became Nigeria's High Commissioner in Britain.

Ojukwu, Emeka, Lt-Col. Igbo. Son of Sir Louis Ojukwu, Military Governor of the Eastern Region, appointed by General Ironsi following the first coup, and leader of the seceded state of Biafra.

Okafor, Ben. Igbo. Playwright and member of BOFF.

Okpara, Michael. Igbo. Former Eastern Region Premier and advisor to Ojukwu.

Von Rosen, Count Carl Gustav. Swedish volunteer and supplier of Minicon aircraft for Biafra.

Sardauna of Sokoto (Sir Ahmadu Bello). Hausa-Fulani. Political leader of the Northern Region, and Nigeria's most powerful politician.

Scott, Robert, Colonel. British High Commission military attaché.

Soyinka, Wole. Yoruba. Writer, political activist, interned by Gowon during the civil war.

Steiner, Rolf. Soldier of fortune, fought for Biafra.

Ujam, Samuel, Igbo. Battalion commander in the Biafran army.

Williams, Taffy. South African mercenary who fought for Biafra.

APPENDIX 1

NIGERIAN ARMS IMPORTS 1967–1969
U.K. shipments against total values, quarterly (*)

Date	Total value	U.K. value	U.K. %age	
Jan.–Sept.	£314,644	£156,655	49·79	*Armoured cars:* Before the outbreak of war sub-group 01– (**) shows an entry for 2 items, total value £14,487 (Ferrets?) *Sources:* West Germany, Netherlands, Israel and Spain sent significant quantities of arms. Communist imports still entered—e.g. ammunition from Poland: £1,803; ammunition from the U.S.S.R.: £18
Oct.–Dec. 1967	£43,582	£14,736	33·81	The most significant entry was a large shipment of Belgian ammunition.
Jan.–Mar. 1968	£N*1,365,838	£N1,181,780	86·51	*Armoured cars* 01– (**) shows an entry in Feb. for 6 items, total value £N180,757. *Ammunition* British imports in Feb. alone worth £N971,174. The only other significant entry was Belgian ammunition.

Appendix 1: Documents showing Nigerian arms imports from Britain 1967–1969. From Cronje, S., *The World and Nigeria*. (London: Sidgwick & Jackson, 1972.)

Date	Total value	U.K. value	U.K. %age	
Apr.–June 1968	£N256,015	£N126,525	49·42	
July–Sept. 1968	£N1,040,722	£N796,661	76·54	*Armoured cars* 01– (**) shows an entry in August for 6 items, total value £N123,000. In July an entry for 2 items, total value £N43,270. *Ammunition* made up the greatest part of imports, with Spain supplying £N125,196 worth— the largest source after Britain. The Belgians shipped £N35,834 worth in July, the last large supply following their embargo.
Oct.–Dec. 1968	£N895,525	£N712,594	79·57	*Ammunition* made up almost the whole total, with Spain (£N178,248) the only supplier except for the U.K., following the embargo by most W. European governments.
Jan.–Mar. 1969	£N2,552,256	£N2,539,367	99·49	*Armoured cars:* 01– (**) shows an entry in Feb. for 6 items, total value £N24,526. *Ammunition* made up almost entire total; ex-U.K. except £N6,816 worth from Sweden and £N113 from W. Germany. The only other source entered was Netherlands (£N5,759) sub-group 04–.
Apr.–June 1969	£N753,786	£N691,295	91·71	*Ammunition* made up almost entire total. Apart from U.K., entries for W. Germany (£N60,486).

Date	Total value	U.K. value	U.K. %age	
July–Sept. 1969	£N1,009,597	£N944,544	93·54	*Ammunition* made up almost entire total. Apart from U.K., entries for W. Germany (£N22,410); Sweden (£N33,988); and Pakistan (£N5,117).
Oct.–Dec. 1969	£N6,217,397	£N6,079,883	99·22	Over two-thirds entered under 03–, hitherto a minor sub-group. (This may be arms in crates.) Belgium entered for £N1,397; W. Germany for £N119,055. (In view of embargos it has been suggested these last represent ports of origin, and that materials were B.A.O.R.) *Ammunition* totalled about £N1·5m., with U.K. the source of almost all. More than 95 per cent of all values received in October and November. The final campaign began in December.

* Post-devaluation £N = £1·17

(*) Source: *Nigerian Trade Summary*, Table B, Group 951 'Firearms of War and Ammunition Therefor', The Chief Statistician, Lagos. See next pages for reproductions of tables from this publication. The contrast between the December 1966 table (the last pre-war year) and the December 1969 table (at the end of the war) is striking in the rise of the totals. *The illustrations give the categories of the various sub-groups mentioned in the above notes.*

(**) Sub group 01– includes armoured fighting vehicles as well as spare parts or weapons for these cars. The number of items shown is therefore not necessarily an accurate guide to the number of vehicles imported. For instance, in April 1968, there is an entry for 4 items totalling £N680— hardly the value of four armoured cars, unless they were given away free and the amount charged represents freight only. Some entries may be fairly assumed to consist of armoured vehicles; for instance in August 1968, 6 items, totalling £N123,000. The armoured cars mentioned above are deduced from such entries; all of them are of British origin.

APPENDIX 2

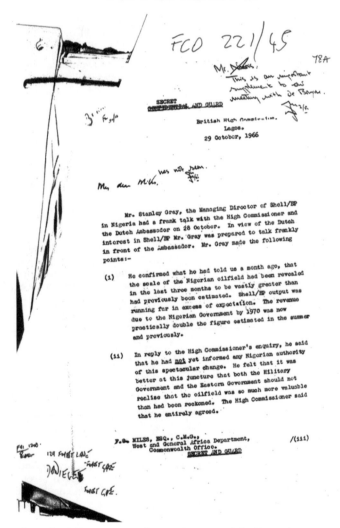

FCO 221/45

78A

Mr. ____
This is an important supplement to our meeting with de Bryar.

SECRET
CONFIDENTIAL AND GUARD

British High Commission,
Lagos.
29 October, 1966

My dear Miles, has not been.

Mr. Stanley Gray, the Managing Director of Shell/BP in Nigeria had a frank talk with the High Commissioner and the Dutch Ambassador on 28 October. In view of the Dutch interest in Shell/BP Mr. Gray was prepared to talk frankly in front of the Ambassador. Mr. Gray made the following points:-

(i)   He confirmed what he had told us a month ago, that the scale of the Nigerian oilfield had been revealed in the last three months to be vastly greater than had previously been estimated. Shell/BP output was running far in excess of expectation. The revenue due to the Nigerian Government by 1970 was now practically double the figure estimated in the summer and previously.

(ii) In reply to the High Commissioner's enquiry, he said that he had not yet informed any Nigerian authority of this spectacular change. He felt that it was better at this juncture that both the Military Government and the Eastern Government should not realise that the oilfield was so much more valuable than had been reckoned. The High Commissioner said that he entirely agreed.

J.O. MILES, ESQ., C.M.G.,   /(iii)
West and General Africa Department,
Commonwealth Office.
SECRET AND GUARD

Appendix 2: Document confirming the potential doubling of Nigerian oil revenue by 1970. The Nigerian authorities were not informed. FCO 221/45, Public Records Office, Kew.

APPENDIX 3

POWER OF ATTORNEY

KNOW ALL MEN by these presents, that
I, LT.-COL. C. ODUMEGWU OJUKWU, Military Governor,
The Republic of Biafra, DO this   day of
July, 1967, APPOINT FRANCIS CHUKWUKA NWOKEDI,
ESQ., of 4, Nwokedi Street, Onitsha, to be
attorney for the Government of the Republic
of Biafra for the purpose hereinafter mentioned,
that is to say:

To negotiate and conclude an
agreement with BARON DU ROURE & J.P. MALLET,
Paris, for the grant of foreign exchange
to the Government of the Republic of
Biafra up to the equivalent of £6,000,000
(six million pounds) sterling in a
currency acceptable to, and to an account
designated by, the Government of the
Republic of Biafra, the first payment
of £1,000,000 (one million pounds) sterling
being made available immediately for the
use of the Government of the Republic of
Biafra on the conclusion of this agreement
in accordance with the terms of the
attached Schedule.

Appendix 3: Documents confirming the proposed sale of Biafran natural resources to Rothschild Bank, Paris. FCO38/244, Public Records Office, Kew.

Appendix 1 — 2 pages

From **THE MILITARY GOVERNOR**
REPUBLIC OF BIAFRA
ENUGU

GRANT OF EXPLOITATION

    KNOW ALL MEN by these presents, that I,
LT. - COL. C. ODUMEGWU OJUKWU, Military Governor,
The Republic of Biafra, DO this da of   1967
GRANT AND CEDE TO THE ROTCHILD Bros BANK, FRANCE,
the exclusive rights of exploitation and extraction
of all deposits of the hereinafter enumerated minerals
within the territorial jurisdiction of the Republic of
Biafra :

        I) COLUMBITE Ore
        2) URANIUM
        3) COAL
        4) TIN CONCENTRATES
        5) NATURAL OIL.
and   6) GOLD ore

    These presents have effect immediately, and
henceforth FOR A DURATION OF IO (TEN) YEARS;ONLY.
    BE IT ALSO KNOWN THAT I, LT. - COL. C. ODUMEGWU
OJUKWU, Military Governor , The Republic of Biafra,

                                   ./.

SECOND   PAGE

HEREBY EMPOWER FRANCIS CHUKWUKA NWOKEDI Esq., of 4 ,
Nwokedi Street, Onisha , TO NEGOTIATE AND CONCLUDE
subsequent renewals. and extentions of the above - granted
rights of extraction and of exploitation.

NOTES

Chapter 1   Introduction

1. James Wilde, *Time Magazine,* 23 August 1968.
2. Daniel Branch and Nic Cheeseman, 'Democratization, sequencing and state failure in Africa: Lessons from Kenya', *African Affairs,* 108/430, Jan. 2009, pp. 1–26, at p. 6.
3. This was particularly true of Sam Ademulegun, commander of the 1ˢᵗ Brigade, Nigerian Army, who became a close confident of the Sardauna of Sokoto, the notional ruler of Nigeria, who paid for that confidence with his life during the first coup.
4. Gbulie, Ben: interview, 14 September 2007. Gbulie was one of the junior officers involved in the first coup.
5. Balogun, Ola, *The Tragic Years: Nigeria in Crisis* (Benin City: Ethiope Publishing Corporation, 1973), p. 86.
6. Balogun (1973), p. 87.
7. De St Jorre, John, *The Brother's War* (Boston: Houghton Mifflin Company, 1972); published in Britain as *The Nigerian Civil War* (London: Hodder and Stoughton, 1972), i.
8. Gbulie, B: interview, 27 March 2007.
9. Gbulie, B., *Nigeria's Five Majors, Coup d'etat of 15ᵗʰ January 1966, First Inside Account* (Onitsha, Nigeria: African Educational Publisher Ltd, 1981), p. 152.
10. Nolte, I., *Obafemi Awolowo and the making of Remo* (Edinburgh University Press, 2009), p. 199.

Chapter 2   Historical Background

11. Cooper (2002), p. 5.
12. Herskovits, J., *Nigeria: Power and Democracy in Africa* (New York: Foreign Policy Association, 1982), p. 8.

13. Herskovits (1982), p. 5.
14. Crowder, M., *The Story of Nigeria* (London: Faber & Faber, 1978), p. 47.
15. Crowder (1978), p. 24.
16. Okpaku, L. (ed.), *Nigeria: Dilemma of Nationhood* (Westport, Connecticut: Greenwood Publishing Company, 1972 and 1987), p. 41.
17. Forsyth (1982), p. 18.
18. Crowder (1978), p. 50.
19. Opia, E., *Why Biafra? Aburi Prelude to the Biafran Tragedy* (San Rafael, California: Leswing Press, 1972), p. 12.
20. Opia (1972), p. 16.
21. Schwarz, W., *Nigeria* (London: Pall Mall Press, 1968), p. 78.
22. Pakenham, T., *The Scramble for Africa* (London: George Weidenfeld & Nicolson, 1991), p.184.
23. Schwarz (1968), p. 79.
24. Miller, C., *The Lunatic Express* (London: Penguin, 2001), p. 203.
25. Crowder (1978), p. 171.
26. Crowder (1978), p. 165.
27. Schwarz (1968), p. 81.
28. Crowder (1978), p. 197.
29. Schwarz (1968), p. 73.
30. Schwarz (1968), p. 83.
31. Opia (1972), p. 31.
32. Opia (1972), p. 34.
33. Okpaku (1972), p. 20.
34. Lynn (2001), p. 329, Doc. 85 Co 537/4625. On the general structure of the constitution, 'We all agreed that unity will not be achieved by attempting to concentrate all power at the centre but rather by further decentralisation of authority to the Regions.'
35. Opia (1972), p. 35.
36. De St Jorre, J., *The Nigerian Civil War* (London: Hodder and Stoughton, 1972), p. 30.
37. Lynn, M., *Nigeria, Part 2* (2001). As evidenced in accounts written in April 1957, the British realised that their influence would wane, but the CO document comments 'The United Kingdom's prestige and reputation are at present high in Nigeria .... If we are to retain all this, and our capacity to influence Nigeria's thinking on international affairs in directions we would wish ... . The best we can hope for, perhaps after independence is that they will for some years continue to ask the United Kingdom to supply them with a Governor-General .... to whom they will look for advice when they get into difficulty', CO 554/1583, p. 397.
38. Balogun (1973), p. 16.

39. Balogun (1973), p. 17.
40. Opia (1972), p. 47.
41. Opia (1972), p. 51.
42. Balogun (1973), p. 18.
43. Opia (1972), p. 54.
44. Opia (1972), p. 55.
45. Opia (1972), p. 55.
46. Balogun (1973), p. 21.
47. Balogun (1973), p. 21.
48. Schwarz (1968), p. 185.
49. Ikeazor, C., *Nigeria 1966, The Turning Point* (London: New Millenium, 1997), p. 37.
50. Schwarz (1968), p. 187.
51. Ikeazor (1997), p. 39.
52. Ikeazor (1997), p. 40.
53. De St Jorre (1972), p. 45.
54. Schwarz (1968), p. 192.
55. Kirk-Greene (1993 edn), p. 27.
56. Ikeazor (1997), p. 65.
57. Ikeazor (1997), p. 66.
58. Luckham (1975), p. 254.
59. Luckham (1975), p. 252.
60. Schwarz (1968), p. 201.
61. De St Jorre (1972), p. 44.
62. Schwarz (1968), p. 199.
63. Adebayo: interview, 12 March 2008.
64. De St Jorre (1972), p. 54.
65. Kirk-Greene (1993), p. 163.
66. Kirk-Greene (1993), p. 48.
67. Schwarz (1968), p. 213.
68. Kirk-Greene (1993), p. 54.
69. De St Jorre (1972), p. 85.
70. Schwarz (1968), p. 220.
71. Cooper (2002), p. 5.
72. *The Times,* 30 May 1966.
73. Cooper (2002), p. 5.
74. Kirk-Greene (1993), p. 414.
75. Gowon: interview, 12 October 2007.

Chapter 3   The Path to War and Its Beginning

76. Omoigui, N., *Nigerian Civil War File: Federal Army Blunders of the Nigerian Civil War.*

77. Lady Iro Hunt: interview, 17 February 2008.

78. Adebayo: interview, 12 March 2008.

79. Cumming-Bruce: interview, 10 April 2007.

80. FCO Prem 13/1661, National Archives, and interview with Gowon. Murtala Mohammed was to continue his challenge for Gowon's position. In November 1966 he sought to depose Gowon as supreme commander with the support of the Northern-based political party, the Northern People's Congress. Gowon was offered command of the army, but he refused because he had the support of the influential Middle-Belt elements of the army as well as young intellectuals from the North. Gowon removed Mohammed as the army's Chief of Staff and sent him to Northern Nigeria. Murtala Mohammed, together with Obasanjo and Danjuma, finally deposed Gowon in a peaceful coup, while Gowon was attending an Organisation of African Unity conference in Kampala in 1975.

81. Gowon: interview, 20 September 2008 and Adebayo: interview, 12 March 2008.

82. Adebayo: interview, 12 March 2008.

83. Whiteman: interview, 22 March 2007.

84. Stremlau, J., *The International Politics of the Nigerian Civil War, 1967–1970* (Princeton University Press, 1977). Although Gowon was the senior Northern military officer, there were other members of the military forces who were senior to him: Commodore Wey, Brigadier Ogundipe and Colonel Adebayo outranked him, and three lieutenant colonels, Bassey, Imo and Hillary Njoku, were senior to him. Interestingly Ojukwu does not feature in this list.

85. Nolte (2009), p. 199.

86. Ojukwu: interview, 25 March 2008.

87. Soyinka, Wole, *You Must Set Forth at Dawn* (London: Methuen, 2007), p. 120.

88. Kirk-Greene (1971), vol. 1, p. 216.

89. Ojukwu: interview, 25 March 2008.

90. Danjuma: interview, 14 April 2007.

91. Whiteman: interview, 22 March 2007.

92. Gowon: interview, 12 October 200. Gowon's whole educational, formative and work experience years involved British influences. His background led him towards the conventional, and the only conventions in which he

had confidence were orientated towards the British establishment. This is important when making comparisons between Ojukwu and Gowon, and was to become decisive as communications between the two disintegrated into open hostility, which in retrospect can be seen as a major contribution to the outbreak of the civil war. For a more detailed account of the two men, their respective backgrounds and their styles of leadership, refer to chapter 5. As both have independently admitted, in hindsight they should have made a greater endeavour to find compromise out of their respective intransigent positions, and thus could have avoided the conflict. Neither man holds any animosity to each other today. Both have stated that when meeting they refer to each other as Jack and Emeka and their relationship is cordial.

93. Cumming-Bruce: interview, 10 April 2007.

94. Cumming-Bruce: interview, 10 April 2007. Cumming-Bruce admitted in his interview that when Gowon came to power, he had no recollection of having met the man. However his wife did recall him as being a guest at one of their dinner parties, and that her memory of Gowon was prompted because he was one of the few of their guests who had written to thank them for the evening.

95. Britain's investment in Nigeria was formidable. Most industries, including trading and exploitation of natural resources, were financed by the British Government, its banks and its corporations. For example, the Bank of England had 45% control of the Commonwealth Development Finance Company, which helped finance development projects in the country. Barclays D.C.O. controlled the largest share of banking activities in the country. Nigeria used the pound as her reserve currency and she was in the Sterling Exchange Area. British corporations had vast interests in the country, notably the United Africa Company, whose roots lay in the early days of European incursion into Nigeria. Britain's investment in Nigeria in 1961 amounted to £48.5 million. Significantly the biggest investment was in oil exploration. By 1967 the Shell–BP Development Company had invested £150 million: Fadahunsi, Olushola, *Nigeria The Last Days of the Republic,* pp. 136–43. It therefore seems strange that the British Government should leave her representative in Lagos to set policy. However perhaps it felt confident that he would create an agenda which would more than adequately look after British interests, as was arguably the case.

96. Cumming-Bruce: interview, 10 April 2007.

97. Clark, Edwin: interview, 8 July 2008.

98. Cumming-Bruce: interview, 2 September 2008.

99. Whiteman in Panter-Brick, *Nigerian Politics and Military Rule* (London: Athlone Press, 1970).
100. Soyinka, Wole (2007), p. 120.
101. Stremlau (1977), p. 37. *New York Times*, 20 August 1966.
102. Forsyth, Frederick, *Emeka* (Ibadan, Spectrum Books, 1982), p. 78.
103. Gowon: interview, 12 October 2008.
104. Forsyth (1982), p. 78.
105. Forsyth (1982), p. 75.
106. Stremlau (1977), p. 36.
107. Hunt, FCO Doc. 51/169, Public Records Office, Kew.
108. Hunt, FCO Doc. 51/169, Public Records Office, Kew.
109. See Appendix 1: pictures of casualties arriving from the north at Enugu railway station. From Enugu National Archives, and Rhodes Library, Oxford, 5 August 2009.
110. FCO Doc. 51/169, Public Records Office, Kew. Hunt report.
111. Okpaku (1972), p. 123.
112. Cumming-Bruce: interview, 10 April 2007. The use of Malcolm Macdonald by Cumming-Bruce is interesting. The two men had had a close working relationship in previous postings. In this case because Cumming-Bruce had been told by the British Govennment to formulate his own policy over Nigeria, he invited Macdonald to Lagos for a holiday.
113. Hunt (1998 and 2006), p. 252.
114. Cumming-Bruce: interview, 10 April 2007.
115. Adebayo: interview, 12 March 2008.
116. Adebayo: interview, 12 March 2008.
117. Cumming-Bruce: interview, 10 April 2007.
118. Stremlau (1977), p. 46.
119. Stremlau (1977), p. 47.
120. Stremlau (1977), p. 34.
121. Opia (1972), Appendix 2, Federal permanent secretaries' recommendations on Aburi, p. 111.
122. Gowon: interview, 12 October 2007.
123. Whiteman in Panter-Brick (1970), p. 41.
124. Panter-Brick (1970), p. 45.
125. Adebayo: interview, 12 March 2008.
126. Forsyth, F., *The Making of an African legend: The Story of Biafra* (London: Penguin, 1969), p. 116. Katsina commented that the Biafran army consisted of 'pen-pushers', and forecast a swift victory by Northern infantry soldiers.
127. Cumming-Bruce: interview, 10 April 2007.
128. Awolowo (1988), p. 636.

129. Awolowo (1988), p. 639.
130. Awolowo (1988), pp. 641–2.
131. Nolte (2009), p. 199.
132. Adebayo, R., *Onward Soldier Marches On* (Ibadan: Evans Brothers, 1998), p. 83. Western Nigeria and particularly Lagos had always been the country's richest and most solvent area. It is interesting to note that from the nineteen-seventies, when Nigeria's revenues became heavily dependent on oil income, the Lagos subsidy from central government was approximately one third of monies allocated to all other states. Elaigwu, J. Isawa, *Gowon: The Biography of a Soldier Statesman* (Ibadan: West Books Publishers, 1986), p. 164. Indeed in Lugard's day the West was always obliged to subsidise the chronically insolvent North. It is therefore hard to see how Gowon could have conducted a campaign against the East without the West's support. At the time Nigeria's largest export commodity was cocoa, and the West, through the Cocoa Marketing Board, had built up large financial reserves. These it put at the disposal of the Federal authorities, in support of the war. As the war progressed Adebayo even introduced more punitive taxation, as well as introducing a compulsory regional savings scheme. These proved very unpopular and culminated in the Agbekoya Riots of 1968.
133. Nolte (2009), p. 200.
134. Stremlau (1977), p. 62.
135. Gowon: interview, 12 October 2007.
136. Stremlau (1977), p. 70.
137. De St Jorre (1972), p. 132.
138. Stremlau (1977), p. 72.
139. Nolte (2009), p. 200.
140. Lynn, *Nigeria, Part 2* (2001), Doc. 232 Co 554/279, no 8, p. 18.
141. Lynn, M. (2001), p. lxxx. Although the Willink Commision recommended various safeguards for minorities, including written guarantees for minority rights, it came down against the creation of new regions, which was not popular with the Action Group who were determined to break the North into two.
142. Balogun (1973), p. 26.
143. Boro (1983) www.unitedijawstates.com/boro.html; last accessed on 1 Nov. 2009.
144. Achuzia: interview 28 March 2008. Gowon concurs with this assessment and admits that at the time the creation of twelve states did much to strengthen the popularity of his government (Gowon: interview 20 September 2008).

145. Biafrans are great traders and entrepeneurs, and the war if anything encouraged many in the community, especially those living on the ever-changing front lines, to trade across the borders for goods and services. Arguably this was one of the factors that enabled Biafra to survive for such a long period. For an analysis of 'attack markets' see interviews with Dr James Eneje and Rev. Fr Nambi Nwanko: Chapter 5, 'Biafra's Longevity'.

146. Eneje, James: interview, 5 November 2008.

147. Achuzia: interview, 28 March 2008. According to Achuzia there was unanimous support by all delegates for the declaration. He was an elected delegate from the Mid-West and attended the meeting.

148. Major-Gen. David Thomson, retired director of the British Defence College, interview, July 2007.

149. Achuzia: interview, 28 March 2008.

150. Cervenka, Z., *The Nigerian Civil War* (Frankfurt: Bernard and Graefe, 1971), p. 138.

151. Danjuma: interview, 12 April 2007.

152. Achuzia: interview, 28 March 2008.

153. FCO Doc. 51/169, Public Records Office, Kew. Copy of a report made by David Hunt, Britain's High Commissioner to Nigeria. This comment confirms Achuzia's statement about the East's early programme for securing arms.

154. Thompson: interview, 20 April 2008.

155. Based on an interview with Achuzia, 12 March 2008.

156. Gowon: interview, 12 October 2008.

157. Oyewole, F., *Reluctant Rebel* (London: Rex Collings, 1975), p. 73. By the end of the war Biafra had commissioned 10,000 officers, of which some 3,000 had been killed or died, and recruited some 150,000 men. There were a number of non-Igbo officers: Col. Banjo, Major Ademoyega, Captains Oyewole, Ola and Adeleke, and Lieutenants Olafimihan, Egbikor and Igbenikaon.

158. Gbulie: interview, 14 September 2008.

159. Gbulie, B., *The Fall of Biafra* (Enugu: Benlie (Nigeria) Publishers, 1989), p. 60.

160. Madiebo, A., *The Nigerian Revolution and the Biafran War* (Enugu: Fourth Dimension Publishing, 1980), p. 130. His comments are interesting, because they are shared by David Hunt, the British High Commissioner, who stated that he did not exclude a quick Federal victory. He thought that the Federal forces should have the capacity to seize the main centres of Igboland. In the event of their capturing Enugu and its radio station, especially if Colonel Ojukwu were eliminated or discredited, most Igbos and the Eastern minorities would in all probability, he felt, resume their places

in a united Nigeria. Conversely, his deputy, still based in Enugu, after the opening of hostilities felt that the East had sufficient men and materials to hold off invasion and even go over to the offensive. Although he thought it possible for the East to be defeated by military force or by the blockade, he felt that the fierceness of the initial fighting and the strength of feelings aroused would make for vicious feeling if defeat should come. FCO 51/169, declassified 2002, Public Records Office, Kew.

161. Forsyth (1969), p. 116. An interesting appraisal of the fighting qualities of the Biafran troops is made by Major Williams, a South African mercenary serving in Biafra at the time; he commented, 'I've seen Africans at war, but nobody can touch these people. Give me 10,000 Biafrans for six months, and we'll build an army which is invincible on this continent.'

162. Njoku, Rose, *Withstand the Storm – War Memoirs of a Housewife* (Ibadan, Heinemann, 1986), p. 251.

163. Achuzia: interview, 28 March 2008.

164. Achuzia: interview, 28 March 2008.

165. Soyinka (2007), p. 144. Omotoso, Kole, *Just Before Dawn* (Ibadan: Spectrum Books, 1998), p. 288.

166. Achuzia: interview, 28 March 2008. Col. Achuzia commented that various names, including his own, had been considered to lead the attack, but because Nzeogwu had been killed, Ojukwu was persuaded, mainly by Banjo, that he was the best man for the job. Interviewing Ojukwu on the subject suggests that Ojukwu chose Banjo because of their very close friendship, but that there was an element of distrust because of Banjo's ambition and because he was Yoruba not Igbo.

167. Adebayo: interview, 4 March 2008. When questioned about Banjo's apparent complicity in compromising the attack, he felt that by that stage Banjo's ability to persuade people to support him and overthrow Gowon was very limited. In his opinion, by then Gowon had gained the backing of most key people in the West and their appetite for change of leadership or compromise with the East was limited.

168. Forsyth: interview, 12 April 2007. See also Forsyth (1969), p. 121.

169. Forsyth (1969), p. 126.

170. Soyinka (2007), pp. 145–72.

171. Gowon: interview, 12 October 2007.

172. Adebayo: interview, 12 March 2008.

173. Gbulie: interview, 14 September 2008.

174. Madiebo (1980), p. 158.

175. Madiebo (1980), p. 161.

176. Forsyth (1969), p. 121.

NOTES 233

177. Stremlau (1977), p. 77.
178. Gowon: interview, 12 October 2008.
179. Appendix: arms list, FCO National Archives, Kew. Archive account of Wilson's visit to Lagos in 1969. There is a very interesting account of Wilson and Gowon riding in the motorcar from Ikeja to Lagos, a distance of some twenty-five miles. Gowon raises the issue of increasing arms supplies and Wilson agrees, but cautions Gowon about mentioning this in any official communiqués.
180. Okpaku (1972; 1987 edn), p. 123.
181. Gowon: interview, 12 October 2008.
182. Forsyth: interview, 12 April 2008.
183. Ojukwu: interview, 25 March 2008.
184. Gbulie: interview, 14 September 2008.
185. Danjuma: interview, 12 April 2007.
186. Stremlau (1977; 1980 edn), p. 79.
187. Gowon: interview, 12 October 2007.
188. *Daily Telegraph,* 15 August 1967.
189. *Sun,* 12 June 1968.
190. *Sun,* 13 June 1968.
191. *Daily Sketch,* 13 June 1968.
192. *Daily Sketch,* 17 June 1967.
193. Leapman: interview, 20 June 2007.
194. Forsyth (1969), p. 203.

Chapter 4 The Second Part of the War: From Mid-1968 to January 1970

195. Kirk-Greene (1971), p.22. Official text quoted in *Morning Post,* 2 January 1968.
196. Lewis, Stephen, *Journey to Biafra* (Canada: Thistle Publishers, 1968). Comment from officers in Biafra's 14th Division. National Archives, Enugu.
197. Achuzia: interview, 28 March 2008.
198. Ojukwu: interview, 25 March 2008.
199. Gbulie: interview, 14 September 2008.
200. Madiebo (1980), p. 176.
201. Ojukwu: interview, 25 March 2008. See also Achuzia, J., *Requiem Biafra* (Enugu: Fourth Dimension Publishing, 1986), for an interesting account of the struggle for control of Onitsha.
202. De St Jorre (1972), p. 211.

203. Gowon: interview, 12 October 2007. However, he reaffirmed that at no time during the campaign did he order attacks on the Biafran civilian population. Conversely, in Ojukwu's eyes this is exactly what Gowon did do, and he was able to make considerable political capital out of the bombings, much to the embarrassment of the Federal Government.
204. Leapman: interview, 20 June 2007.
205. Perham, Dame Marjorie, *Oxfam News*, April 1968.
206. FCO 51/169/157, Public Records Office, Kew.
207. Brierly, T., Oxfam's Director for Equatorial and West Africa: interview, 21 February 2008.
208. De Jorre (1972), p. 208.
209. Gowon: interview, 12 October 2007.
210. Report by Major-Gen. H.T. Alexander, British representative on the International Observer Team in Nigeria, January 1970; Liddell Hart Centre for Military Archives, King's College London.
211. Report by international commission of jurists on evidence of genocide brought by the Biafran Government. The committee met in Paris on 22–3 March 1968, and was chaired by Prof. Lopez-Ray. The committee found that there was a prima facie case of genocide against the Biafran people. MSS Afr s 2399, Britain–Biafra Association, Rhodes House Library, Oxford.
212. Ojukwu: interview, 12 March 2008.
213. Achuzia: interview, 28 March 2008.
214. Kirk-Greene (1971), p. 399; Ojukwu interprets the Kwale incident, Doc. 205.
215. Achuzia: interview, 28 March 2008.
216. Ojukwu: interview, 12 March 2008.
217. Ojukwu: interview, 25 March 2008.
218. Gbulie: interview, 14 March 2008.
219. Ojukwu: interview, 25 March 2008.
220. *Daily Telegraph*, 3 June 1969.
221. *Africa Confidential*, No 12, 6 June 1969, p. 1.
222. Gowon: interview, 12 October 2008.
223. Col. R.E. Scott, 'Appreciation of the Nigerian Conflict' (Scott Report): 'The Nigerian soldier is inherently superstitious. To him ju-ju {witchcraft} is a terrifying medium. It was for this reason that night operations were rarely employed.'
224. James Eneje: interview, 19 June 2008, and Rev Fr Nambi Nwankwo: interview, 27 March 2008.
225. *Daily Telegraph*, 4 November 1969, by Brian Silk.

226. Njoku (1986), p. 248.

227. Madiebo (1980), p. 104. Madiebo says that he planned this force and that it was actioned by Colonel Aghanya. Madiebo felt that such a force would be most effective operating in Federal-held territory where it would help to pin down substantial numbers of troops. He said that it should plan to live mainly off the land, be given limited arms, and should rely on capturing sufficient arms for its use from Federal soldiers. He felt that if it operated within Biafran territory it could lead to reprisals on the local population should territory be overrun by Federal troops.

228. Ben Okafor: interview, 20 February 2008.

229. De St Jorre (1972), p. 188.

230. Interviews: Dr James Eneje, 5 February 2008, recruited into BOFF, and Rev Fr. Nambi Nwankwo, 27 March 2008, recruited into the boys' company.

231. Eneje: interview. April 2008.

232. Achuzia: interview, 22 March 2008.

233. Two examples of Igbo democracy in action were recently witnessed by the author. One at Npanator, near the university town of Nsukka, and the other in a rural community north of Asaba, in the Delta Region. At Npanator the proposed election of an individual to a responsible position within the community was open to comment by any community member and required the majority support of all those who attended the meeting. The meeting was open to all members of the community. At the community north of Asaba a similar democratic solution was required.

234. Oyewole (1975), p. 146.

235. Forsyth (1969), p. 115.

236. Njoku (1986), p. 99.

237. Gbulie: interview, 14 September 2007; Achuzia: interview, 28 March 2008.

238. Capt Ujam: interview, 19 September 2007.

239. Madiebo, A., *The Nigerian Revolution and the Biafran War* (Enugu: Fourth Dimension, 1980), pp. 110–12.

240. Ojukwu: interview, 25 March 2008.

241. Madiebo (1980), p. 145.

242. Adekunle: interview, 28 September 2008.

243. Gbulie: interview, 14 September 2007.

244. Achuzia: interview, 28 March 2008.

245. Gbulie: interview, 14 September 2007.

246. James Wilde, *Time Magazine*, 26 January 1970.

247. Forsyth (1969), p. 116.

248. Cervenka (1971), p. 150.

249. Achuzia: interview, 28 March 2008.

250. Scott Report (1986).

251. Achuzia: interview, 28 March 2008.

252. Cervenka (1971), p. 150.

253. Scott Report.

254. Forsyth: interview, 12 April 2007.

255. Forsyth (1969), p. 133.

256. Ojukwu: interview, 25 March 2008.

257. Achuzia: interview, 28 March 2008.

258. Kalu had joined the Nigerian army in 1959, served as a non-commissioned officer and was commissioned in 1961. He attended and passed his staff college course at Camberley, England. When the civil war started he was a major in the Nigerian army, stationed in Port Harcourt. He was an associate of Achuzia in the town, and gave support to Achuzia's idea of a militia force at the start of hostilities. By mid 1968 he had become a divisional commander in the Biafran army with the rank of Brigadier. See Luckham (1975), Gbulie (1989) and Achuzia (1986).

259. Enugu, National Archives FRP/1. Lewis (1968).

260. Soyinka (2007), p. 217.

261. Gowon: interview, 12 October 2007.

262. Adekunle: interview, 28 September 2008.

263. Adekunle: interview, 28 September 2008. He also explained that he had an excellent Igbo cook.

264. De St Jorre (1972), p. 261.

265. Col. R.E. Scott, 'Appreciation of the Nigerian Conflict', 13 December 1969, Liddell Hart Centre for Military Archives. Also reproduced in the *Sunday Telegraph*, 11 January 1970. The report was extremely derogatory about the fighting capabilities of the Nigerian Army. The report, confidential at the time, was leaked to the *Sunday Telegraph*, causing deep embarrassment to the British Government, who had hoped to retain a strong influence over Gowon's administration after the war. Publication in the *Sunday Telegraph* occurred as the war came to an end. Scott, who had been a squash-playing companion of Gowon, was hastily expelled from Nigeria. Scott finally comments on the quantity of small arms demanded by the Federal forces. He says that their logicians assessed the need for 5 million rounds of 7.62 mm for each division and 5 million rounds in reserve in Lagos, in the autumn of 1968. By the time of his report this figure had trebled!

266. Achuzia: interview, 28 March 2008.

267. Achuzia: interview, 28 March 2008.

268. De Jorre (1972), p. 194.

269. Cervenka (1971), p. 74.
270. Sqd-Leader Alfred Anowai: interview, 14 September 2007.
271. FCO 8239/5/6/8, Sunday, 30 March 1969.
272. Scott Report.
273. Gowon: interview 12 October 2007.
274. Adekunle: interview, 28 September 2008.
275. Adekunle: interview, 28 September 2008.
276. De St Jorre (1972), p. 274.
277. De St Jorre (1972), p. 278.
278. Gowon: interview, 12 October 2007.
279. *Africa Confidential*, No 12, 6 June 1969.
280. Adekunle: interview, 28 September 2008.
281. *New Nigerian*, 17 Jan. 1970, p. 12.
282. Achuzia: interview, 28 March 2008.
283. Gbulie: interview, 14 September 2007.
284. Cervenka (1971), p. 80.
285. Ojukwu: interview, 25 March 2008.
286. Achuzia: interview, 28 March 2008.
287. Hunt, 6 November 1970, FCO, 51/169, Public Records Office, Kew.
288. Scott Report, *Sunday Telegraph*, 11 January 1970.
289. FCO 51/169, Public Records Office, Kew.
290. FCO 51/169, Public Records Office, Kew.
291. Achuzia: interview, 28 March 2008. It has proved difficult to obtain supportive evidence of these meetings. Gowon says he was unaware of these encounters and Ojukwu simply made no comment on them.
292. Ojukwu: interview, 25 March 2008.
293. Ojukwu: interview, 25 March 2008.
294. Josephine Achuzia: interview, 21 November 2008.
295. De St Jorre (1972), p. 369.
296. De St Jorre (1972), p. 368.

Chapter 5   Biafra's Longevity

297. Forsyth (1969), p. 108.
298. Balogun (1973), p. 73.
299. Ojukwu: interview, 25 March 2008.
300. De St Jorre (1972), p. 192.
301. Ojukwu: interview, 25 March 2008; De St Jorre (1972), p. 193.
302. Ojukwu: interview, 25 March 2008.

238 THE BIAFRAN WAR

303. Ojukwu: interview, 25 March 2008. Onyegbula, Godwin, *The Nigeria – Biafran Bureaucrat* (Ibadan: Spectrum Books, 2005).
304. Uwechue, Ralph, *Reflections on the Nigerian Civil War* (New York: Africana Publishing Corporation, 1971), pp. 127–8.
305. Gowon: interview, 12 October 2007.
306. De St Jorre (1972), p. 229; Achuzia: interview, 28 March 2008.
307. Kirk-Greene (1971), p. 348.
308. Kirk-Greene (1971), p. 445, Document 200.
309. Kirk-Greene (1971), p. 445, Document 200.
310. Danjuma: interview, 12 April 2007.
311. Gowon: interview, 12 October 2007.
312. *Daily Telegraph*, 4 November 1969, from a report by Brian Silk, who had just spent four months in Nigeria.
313. *Daily Telegraph*, article by E.V. Gatacre who had just returned from Biafra, 2 June 1969.
314. Ironsi's ill-fated attempts at centralising control of government, which helped create the impetus for the second coup.
315. Cooper (2002), p. 156. Nigeria's regions had been built on a set of institutions – bureaucracies, militaries, post offices and, initially, legislatures.
316. Ojukwu, O., *Biafra* (New York: Harper and Row, 1969), p.240: Ojukwu addressing a joint meeting of the Consultative Assembly and Elders, 27 January 1968.
317. The author had many meetings with Easterners who had experienced the war, and without exception they all had a respectful admiration for Ojukwu.
318. Ojukwu: interview, 25 March 2008.
319. Achuzia: interview, 28 March 2008. He recounts using these rockets during the defence of Onitsha and also during his successful attack on a Federal supply column at Abagana.
320. *The Times,* 5 March 1969.
321. Oyewole (1975), p. 88.
322. Onyegbula (2005), p. 153.
323. *The Times*, 5 March 1969, article by Winston Churchill Jr.
324. Ojukwu: interview, 25 March 2008.
325. Ojukwu: interview, 25 March 2008. He confirmed that some of his family money was contributed, alongside other people's contributions, to support the fledgling state's finances.
326. Symes, P., *Bank Notes of Biafra* (International Bank Notes Society, Vol. 36, No 4, 1997).
327. Symes (1997), p. 4.

328. Appendix FCO 38/214, National Archives.

329. FCO 38/244, National Archives. Letter and memorandum to the Secretary of State for Commonwealth Affairs from the British High Commissioner, October 1967.

330. Achuzia: interview, 28 March 2008. An interesting event was to occur to the author when interviewing Achuzia. He was invited to Achuzia's home village and community near Asaba and presented to the community's chief and his cabinet. The chief's minister of finance turned out to be Lt-Col. Morah, who recognising the author's surname, enquired if he was related to John Gould. It appears that Morah had been a protégé of the author's father during Morah's early days in the Nigerian army. The author felt that it was not an opportune time to discuss misappropriation of funds during the civil war, an opportunity lost, but Achuzia's comments did seem to have substance in view of comments made by Symes.

331. Symes (1997), p. 4.

332. Symes (1997), p. 5.

333. Symes (1997), p. 6.

334. Eneje: interview, 5 November 2008.

335. Symes (1997), p. 11.

336. See Appendix for photograph of Biafran currency.

337. Symes (1997), p. 11.

338. De St Jorre (1972), p. 306.

339. During the author's many visits to Eastern Nigeria it was always amazing to see the degree of attention which is paid to the repair of even the most decrepit pieces of equipment. Nothing, it seems, is beyond redemption.

340. FCO Doc. 221/45, National Archives.

341. FCO Doc. 38/267, National Archives. There was a difficult period for Shell/BP, just before the start of hostilities, when the East demanded 57.5 percent of oil revenues, the remainder going into a suspense account. Shell/BP agreed, but the Federal Government countered by extending the blockade to oil tankers and the main oil terminal at Bonny. Ojukwu's comment was 'If you are operating in Biafra you pay Biafra – it's as simple as that.' Shell/BP then made a token payment of £250,000, which caused much diplomatic activity between the FCO and the High Commission and Shell/BP; the British Government owned 49 percent of Shell/BP, which meant she was hardly a disinterested party. In Biafra the Bonny blockade by the Federal Government caused much anti-British feeling, and Ojukwu and his government took over all Shell/BP oil installations and arrested Shell/BP's Managing Director, Mr Stanley Grey. However, at this point there were other more pressing matters exercising the minds of the Biafran

Government: the war had started on 5 July and this inevitably took priority. Grey was released and no royalties from Shell/BP were paid to the Biafran Government. Indeed it seems that even the £250,000 failed to be paid to the Biafran authorities, due to them prevaricating over which account should receive it, either in London or in Geneva. The FCO, together with the Treasury and the Bank of England, effectively stopped payment because of exchange-control permission. No further claims for payments were made by the Biafrans, and although attempts were made by Biafra to disrupt the flow of oil throughout the war, culminating in Von Rosen's successful disruptions toward the end of hostilities, oil was never the priority for Biafra or the Federal Authorities as it was for Britain and France. De St Jorre (1972), p. 140.

342. FCO Doc.38/267, National Archives, 1 September 1967.
343. FCO Doc. 38/268, 29 September 1967. The Nigerian High Commissioner, Brigadier Ogundipe, bought 10,000 rifles from Spain and 15,000 rifles from Germany as well as a large quantity of ammunition. Aircraft carrying these supplies to Nigeria were subject to clearance by the British authorities and his supply was contrary to the British Government.
344. Appendix 2: Arms supply. There were times during the war when Britain was supplying 90% of all the Federal Government's arms.
345. *The Times*, 6 March 1969.
346. *Oxfam News*, April 1968.
347. Michael Leapman: interview, 10 June 2007.
348. Questionnaire carried out by the author at random with members of the British public, 2008.
349. FCO Doc. 38/211, National Archives. Part of a telegram sent by Wilson to Gowon on 19 July 1967.
350. FCO Doc. 38/211, National Archives. Part of a telegram sent by Wilson to Gowon on 19 July 1967.
351. Brierly: interview, 21 February 2008.
352. Ojukwu: interview, 25 March 2008; Gbulie: interview, 12 October 2007.
353. Ojukwu: interview, 25 March 2008.
354. Brierly: interview, 21 February 2008; Josephine Achuzia: interview, 25 January 2007.
355. Ojukwu: interview, 25 April 2008.
356. Brierly: interview, 25 April 2008.
357. Smith, M., *A Cause For Our Time, Oxfam the First Fifty Years* (Oxford University Press, 1992), p. 122.
358. Gowon: interview, 12 October 2007.
359. Ojukwu: interview, 25 March 2008.

360. *World Medicine*, 12 November 1968: part of an article by Dr Noel Moynihan, working in Nigeria for the Save the Children Fund.
361. Ojukwu: interview, 25 March 2008.
362. Sqd-Ldr Alfred Anowai: interview, 14 September 2007.
363. Brierly: interview, 21 February 2008.
364. Fred Cuny (a foreign pilot who flew transport aircraft for different organisations): interview. BBC *Timewatch*, 15 June 2000.
365. *New York Herald Tribune*, 17 August 1968.
366. *New York Herald Tribune*, 17 August 1968.
367. *The Times,* 28 May 1969.
368. *The Times,* 28 May 1969.
369. De St Jorre (1972), p. 339.
370. Forsyth: interview, 12 April 2007. Forsyth and Ojukwu remain friends to this day. Forsyth was instrumental in looking after and educating Ojukwu's children, during and after the war, in England. During his time in Biafra he was to write a successful account of the war, which even Ojukwu felt was too biased in Biafra's favour (Ojukwu: interview, 25 March 2008), and this account was to lead him to write his first successful novel, *The Dogs of War.*
371. *Daily Telegraph,* 17 July 1968, interview with Chinua Achebe.
372. *Daily Telegraph,* 17 July 1968, interview with Dr Garrick Leton, the principal of the Advanced Training College in Owerri.
373. *Guardian,* 13 June 1968.
374. *The Times,* 6 March 1968.
375. Gowon: interview, 12 October 2007.
376. FCO Doc. 38/270, 7 March 1968, National Archives.
377. FCO Doc. 38/268, 20 November 1968, National Archives.
378. Ojukwu: interview, 25 March 2008. He admitted that this figure of 50,000 had been a useful exaggeration to help promote Biafra's cause, but that it had grown from the original reports at the time which suggested a figure of nearer 5,000.
379. *Daily Telegraph*, 12 December 1968.
380. Major-Gen. H.T. Alexander, British representative on the International Observer Team in Nigeria, January 1970; Liddell Hart Centre for Military Archives, King's College London.
381. Gowon: interview, 12 October 2007.
382. *The Sun,* 6 September 1968; *The Times, Daily Telegraph,* and *Daily Express* also recorded the incident.
383. *Daily Sketch,* 20 August 1968.
384. *Daily Telegraph,* 6 September 1968. ITN also filmed the execution of the officer responsible. According to Michael Leapman, the execution was

delayed to allow Michael Nicholson and his team from ITN to get their equipment in place to record the detail. Michael Leapman: interview.

385. Gowon: interview, 12 October 2007.

386. Report by Major-Gen. H.T. Alexander, British Representative on the International Observer Team in Nigeria, January 1970; Liddell Hart Centre for Military Archives, King's College London.

387. Observer Team to Nigeria, report to Federal Government of Nigeria, 12 February 1970; Liddell Hart Centre for Military Archives, King's College London.

388. De St Jorre (1972), p. 306.

389. Ojukwu: interview, 25 March 2008.

390. *Newsweek,* 24 March 1969.

391. *The Times,* 12 March 1969: A British Observer's view of the Nigerian War.

392. *Daily Telegraph,* 12 March 1969.

Chapter 6 Gowon and Ojukwu: An Appraisal of the Two Leaders

393. Gowon: interview, 20 September 2008.

394. FCO/Prem13/1661, 11 November 1966.

395. Gbulie: interview, 14 September 2007. Also quoted in Gbulie (1981), p. 71.

396. Gowon interview, 12 October 2007 His comments were that, although hindsight is a wonderful thing, he would definitely have tried to accommodate the East's objectives more sympathetically. Ojukwu interview, 25 March 2008. He said that, in retrospect his reactions at the time were too impulsive, but in his defence he was carried along by the attitude for secession by the East's Consultative Committee.

397. W.F. Gutteridge, *Military Regimes in Africa 1966–1974* (Ibadan: Spectrum Books, 1979), pp. 133–7.

398. Gowon: interview, 12 October 2007. I first met Gowon when I was a young man of 17, when I was asked to collect him from his military mess and drive him to our home so that he could babysit for my sister. We struck up a good friendship and we would frequently challenge each other to a game of squash.

399. Kirk-Greene: interview, 2008.

400. Gowon: interview, 12 October 2007.

401. Gowon: interview, 5 November 2008. Dr James Eneje, an Igbo contemporary at Warwick University, confirmed this story. He also went on to confirm Nigeria's indignation when a press report featured Gowon in a refectory queue with other undergraduates for lunch, indicating the modesty of the man.

402. Last: interview, 8 April 2008.
403. Uwechue (1971), p. 94.
404. Ojukwu: interview, 25 March 2008.
405. Ojukwu: interview, 25 March 2008.
406. Forsyth: interview, 12 April 2007.
407. Forsyth: interview, 12 April 2007; Hunt, Lady Iro: interview, 27 April 2008.
408. Uwechue (1971), p.132.
409. Oyewole (1975), p.183.
410. Elaigwu, *Gowon* (1986), p. 27.
411. Elaigwu, *Gowon* (1986), p. 27.
412. Gowon: interview, 12 October 2007.
413. Cabinet Office, 7933(a) 1968; National Archives, Kew. From a letter by Martin Dent, lecturer at Keele University, and formerly a District Officer in the Tiv Region of Nigeria; dated 17 March 1968.
414. Gowon (1986), p. 21.
415. Gowon (1986), p. 31.
416. Gowon: interview, 12 October 2007. He commented that a certain regimental sergeant-major found 'Yakabu' just too tongue-twisting and 'Jack' much easier.
417. Gowon: interview, 12 October 2007.
418. Elaigwu, *Gowon* (1986), p. 72.
419. Danjuma: interview, 12 April 2007.
420. Gowon: interview, 12 October 2007.
421. Ojukwu (1969), p. 11.
422. Gowon: interview, 12 October 2007.
423. Gowon: interview, 12 October 2007.
424. Burrows: interview, 22 March 2009.
425. Burrows: interview, 22 March 2009.
426. Ojukwu: interview, 25 March 2008.
427. Burrows: interview, 22 March 2009.
428. Ojukwu: interview, 25 March 2008.
429. Ojukwu: interview, 25 March 2008.
430. Ojukwu: interview, 25 March 2008.
431. Ojukwu: interview, 25 March 2008.
432. Ojukwu: interview, 25 March 2008. Even today he blames Gowon for his inability to suppress the riots and killings of Igbo people following the second coup.
433. Ojukwu: interview, 25 March 2008; Gowon: interview, 12 October 2007.

434. Gowon: interview, 12 October 2007. He said that the Nigerian Army was his life and it was obvious from his tone that he has great affection for it. He said that he was really very ill-suited for career in politics, it did not motivate him and he found the intrigue and compromise did not suit his straightforward temperament.

435. Gbulie: interview, 14 September 2007.

436. FCO, Doc 25/232, National Archives, Kew.

437. Iro Hunt: interview. In view of her own disparaging comments about Ojukwu, a question should perhaps be posed about the triangular relationship between Hunt, Lady Hunt and Ojukwu. Could it have been that Hunt, the British High Commissioner, had allowed personal relationships to interfere with his professional life? This suggestion is based on the fact, mentioned before, of the close relationship this small group of elite people had in the mid-1960s in Nigeria; it was perhaps almost incestuous.

438. Ojukwu (1989), p. 5.

439. Kirk-Greene (1971), Vol. 1, Doc 37.

440. Gowon: interview, 20 September 2008.

441. Cumming-Bruce: interview, 12 April 2007.

442. Ojukwu: interview, 25 March 2008.

443. Ojukwu (1969), p. 177.

444. Kirk-Greene (1971), p. 318. It is interesting to note that it was not until the Aburi meeting that discussion took place about the fate of General Ironsi. Ojukwu informed the writer that in fact he had already been told about Ironsi's and Fajuyi's fates.

445. Ojukwu: interview, 25 March2008.

446. Gowon: interview, 20 September 2008.

447. Gowon and Cumming-Bruce: interview, 10 April 2007.

448. FCO Doc 38/213, National Archives, Kew.

449. Ojukwu: interview, 25 March 2008.

450. Forsyth (1969), p.110.

451. Ojukwu: interview, 25 March 2008.

452. Achuzia: interview, 28 March 2008.

453. Ojukwu: interview, 25 March 2008.

454. Achuzia: interview, 28 March 2008.

455. Madiebo (1980), p.167.

456. Dent, Martin, lecturer at Keele University, former District Officer, Tiv, Nigeria: letter to Wilson, British Prime Minister, 17 March 1968; National Archives, Cabinet Office Doc 7933(a).

457. Address given by Dr V.S.O. Olunloyo at a reception for Brig.-Gen. Benjamin Adekunle, at Lautech, Ogbomoso, Nigeria, on Saturday 11 April 2009.

Quoted from *A Combatant in Government*, Chapter 3, by Major-Gen. David Jemibewon.

458. De St Jorre (1972), pp. 282, 283.
459. Gowon: interview, 12 October 2007.
460. Dent, letter to Wilson.
461. Gowon: interview, 20 September 2008.
462. Elaigwu, *Gowon* (1986), p. 120.
463. Gowon: interview, 20 September 2008.
464. Cronje, S., *The World and Nigeria* (London: Sedgwick and Jackson, 1972), p. 221.
465. Saro-Wiwa (1989), p. 203.
466. FCO 38/267, file note 16, National Archive, Kew.
467. Ojukwu: interview, 25 March 2008; Leapman: interview, 10 June 2007.
468. Ojukwu: interview, 25 March 2008.
469. Gowon: interview, 12 October 2007.
470. Dent, letter to Wilson, 17 March 1968. National Archives, Kew.
471. Writer's visits to Ojukwu's home: he was very conscious of the regular presence of Holy Fathers from the local Christian community.
472. Gowon: interview, 12 October 2007; Ojukwu: interview, 25 March 2008.

Chapter 7   Conclusion

473. Kirk-Greene (1971), vol. 1, p. 5.
474. See Appendix.
475. Ojukwu: interview, 25 March 2008.
476. Achuzia: interview, 28 March 2008.
477. British High Commission, Lagos, to FCO, 14 December 1967. FCO Doc 51/169, Public Records Office, Kew.
478. Perkins, N.C. and James, E.S., *The Nigeria-Biafra War; Minorities in Biafra* (two memoranda, typewritten, 1969), MS Afr.S. 1927/1/2, Rhodes House Library, Oxford, p. 63.
479. Anowai, Alfred, Sqd-Ldr: interview, 18 February 2007.
480. Cumming-Bruce: interview, 10 April 2007.
481. Adebayo: interview, 12 March 2008.
482. Kirk-Greene (1971), p. 54.
483. See photograph in Appendix.
484. Ojukwu: interview, 25 March 2008.
485. Gowon: interview, 12 October 2007.
486. Dike, *100 Years of British Rule in Nigeria 1851–1951* (Lagos: 1957), p. 43.

487. From a conversation between Sam Ademulegun , an indigenous Nigerian Army officer, and John Gould, the author's father, held in 1958.

488. Gbulie: interview, 14 September 2007.

489. See Appendix, copy document.

490. Question asked of many interviewees from the East, 2007–8.

491. British High Commission, Lagos, to FCO, London, 14 December 1968. FCO Doc. 38/285, National Archives, Kew.

492. Achuzia, Gbulie and Ojukwu: interviews, 2008.

493. FCO 38/247, Public Records Office, Kew.

494. Gowon: interview, 12 October 2007.

495. FCO Report on Nigeria, 9 November 1968. FCO 186/9, Public Records Office, Kew.

496. Hunt (1990), p. 261.

497. Hunt (1990), p. 261.

498. Gowon: interview, 12 October 2007.

499. Hunt (1990), p. 256; conversation between Jim Parker, British Assistant High Commissioner, and Ojukwu, Enugu.

500. Forsyth (1969), p. 116.

501. Within the first year and a half of the war the official contributions to Nigerian relief aid made by eighteen governments, mainly from Western Europe and America, amounted to £20,812,000. Throughout the entire war period the British Government subscribed nearly £3.49 million to the cost of relief in Nigeria, and considerable sums were also received from British voluntary organisations. FCO Doc. 51/169, Public Records Office, Kew.

502. FCO Doc. 38/246, Public Records Office, Kew.

503. *The Guardian,* 3 October 1968.

504. *The Guardian,* 3 October 1968.

505. FCO Doc. 38/246, Public Records Office, Kew.

506. Report by International Observer Team, January 1970; Liddell Hart Centre for Military Archives, King's College London.

507. Report by international commission of jurists on evidence of genocide, brought by the Biafran Government. The report was made in Paris on 22–3 March 1968, and was chaired by Professor Lopez-Ray, a distinguished international jurist. The committee said there was a prima facie case of genocide against the Biafrans; MS Afrs 2399, Britain-Biafra Association, Rhodes House Library, Oxford, pp. 81–9.

508. *Genocide: a documentary diary*, Directorate of Propaganda, November 1968; Enugu Archives PD/X13.

509. Ojukwu: interview, 25 March 2008.

510. Gowon: interview, 12 October 2007.

Epilogue

511. Emezue, Sydney: interview, 25 August 2007; lecturer in politics at Enugu University, and Biafran war veteran.
512. Ikeazor (1997), p. 3.
513. Gowon: interview, 12 October 2007.
514. *The Times*, 14 October 2009.
515. Ojukwu: interview, 25 March 2008.
516. FCO Doc. 51/169, Public Records Office, Kew.
517. Achuzia: interview, 28 March 2008, and Adekunle: interview, 28 September 2008.
518. Brierly: interview, 18 January 2008.
519. Last: interview, 12 February 2008.
520. Hunt (1990), p. 264.
521. Danjuma: interview, 2007.
522. Email from Ben Gbulie to author, 2009.
523. Achuzia: telephone interview, August 2009.
524. *The Daily Sun*, Lagos, Friday 24 August 2007.

Postscript

525. This state of affairs was confirmed during a meeting of teachers and administrators, in Enugu, with the author, during a visit, in June 2007 and confirmed by Dr James Eneje, an Igbo and boy soldier during the civil war May 2011.
526. *Daily Independent*, 15 January 2006.
527. *Daily Independent*, 23 December 2003.

BIBLIOGRAPHY

PRIMARY SOURCES

Unpublished Oral Interviews

Achuzia, Joe. Col. Biafran Army. Interviewed on 28 March 2008.

Achuzia, Joesephine. Ex-wife of Joe Achuzia. Interviewed on 25 January 2007.

Achuzia, Simon. Son of Joe Achuzia. Interviewed 20 November 2008.

Adebayo, Robert, Maj-Gen. Nigerian Army and Governor of Western Region during the war . Interviewed on 12 March 2008.

Adekunle, Benjamin, Brig.-Gen. Nigerian Army. Interviewed on 28 September 2008.

Anowai, Alfred, Sqd-Ldr. Biafran Airforce. Interviewed on 14 September 2007.

Brierly, Tim. West African Field Director, Oxfam. Interviewed on 21 February 2008.

Bell, Martin. BBC correspondent. Interviewed on 16 April 2007.

Burrows, Julia. Daughter of the managing director of Richard Costain Ltd. Interviewed on 22 March 2009.

Clark, Edwin, Chief. Former minister in Gowon's administration and Delta Region activist. Interviewed on 8 July 2008.

Cummings-Bruce, Francis, Lord Thurloe. British High Commisioner, during first and second coup. Interviewed on 10 April 2007.

Danjuma, T.Y, Lt-Gen. Nigerian Army. Interviewed on 14 April 2007.

Doble, Denis. FCO official in Biafra in 1970. Interviewed on 10 April 2007.

Edwards, Pamela. School friend of Ojukwu's. Interviewed on 20 February 2009.

Emezue, Sydney. Professor and soldier in Biafran Army. Interviewed on 25 August 2007.

Eneje, James, Dr. Boy recruit to Biafran Organisation of Freedom Fighters. Interviewed on 5 November 2008.

Gowon, Jack, Maj-Gen. Nigerian Army and Nigerian Head of State. Interviewed on 12 October 2007.

Hunt, Iro, Lady. Wife of Sir David Hunt, British High Commissioner after Cummings-Bruce. Interviewed on 17 February 2008.

Ferreira, Dr. Lt-Col. Nigerian Army. Chief medical officer for 4th division Nigerian Army. Interviewed on 20 September 2007.

Forsyth, Frederick. Writer and journalist. Interviewed on 12 April 2007.

Gbulie, Ben, Lt-Col. Biafran Army and writer. Interviewed on 14 September 2007.

Ikeazor, Chukwudum. Writer and ex-Nigerian policeman. Interviewed on 15 May 2007.

Kirk-Greene, Tony. Fellow St Anthony's College, Oxford. Interviewed on 12 February 2008.

Last, Murray. Emeritus Professor, London University. Interviewed 8 March 2008.

Leapman, Michael. Reporter, *The Sun*. Interviewed on 20 June 2007.

Nwankwo, Rev. Fr. Boy recruit to Biafran Organisation of Freedom Fighters. Interviewed on 19 June 2008.

Nwobosi, Emanuel, Col. Biafran Army. Interviewed on 24 March 2008.

Ojukwu, Emmeka, General. Biafran Army and Biafran Head of State. Interviewed on 25 March 2008.

Okafor, Ben. Actor, writer, Boy recruit to Biafran Organisation of Freedom Fighters. Interviewed on 20 February 2008.

Okafor, David, Col. Biafran Army. Interviewed on 21 September 2007.

Onyefueu, Godwin, Major. Biafran Army. Interviewed on 21 September 2007.

Thomson, David. Retired Maj-Gen British Army. Interviewed on 20 April 2008.

Ujam, Chief, Capt. Biafran Army. Interviewed on 19 September 2007.

Whiteman, Kaye. Writer, journalist. Interviewed on 22 March 2007.

Watson, Simon. Retired bank manager. Employee of Bank of British West Africa, Kaduna. Interviewed on 20 March 2007.

Unpublished documents

Foreign and Commonwealth documents from the National Archives Kew.
FCO 13/1661
FCO 25/232
FCO 51/157/159
FCO 38/211/213/214/244/246/247/268/270/285
FCO 186/9
FCO 221/45
FCO 8239/5/6/8

Cabinet Office 7933(A)

Federal Republic papers, National Archives, Enugu.
FRP/1 Lewis (1968)
PD/X13

Published documents

James Wild, Time Magazine 23 August1968/26 Jan 1970

Kaye Whiteman, *A Last Look at Biafra* (London: Inter play, 1070)

Stephen Lewis, *Journey To Biafra* (Canada: Thistle Publisher, 1968) National Archives Enugu.

Peter Symes, *Bank Notes of Biafra* (International Bank Note Society, Vol36, No4, 1997)

Report by Maj-Gen HT Alexander on The International Observer Team. Liddell Hart Centre for Military Archives, Kings College, London

Report by Lt-Col RE Scott, *Appreciation of the Nigerian Conflict* 13 December 1969. Liddell Hart Centre for Military Archives, Kings College, London

Address given by Dr VSO Olunloyo on 11 April 2009 for Brig B Adekunle's birthday, from the personal collection of Michael Adekunle. Quoted from *A Combatant in Government*. Ch3 by Maj-Gen. Jemibewon.

Report by international commission of jurists on genocide, during the Nigerian Civil War. MSS Afrs 2399 Britain-Nigeria Association, Rhodes House Library, Oxford.

Memoranda by NC Perkins and ES James, *The Nigeria-Biafran War 1969*. MS Afrs 1927/1/2 Rhodes House Library, Oxford

SECONDARY SOURCES

Autobiographies of Participants in the War

Achuzia, JOG., *Requiem Biafra* (Enugu: Fourth Dimension, 1986)

Adebayo, R., *Onward Soldier Marches On* (Ibadan: Evans Brothers, 1998)

Awolowo, O., *Awo The Autobiography of Chief Obafemi Awolowo* (Cambridge University Press, 1960)

Efiong, I., *Reintegration True or False* (Enugu: Star Printing and Publishing Company Ltd, 1983)

Ejoor, D., *Reminiscences* (Lagos: Malthouse Press, 1989)

Gbulie, B., *Nigeria's Five Majors, Coup d'etat of 15 January 1966, First Inside Account* (Onitsha: African Educational Publisher Ltd, 1981)

Gbuli, B., *The Fall of Nigeria* (Enugu: Benlie Publishers, 1989)

Hunt, D., *Sir David Hunt, Memoirs Military and Diplomatic* (London: Trigraphltd, 1990 and 2000)

Madiebo, A., *The Nigerian Revolution and the Biafran War* (Enugu: Fourth Dimension Publishing, 1980)

Njuku, R., *Withstand the Storm-War: Memoirs of a Housewife* (Ibadan: Heinemann, 1986)

Newspapers

Daily Telegraph: 15 August 1967/17 July 1968/6 September 1968/12 December 1968/12 March 1969/2 June 1969/3 June1969/4 November 1969

The Sun: 12 June 1968/13 June 1968/6 September 1968

Daily Sketch: 13 June 1968/17 June 1968/20 August 1968

The Times: 30 May1966/6 March 1969/12 March 1969/28 May 1969/14 October 2009

Guardian: 13 June 1968/3 October 1968

Daily Sun (Lagos): 24 August 2007

New York Herald Tribune: 17 August 1968

Africa Confidential, no 12: 6 June 1969

New Nigerian: 17 January 1970

World Medicine: 12 November 1968

Newsweek: 24 March 1969

BBC Timewatch: 15 June 2000

Books

Achebe, C., *The Trouble with Nigeria* (London: Heinemann, 1983)

Adechie, C. N., *Half a Yellow Sun* (London: Harper Collins, 2006)

Aluka, S., *1964 Federal election crisis – an analysis* (Onitsha: Etudo Limited, 1965)

Amadi, E., *Sunset in Biafra* (Ibadan: Heinemann, 1973)

Anthony, D. A., *Poison and Medicine, Ethnicity, Power, and Violence in a Nigerian City 1966–1986* (Oxford: James Currey, 2002)

Armstrong, R., *The Issues at Stake Nigeria 1967* (Ibadan: Ibadan University Press, 1976)

Balogun, O., *The Tragic Years: Nigeria in Crisis 1966–1970* (Benin City: Ethiope Publishing Corporation, 1973)

Birch, G. and Dominic St George, *Biafra: The Case for Independence* (London: Britain-Biafra Association, 1968)

Cervenka, Z., *The Nigerian Civil War* (Frankfurt: Bernard and Graefe, 1971)

Chima, A., *The Future Lies in a Progressive Biafra* (London: Citadel Press, 1968)

Collis, R., *Nigeria in Conflict* (London: Secker and Warburg, 1970)

Cooper, F., *Africa Since 1940: The Past of the Present* (Cambridge University Press, 2002)

Cronje, S., *The World and Nigeria* (London: Sedgwick & Jackson, 1972)

Crowder, M., *The Story of Nigeria* (London: Faber and Faber, 1978)

Dike, K., *A Hundred Years of British Rule in Nigeria 1851–1951* (Lagos: Tollbrook, 1957)

Dudley, V. J., *An Introduction to Nigerian Government and Politics* (London: Macmillan Press, 1972)

Elaigwu, J., *Gowon: The Biography of a Soldier Statesman* (Ibadan: West Books Publishers, 1986)

Emecheta, B., *Destination Biafra* (Glasgow: Collins, 1982)

Essien, J., *In The Shadow of Death* (Ibadan: Heinemann, 1987)

Ezenwa-Ohaeto, *Chinua Achebe: A Biography* (Oxford, James Currey, 1997)

Fadahunsi, O., *Nigeria: The Last Days of the Federal Republic* (Ibadan: Ibadan Press, 1970)

Fage, J. A., *A History of Africa* (London: Hutchinson & Co., 2002)

Forsyth, F., *Emeka* (Ibadan: Spectrum Books, 1982)

Forsyth, F., *The Making of an African Legend: The Story of Biafra* (London: Penguin, 1969)

Graham-Douglas, N., *Ojukwu's Rebellion and World Opinion* (London: Galitizene, Chant, Russell and Partners, 1970)

Gutteridge, W., *Military regimes in Africa* (Ibadan: Spectrum Books, 2005)

Harneit-Sievers, A., Ahazuem, J. and Emezue, S., *A Social History of the Nigerian Civil War* (Enugu: Jemezie Associates, 1997)

Herskovits, J., *Nigeria: Power and Democracy in Africa* (New York: Foreign Policy Association, 1982)

Idahosa, P., *Truth and Tragedy: A Fighting Man's Memoir of the Nigerian Civil War* (Ibadan: Heinemann, 1989)

Ihonvbere, J. and Shaw, T., *Illusion of Power: Nigeria in Transition* (New Jersey: Trenton, 1998)

Ike, C., *Sunset at Dawn: A Novel of the Biafran War* (Ibadan: University Press, 1976)

Ikeazor, C., *Nigeria 1966: The Turning Point* (London: New Millennium, 1997)

Isichei, E., *Igbo Worlds* (London: Macmillan Education Limited, 1978)

Jacobs, D., *The Brutality of Nations* (New York: Alfred A. Knopf, 1987)

Kirk-Greene, A., *Crisis and Conflict in Nigeria, vols 1 and 2* (Oxford University Press, 1975)

Lewis, S., *Journey to Biafra* (Canada: Thistle Publishers, 1968)

Luckham, R., *The Nigerian Military: A Sociological Analysis of Authority and Revolt 1960–67* (Cambridge University Press, 1975)

Lynn. M., ed., *British Documents on the End of Empire, vols 1 and 2* (London: The Stationery Office, 2001)

Mainasara, A., *The Five Majors – Why We Struck* (Zaria: Hudahuda Publishing Company, 1982)

Meredith, M., *The State of Africa: A History of Fifty Years of Independence* (London: Free Press, 2005)

Metrowich, F., *Nigeria: The Biafran War* (Pretoria: Institute of South Africa, 1969)

Miller, C., *The Lunatic Express* (London: Penguin, 2001)

Miners, N. J., *The Nigerian Army 1956–1966* (London: Methuen & Co. Ltd 1971)

Muffett, D., *Empire Builder Extraordinary: Sir George Goldie* (Douglas, Isle of Man: Shearwater Press, 1978)

Niven, R., *The War of Nigerian Unity* (Ibadan: Evans Brothers, 1970)

Nolte, I., *Obafemi Awolowo and the Making of Remo* (Edinburgh University Press, 2009)

Nwankwo, A., *Nigeria: The Challenge of Biafra* (London: Rex Collings, 1972)

Obi-Ani, P., *Post War Social and Economic Reconstruction of Igboland: 1970–1983* (Enugu: Mikon Press, 1998)

Obumselu, B., *Massacre of Ndiigbo in 1966* (Lagos: Tollbrook Ltd, 1976)

Odogwu, B., *No Place to Hide: Crisis and Conflicts Inside Biafra* (Enugu: Fourth Dimension Press, 1985)

Ogunsheye, F. A., *A Break in the Silence; Lt. Col. Adebulunla Victor Banjo* (Ibadan: Spectrum Books Ltd, 2001)

Ojukwu, O., *Biafra: Selected Speeches and Random Thoughts* (New York: Harper and Row, 1969)

Okadigbo, O., *Power and Leadership in Nigeria* (Enugu: Fourth Dimension Press, 1987)

Okocha, E., *Blood on the Niger: An Untold Story of the Nigerian Civil War* (Port Harcourt: Sunray Publications, 1994)

Okpaku, L., ed., *Nigeria: Dilemma of Nationhood* (Westport, Connecticut: Greenwood Publishing Company, 1972 and 1987)

Olushola, Fadahunsi, *Nigeria The Last Days of the Republic* (Ibadan: A-O.F. Press, 1970)

Omotoso, K., *Just Before Dawn* (Ibadan: Spectrum Books, 1998)

Onyegbula, G., *The Nigerian-Biafran Bureaucrat* (Ibadan: Spectrum Books, 2005)

Opia, E., *Why Biafra? Aburi Prelude to the Biafran Tragedy* (San Rafael, California: Leswing Press, 1972)

Osaghae, E. E., *Crippled Giant: Nigeria Since Independence* (London: Hurst & Co., 1998)

Oyeweso, S., *Perspectives on the Nigerian Civil War* (Lagos; OAP Publications, 1982)

Oyeweso, S., *From Neutrality to Active Involvement: Awolowo and the Nigerian Civil War, The End of an Era* (Ife Ife: Obafemi University Press Ltd, 1988)

Oyewole, F., *Reluctant Rebel* (London: Rex Collings, 1975)

Pakenham, T., *The Scramble for Africa* (London: George Weidenfeld & Nicolson, 1991)

Panter-Brick, ed., *Nigerian Politics and Military Rule* (London: Athlone Press, 1970)

Perham, M., *Lugard, vols 1 and 2* (London: Collins, 1955–69)

Saro-Wiwa, K., *On Darkling Plain: An Account of the Nigerian Civil War* (Port Harcourt: Saros International Publishers, 1989)

Schwarz, W., *Nigeria* (London: Pall Mall Press, 1968)

Smith, M., *A Cause for our Time: Oxfam the First Fifty Years* (Oxford University Press, 1992)

Soyinka, W., *You Must Set Forth at Dawn* (London: Methuen, 2007)

Stremlau, J., *The International Politics of the Nigerian Civil War, 1967–1970* (Princeton University Press, 1977 and 1980)

St Jorre, J. de, *The Nigerian Civil War* (London: Hodder and Stoughton, 1972)

St Jorre, J. de, *The Brothers' War Biafra and Nigeria* (Boston: Houghton Mifflin Company 1972)

Uwechue, R., *Reflections on the Nigerian Civil War* (New York: Africana Publishing Corporation, 1971)

Waugh, A. and Cronje, S., *Biafra: Britain's Shame* (London: Michael Joseph, 1969)

Whiteman, K., *A Last Look at Biafra* (London: Interplay, 1970)

INDEX